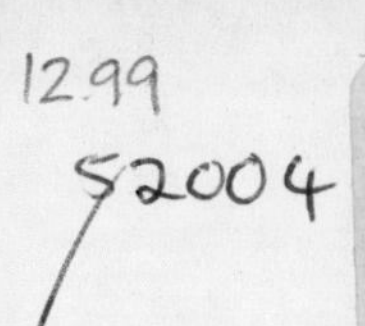

Materials in construction

G. D. Taylor

B.Sc., Ph.D., MCIOB., Cert. Ed. AKC

B. J. Smith

B.Sc., Ph.D., M.C.I.O.B., M.C.I.B.S., M.Inst.P.

Materials in construction

Longman Scientific & Technical
Longman Group UK Limited,
Longman House, Burnt Mill, Harlow,
Essex CM20 2JE, England
and Associated Companies throughout the world

First published 1985
Seventh impression 1994

British Library Cataloguing in Publication Data

Taylor, Geoffrey
Materials in construction.
Level 2.
1. Building materials
I. Title II. Smith, B.J., 1945–
624.1′8 TA403

ISBN 0-582-41322-2

Produced by Longman Singapore Publishers (Pte) Ltd
Printed in Singapore

Contents

Chapter 7 Plastics 187

Chapter 8 Paints 219

Chapter 9 Plastics 227

Answers to numerical questions 236

Acknowledgements

We are grateful to the following for permission to reproduce copyright material:

B. T. Batsford Ltd for fig 2.6 from p 137 *Components and Finishes* by Everett; British Standards Institution for extracts, figs 5.7, 5.9, 5.17–18 Tables 1.2, 1.11–1.14, 6.1–6.5, 9.1. all *B.S. Specifications*, copies of the Documents can be obtained from BSI at Linford Wood, Milton Keynes, MK14 6LE; Granada Publishing for fig 5.2 from fig 6, p 12 *Timber Properties and Uses* by W. P. K. Findley; the Controller of Her Majesty's Stationery Office for figs 1.13–1.18, Tables 1.8–9 from *Design of Normal Concrete Mixes*, BRE, fig 5.11 from *The Strength Properties of Timber*, Princess Risborough Lab. of BRE, Tables 7.3–4, 7.7 from pp 3, 2, 1/3 *BRE DIGEST* 69, 224. All Crown Copyright.

We have unfortunately been unable to trace the copyright holder of Table 7.5 and would appreciate any information which would enable us to do so.

Chapter 1

Concrete

Concrete is essentially a mixture of cement, aggregates and water. Other materials added at the mixer are referred to as 'admixtures'.

Cements

The most important cements are Portland cements; so named because of a similarity in appearance of concrete made with these cements to Portland stone. Portland cements are hydraulic – that is, they set and harden by the action of water only.

Portland cements are made by heating a finely-divided mixture of clay or shale and chalk or limestone in a kiln such that chemical combination occurs between them. About 5 per cent gypsum (calcium sulphate) is added to the resulting clinker in order to prevent 'flash' setting and the final stage involves grinding to a fine power.

Although the familiar grey powder may appear to have a high degree of uniformity, it is important to appreciate that Portland cement is a complex combination of the minerals contained originally in the clay or shale and the calcium carbonate which constitutes limestone or chalk. These compounds are listed below, together with commonly-used abbreviations.

Clay or Shale	SiO_2	Silica (silicon oxide)	abbreviated S
	Fe_2O_3	Ferrite (iron oxide)	abbreviated F
	Al_2O_3	Alumina (aluminium oxide)	abbreviated A
Limestone or Chalk	$CaCO_3$	(calcium carbonate) on heating gives CaO (quicklime)	abbreviated C

Chemical analysis or microscopic examination of cement clinker shows that there are four chief compounds present. Table 1.1 summarises the properties of these compounds, including their heat

Table 1.1 Properties of the four chief compounds in Portland cements

Name	Abbreviation	Approximate percentage in OPC	Properties	Heat of hydration J/g
Dicalcium silicate	C_2S	30	Slow strength gain – responsible for long-term strength	260
Tricalcium silicate	C_3S	45	Rapid strength gain – responsible for early strength (e.g. 7 days)	500
Tricalcium aluminate	C_3A	12	Quick setting (controlled by gypsum) susceptible to sulphate attack	865
Tetracalcium alumino ferrite	C_4AF	8	Little contribution to setting or strength. Responsible for grey colour of OPC	420

emission on hydration and typical percentages in ordinary Portland cement. The percentages do not add up to 100 because small quantities of other compounds are also present.

The properties of Portland cements vary markedly with the proportions of the four compounds, reflecting substantial differences between their individual behaviour. The proportion of clay to chalk (usually approximately 1 : 4 by weight respectively) must be very carefully controlled during manufacture of the cement, since quite small variations in the ratio produce relatively large variations in the ratio of dicalcium silicate to tricalcium silicate. A greater proportion of chalk favours the formation of more of the latter, since it is richer in lime. The tricalcium aluminate and the tetracalcium alumino-ferrite contribute little to the long-term strength or durability of Portland cements but would be difficult to remove and, in any case are useful in the manufacturing process, since they act as fluxes, assisting in the formation of the silicate compounds.

There will also be variations in cement properties from one works to another as a result of differences in the composition of the clay or shale so that, if maximum uniformity is to be achieved in a concreting job, cement from the same works is essential.

The properties of a cement are dependent not only on its composition but also on its fineness. This is because cement grains have very low solubility in water, so that the rate of reaction and hence setting and hardening increase as the surface area of grains increases – that is, as they become finer. Fineness is measured by the term 'specific surface', which is defined as:

$$\frac{\text{Surface area of the grains in a sample}}{\text{Mass of that sample}}$$

The units of specific surface are m^2/kg, that of ordinary Portland cement (OPC) being required by BS 12 to be not less than 225 m^2/kg.

Ordinary Portland cement is the cement best suited to general concreting purposes; it is the lowest priced cement and combines a reasonable rate of hardening with moderate heat output. Other types of cement are, however, available, each being recommended for specific applications. The chief variants on ordinary Portland are as follows:

Rapid-hardening Portland cement

This is specified by the same British Standard as OPC, being only essentially different in respect of fineness – BS 12 requires a minimum fineness of 325 m^2/kg. Rapid-hardening Portland cement (RHPC) therefore tends to set and harden at a faster rate than OPC. The rate of set is controlled by the addition of slightly more gypsum during manufacture, since it is the hardening properties and heat emission rather than setting rate which form the basis of applications. Early strength development is considerably higher than that of OPC, while long-term strength is similar. Applications include the following.

1. To permit increased speed in construction – for example subsequent lifts of concrete can proceed more rapidly on account of its increased early strength.
2. In frosty weather there is less risk of the concrete freezing, since the cement has a higher early heat output.
3. Concrete made with rapid-hardening cement can be safely exposed to frost sooner, since it matures more quickly.

Sulphate-resisting Portland cement BS 4027

This cement (SRPC) has better resistance to sulphate attack than OPC (see 'Sulphate attack', p. 9). The percentage of the sulphate-susceptible tricalcium aluminate is limited to 3.5 per cent in BS 4027 in order to minimise chemical combination with sulphates in solution. Sulphate-resisting cement may be produced by the addition of extra iron oxide before firing; this combines with alumina which would otherwise form C_3A, instead forming C_4AF, which is not affected by sulphates. Hence sulphate-resisting cement may be slightly darker in colour than OPC. Applications include foundations in sulphate-bearing soils, in mortar for flues in which sulphur may be present from fumes and in marine structures, since sea water contains sulphates.

Low-heat Portland cement BS 1370

The heat output of this cement (LHPC) is limited by BS 1370 to 250 J/g at the age of 7 days and 290 J/g at the age of 28 days. These may be compared to typical heat outputs of 330 J/g and 400 J/g at the same ages for OPC. The reduction in heat output is obtained by means of lower quantities of the rapidly hydrating compounds C_3S and C_3A. In order to produce satisfactory development of strength with time, the fineness of this cement is higher than that of OPC – it must not be less than 320 m^2/kg. Although early strength is slightly less than that of OPC, long-term strength is similar.

The chief use of LHPC is in mass concrete, since there is a tendency for the heat to build up internally in such structures, causing cracking due to the temperature differential between inner and outer layers. Typical applications include large raft foundations and dams.

Portland blast-furnace cement BS 146

This cement (PBFC) comprises a mixture of OPC and ground blast-furnace slag, the proportion of the latter not exceeding 65 per cent of the total. The slag contains mainly lime, silica and alumina (in order of decreasing amounts), which exhibit hydraulic action in the presence of calcium hydroxide liberated by the Portland cement.

Early strength is lower than that of OPC but PBFC liberates less heat than OPC and produces better sulphate resistance. Ultimate strength is similar to that of OPC concrete and PBFC may be competitive in cost in regions in which the slag is produced. Ground blast-furnace slag may also be used in part replacement of cement, reducing cost and modifying properties as above.

White Portland cement

This contains not more than 1 per cent of iron oxide, which is responsible for the grey colour of OPC. China clay, which is almost iron-free, is used instead of ordinary clay. Firing and grinding are also modified to prevent coloured matter being introduced. In consequence the cement costs approximately twice as much as OPC. Setting is similar to OPC but long-term strength is slightly lower (though within the limits of BS 12). The cement is used to produce white or coloured concretes – for the latter, pigments would be incorporated. These concretes may be employed for their aesthetic or light-reflecting qualities.

British Standard test for setting time

In this test a sample of cement is mixed with water to form a paste of standard consistency. A 40 mm thick sample of this paste is then subjected to two types of penetration test, using the Vicat apparatus. In the first, the penetration of a 1.13 mm diameter round needle is measured (Fig. 1.1). When this is between 4 and 6 mm from the base, the cement is said to have reached its 'initial set' This would be related, for instance, to the time available for placing the concrete and must be not less than 45 min (BS 12).

At a much later stage, a 1.13 mm diameter round needle projecting 0.5 mm from a small brass cylinder is applied (Fig. 1.2) and, when the brass cylinder fails to mark the cement paste, the 'final set' has occurred. This according to BS 12, should be not later than 10 h after adding the water and would be related to the time after which concrete could be treated as 'solid'. It should be emphasised that both 'initial' and 'final' sets are arbitrarily selected points on a smooth and continuous curve relating stiffness to time.

British Standard test for soundness

This test is primarily designed to detect the presence of any free lime which might be present in cement clinker. Such lime would, if present, gradually become exposed on hydration of the cement and, since it expands on 'slaking' with water, would cause overall expansion (unsoundness) in concrete. Since the exposure of the lime

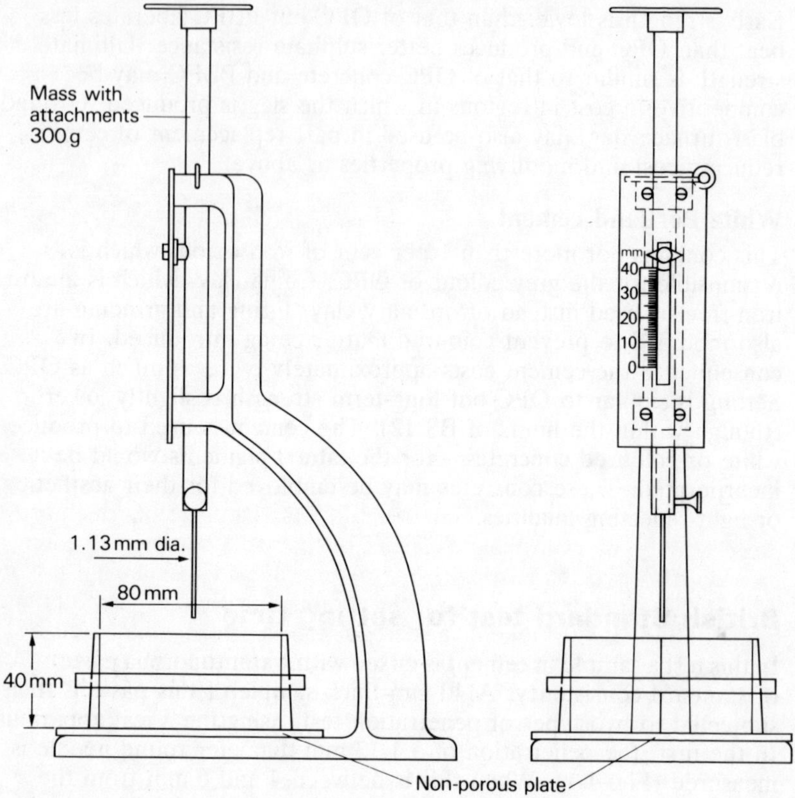

Mass with
attachments
300 g
mm
40
30
20
10
0
1.13 mm dia.
80 mm
40 mm
Non-porous plate

Fig. 1.1 Vicat apparatus fitted with initial set needle

1.13 mm dia.
3.3 mm
Air vent
6.4 mm
0.5 mm
0.5 mm
5 mm

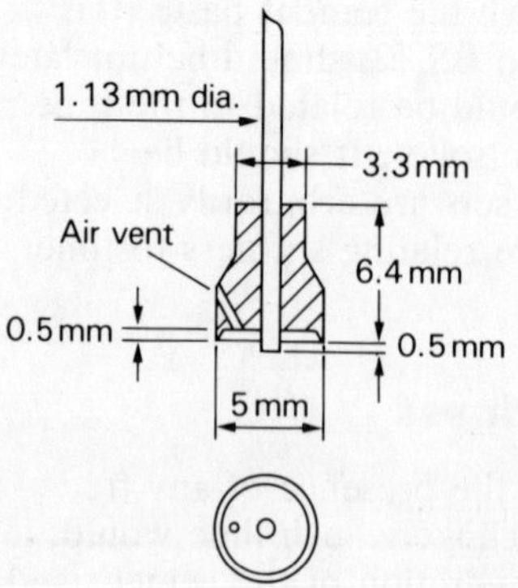

Fig. 1.2 Enlarged view of final set needle for Vicat test

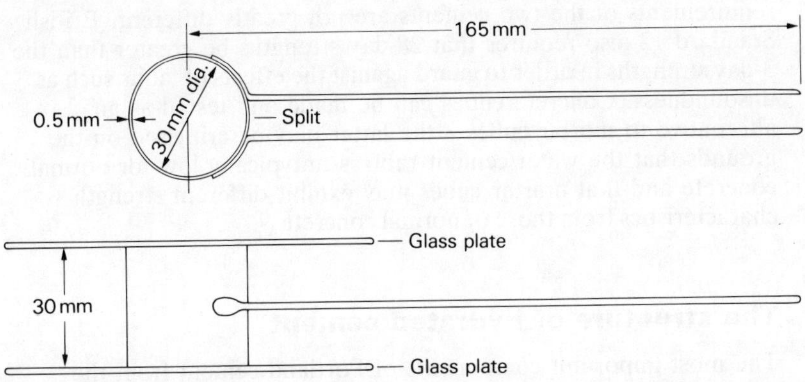

Fig. 1.3 Le Châtelier apparatus for measuring soundness of cement

takes some months to occur, an accelerated test is used to detect its presence. The Le Châtelier apparatus (Fig. 1.3) is used, consisting of a small brass cylinder containing a split, on each side of which are fixed long pointers to magnify any movement. A sample of cement mortar is allowed to harden in the apparatus and then boiled for one hour. The expansion is noted after cooling and should not be greater than 10 mm. If the cement fails to comply, a sample is aerated by exposure to air of humidity between 50 per cent and 80 per cent for 7 days. This causes slaking of any lime to which air has ready access. The expansion of the cement on repeating the soundness test should not exceed 5 mm.

British Standard test for mortar cubes

This test ensures satisfactory strength development of concrete; the average strength of groups of three 70.7 mm cubes being required to be not less than the values given in Table 1.2 for OPC and RHPC. The tests relate to 3 : 1 mixtures of Leighton Buzzard sand and the cement concerned, with a water/cement ratio of 0.4. Note that the 3-day strength compared to 28-day strength is greater in the case of RHPC (63%) than OPC (56%) and that the 28-day strength

Table 1.2 BS 12 requirements for the strength of 70.7 mm mortar cubes

Age	Strength requirement (N/mm²)	
	Ordinary Portland cement	Rapid-hardening Portland cement
3 days	23	29
28 days	41	46

requirements of the two cements are not greatly different. British Standard 12 also requires that 28-day strengths be greater than the 3-day strengths in order to guard against the effects of faults such as unsoundness. Concrete cubes can be made and tested as an alternative to mortar cubes – the latter may be criticised on the grounds that the water/cement ratio is untypically low for normal concrete and that mortar cubes may exhibit different strength characteristics from those of normal concrete.

The structure of hydrated cement

The most important components of Portland cement from the strength development point of view are C_2S and C_3S and on hydration they form the same compounds:

$$2\,(2CaOSiO_2) + 4\,H_2O \rightarrow 3\,CaO.2SiO_2.3H_2O + Ca(OH)_2$$
$$2\,(3CaOSiO_2) + 6\,H_2O \rightarrow 3\,CaO.2SiO_2.3H_2O + 3Ca(OH)_2$$

Calcium silicate hydrate — Calcium hydroxide

(Note that the full formulae for C_2S and C_3S have been given here to enable the equations to be balanced.)

However, it is the *physical* form of these compounds which is most important to an understanding of the behaviour of concrete. The calcium silicate hydrate forms extremely small fibrous, platey or tubular crystals, which can be regarded as a sort of rigid sponge, referred to as cement 'gel'. This gel must be saturated with water if hydration is to continue. The calcium hydroxide forms much larger platey crystals. These dissolve in water, providing hydroxyl (OH^-) ions, which are important for the protection of steel in concrete. As hydration proceeds, the two crystal types become more heavily interlocked, increasing the strength of the concrete.

Shrinkage and moisture movement

Shrinkage, or to use a fuller description *drying* shrinkage, is a contraction occurring when concrete is dried for the first time. This should be distinguished from subsequent movements resulting from moisture changes and referred to as 'moisture movement' because the initial shrinkage is partly irreversible and is much more likely to result in damage to the concrete than subsequent movements. Figure 1.4 gives a schematic representation of typical volume changes of concrete with time. During wet curing there is a slight expansion – indeed it should be noted that cement expands on hydration by over 100 per cent, filling at least part of the space previously occupied by

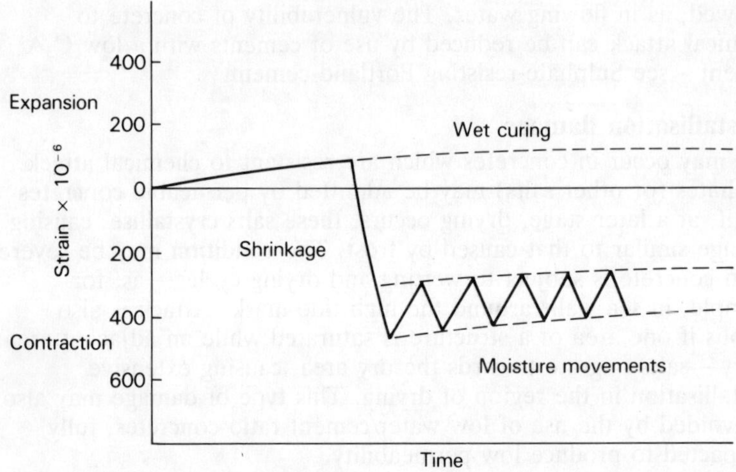

Fig. 1.4 Shrinkage and moisture movements in concrete

water. Shrinkage occurs when, on drying, water from within the cement' 'gel' is removed, causing gel surfaces to approach slightly. Hence the origin of shrinkage lies within the hydrated cement and it follows that rich, wet mixes, which contain more cement gel, shrink more. Long-term shrinkage strains vary from 200×10^{-6} for lean, low-workability mixes to over 700×10^{-6} for rich, wet concretes. Approximately 40 per cent of this movement is irreversible. Moisture movement does, however, occur on each subsequent wetting and drying, as water is admitted to and removed from the cement gel. Even the lower shrinkage value given above could cause tensile failure in the concrete if shrinkage is restrained or if differential shrinkage occurs between different parts of a structure. Hence it is important to cure concrete until it has some ability to withstand the strains occurring due to shrinkage.

Sulphate attack

This occurs when concrete is exposed to sulphates in solution. There are two mechanisms by which damage can be sustained

Chemical attack

Tricalcium aluminate (C_3A) reacts chemically with sulphates in solution to form calcium sulphoaluminate, expansion occurring during the reaction. Hence, where sulphates can penetrate the concrete, disruption may result, leading, ultimately, to failure. The problem is particularly severe where the source of sulphates can be renewed, as in flowing water. The vulnerability of concrete to chemical attack can be reduced by use of cements with a low C_3A content – see Sulphate-resisting Portland cement.

Crystallisation damage

This may occur in concretes which are resistant to chemical attack. Sulphates (or other salts) may be admitted by permeable concretes and if, at a later stage, drying occurs, these salts crystallise, causing damage similar to that caused by frost. The condition may be severe when concrete is subject to wetting and drying cycles – as, for example, in sea walls around the high tide mark. Attack is also serious if one area of a structure is saturated while an adjacent area is dry – salts migrate towards the dry area, causing extensive crystallisation in the region of drying. This type of damage may also be avoided by the use of low water/cement ratio concretes, fully compacted to produce low permeability.

Aggregates for concrete

Aggregates are used in concrete for the following reasons:

1. They greatly reduce cost.
2. They reduce the heat output per unit volume of concrete and hence reduce thermal stresses.
3. They reduce the shrinkage of the concrete.
4. They help produce a concrete with satisfactory plastic properties.

There may be other reasons for which 'special' aggregates would be employed; for example:

1. Low-density concretes to decrease foundation loads, increase thermal insulation and reduce thermal inertia (lightweight aggregates).
2. High-density concrete as required, for example, for radiation shielding (barytes – barium sulphate – or iron-based aggregates).
3. Abrasion-resistant concretes for floors (granite or carborundum aggregates).
4. Improved fire resistance (limestone, lightweight aggregates such as expanded pulverised fuel ash).

Maximum aggregate size

As a general rule, the maximum size of an aggregate should be as large as possible, since larger aggregates result in a lower fine aggregate requirement, hence a lower specific surface of the aggregate overall and consequently reduced water and cement requirements. The resulting concrete should therefore be more economical and exhibit lower shrinkage for a given strength. There are, of course, constraints on the maximum size that can be employed; first, the maximum aggregate size should not exceed approximately one-fifth of the minimum dimension in the structure, consideration also being given to spacings between reinforcing bars. Secondly, the aggregate size chosen will need to be a size that is readily available. The standard sizes, together with typical applications, are given in Table 1.3.

Table 1.3 British Standard maximum aggregate sizes with typical applications

Nominal max. size (mm)	Application
40	Mass concrete, road construction
20	General concrete work, including reinforced and prestressed concrete
10	Thin sections, screeds over 50 mm thickness
5	Screeds of 50 mm thickness or less

Aggregates which are largely retained on a 5 mm mesh sieve are described as coarse aggregates – these may comprise uncrushed gravels which result from the natural disintegration of rock or crushed stones and crushed gravels, produced by crushing hard stone and gravel respectively. Aggregates that largely pass a 5 mm sieve are referred to as fine aggregates. The latter may comprise natural sands – that is, sands resulting from natural disintegration of rock or crushed stone or crushed gravel sands.

Grading of aggregates

It is customary for aggregates for concrete to be *continuously graded* from their maximum size down to the size of the cement grains, since this ensures that all voids between larger particles are filled without an excess of fine material. (It will be recalled that an excess of fine material results in increased water and cement requirements, as explained under the heading of 'Maximum aggregate size'.) This effect is illustrated in Fig. 1.5.

Aggregates occurring in the form of natural gravels (uncrushed) and those obtained by crushing rock both have naturally continuous gradings, but to comply with BS 812 the gradings must be within certain limits. Gradings are determined by passing aggregates through a set of standard sieves, the particular sieves used depending on the maximum aggregate size (Experiment 1.1). The grading is then defined by the percentage of the total sample used which passes

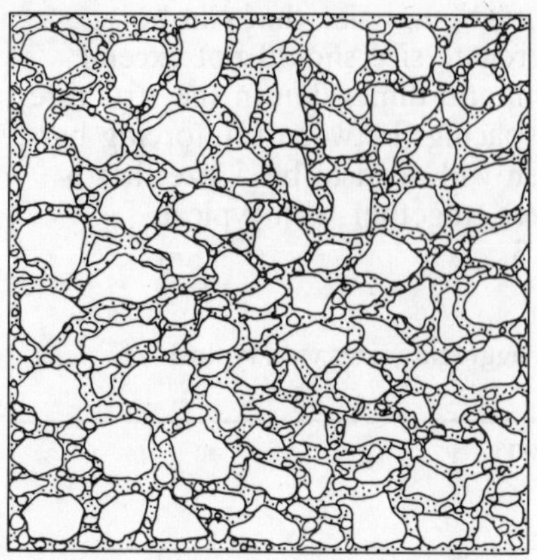

Fig. 1.5 Simple illustration of the use of graded aggregate in concrete. Spaces between larger particles are filled by progressively smaller particles

Table 1.4 Example of a sieve analysis for a fine aggregate for concrete

Sieve size mm/μm	**Mass retained (g)**	**Cumulative mass retained (g)**	**Mass passing (g)**	Percentage passing
10 mm	0	0	287	100
5	6	6	281	98
2.36	17	23	264	92
1.18	32	55	232	81
600 μm	48	103	184	64
300	81	184	83	29
150	86	270	17	6
passing 150	17	287	—	—

each sieve. Table 1.4 shows the sieve sizes used for fine aggregate, together with specimen results.

These are plotted in Fig. 1.6. Note that the sieve sizes are not plotted to a linear scale, successive sizes being spaced equally instead. Points are joined by straight lines. Figure 1.6 also includes the limits of zone 3 into which this particular fine aggregate fits. A rapid assessment as to which of the four zones a fine aggregate fits may be obtained by passing a sample through a 600 μm sieve, this being the only sieve in which there is no overlap between the zones. Figure 1.7 shows the four grading zones for fine aggregate, zone 1 being the coarsest and zone 4 the finest.

Coarse aggregates are not assigned 'zones', since the range of

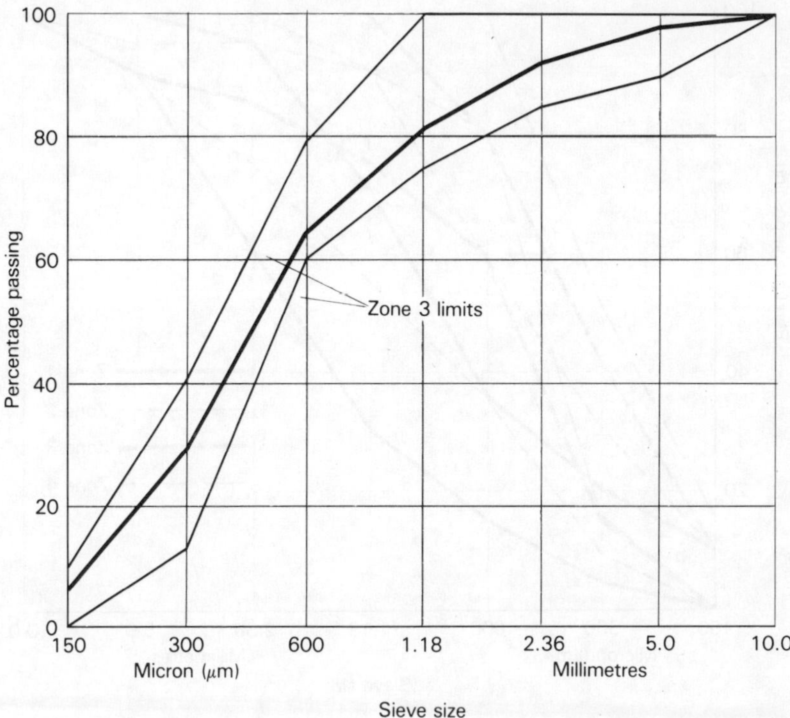

Fig. 1.6 Aggregate grading corresponding to sieve analysis results given in Table 1.4. The zone 3 grading envelope into which this aggregate fits is also indicated

particle sizes is, in general, smaller than that of fine aggregates. They should, however, fit into a BS grading envelope for that particular size and type.

Table 1.5 indicates that there are three ways in which a continuously-graded aggregate of maximum size 20 mm may be stockpiled and batched. The simplest method would be to have single stockpile of 20 mm 'all in' aggregate, sometimes referred to as 'ballast', since this material is relatively cheap and only a single quantity then needs to be batched. This method gives, however, only poor control over the distribution of particle sizes within each batch quantity – coarse particles are prone to separation from fine material, especially if stockpiling technique is poor. Successive batches of the resulting concrete would therefore tend to have variable water requirements for a given workability, depending on the fineness of individual batches of aggregate. While this method of batching is satisfactory for lightly stressed concrete – such as foundations and ground floor slabs in domestic dwellings – it would

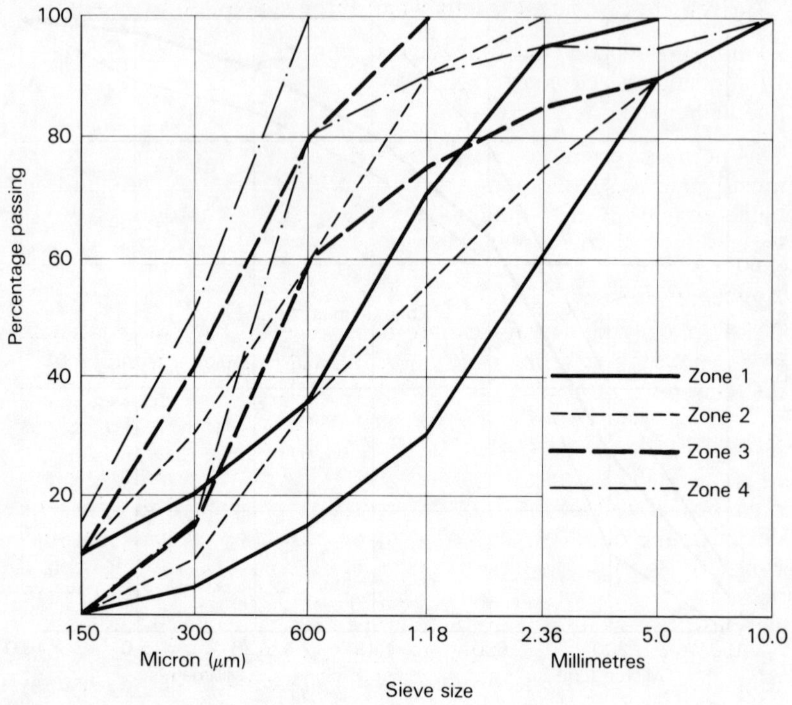

Fig. 1.7 Grading zones for fine aggregates for concrete

Table 1.5 Three alternative ways of batching graded aggregate of maximum size 20 mm

No. of Stockpiles	Aggregate size 20 mm	10 mm	5 mm	150 μm
1	20 mm 'all in' aggregate (ballast) ←→			
2	20 mm graded course aggregate ←→			fine aggregate ←→
3	20 mm single size coarse aggregate ←→	10 mm coarse aggregate ←→		fine aggregate ←→

not be recommended for structural quality concrete. The second alternative is to use '20 mm graded coarse aggregate' and fine aggregate, thereby ensuring that the ratio of quantities of aggregate of sizes above and below 5 mm is maintained accurately constant. This 'two stockpile' method is widely used in concrete production.

Even closer control results when three stockpiles are used:

20 mm single sized coarse aggregate;
10 mm single sized coarse aggregate;
fine aggregate.

This permits very close control over the coarser sizes which are most prone to segregation. The extra cost of material and additional batching may, in high-quality work, be offset by the reduced variability of the resultant concrete.

Aggregate density

Before classifying aggregates into density groups, it is necessary first to examine the meaning of the term 'density', since a number of differing definitions exist, according to context of use.

Relative and solid density

Most aggregates comprise a mass of solid material containing air pores which may or may not be accessible to water. The term which describes the density of the solid material itself is 'relative density' (formerly specific gravity), though several definitions are possible according to the way in which accessible pores are treated. Perhaps the most important of these is relative density in the 'saturated surface dry' (SSD) state – that is when all accessible pores are full of water but the aggregate surface is dry. This relative density usually forms the basis of mix design methods and is defined:

$$\begin{array}{l}\text{Relative density} \\ \text{(saturated surface dry)}\end{array} = \frac{\begin{array}{c}\text{Mass of given sample of SSD aggregate} \\ \text{particles, including absorbed water}\end{array}}{\begin{array}{c}\text{volume of water displaced} \\ \text{by saturated surface dry} \\ \text{sample}\end{array} \times \begin{array}{c}\text{density of} \\ \text{water}\end{array}}$$

Relative density could be defined in other ways – for example by taking the mass of *dry* aggregate with the same volume as given above. (This is referred to as the 'oven dry' relative density in BS 812.) However, in the case of most natural aggregates, void contents are small, so that differences between the various definitions of relative density are correspondingly small. The term 'solid density' will be taken to mean 1000 × relative density (say on a saturated surface dry basis).

Bulking and bulk density

When aggregates are loosely packed together or stockpiled, large volumes of air are trapped between particles – usually many times the volume of air present *within* particles. This is referred to as 'bulking' and for coarse aggregates it amounts to between 30 and 50 per cent of the total space occupied. The extent of bulking of fine aggregates depends very much on their moisture content; the void content of dry fine aggregate may be quite small – say 20 per cent; this can increase to 40 per cent when 5 to 10 per cent moisture is present, thereafter decreasing as further moisture tends to cause particles to consolidate. The bulking at intermediate moisture contents is the result of thin water films increasing friction between fine aggregate particles. The situation is illustrated in Fig. 1.8. (see experiment 1.2).

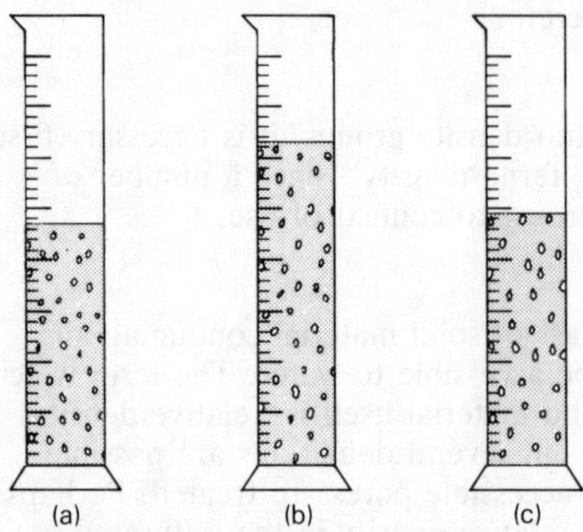

Fig. 1.8 Volume occupied by a given mass of fine aggregate when (a) dry (b) damp (c) wet

Bulking of aggregates produces uncertainty in the solid content of aggregates batched by volume and for this reason batching by weight (mass) is much preferred, except for concrete having only nominal performance requirements. Hence most concrete production equipment is geared to weight batching.

Low-, medium- and high-density aggregates

Most natural aggregates have solid densities within quite a narrow range of values – between 2400 and 2700 kg/m^3 (corresponding to relative densities between 2.4 and 2.7). These would result in concrete having densities normally in the range 2200 to 2500 kg/m^3 – slightly lower than the corresponding aggregate densities on account of the water content of the former.

Widely used now in the construction industry are lightweight aggregates, which comprise highly porous particles. Examples of synthetic lightweight aggregates are sintered pulverised fuel ash, expanded clay, blast furnace slag and expanded slate. Natural lightweight aggregates such as pumice may also be used. These can be used to produce concrete having densities of as low as 500 kg/m^3 (see 'Lightweight concretes').

There are certain situations in which high-density concretes are required – for example, for radiation shielding for nuclear reactor vessels. Such concretes are produced by use of high-density aggregates such as barytes (barium sulphate), relative density 4.1 magnetite (iron ore) relative density 4.5 or even metallic aggregates such as steel shot. The latter may have relative densities of over 7.0, resulting in concrete having over twice the normal density.

Silt and clay

These may be defined as mineral materials passing a 75 μm sieve (compare with to the smallest BS sieve size for fine aggregate – 150 μm). They are harmful to concrete if present in substantial amounts, since they increase the specific surface and hence the water requirement of a mix, resulting in lower strength unless cement content is also increased.

Fine aggregates are likely to contain more silt than coarse aggregates and BS 812 describes a field settling test, by means of which a rapid estimate of the silt/clay content of fine aggregate (other than crushed stone sands) can be made. The test involves shaking a measuring cylinder containing a mixture of 1 per cent salt solution and fine aggregate (experiment 1.3). The salt helps to separate the silt into a separate layer whose volume can be measured after allowing to stand for 3 hours (Fig. 1.9). If the amount is more than approximately 8 per cent by volume, separate tests are necessary to determine whether the silt and clay content *by weight* are in excess of BS 882 limit of 3 per cent for natural sand and crushed gravel sand.

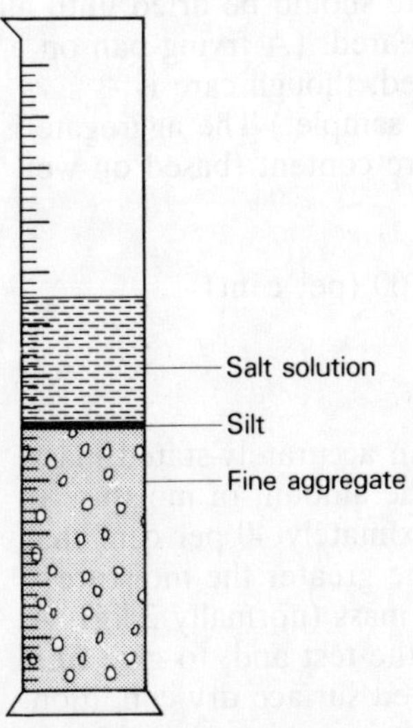

Fig. 1.9 Field settling test for detection of silt/clay in fine aggregate

Coarse aggregates can be checked for silt and clay by visual inspection. When in doubt, a decantation test (BS 812) should be used to ascertain whether the silt content is in excess of the BS 882 limit of 1 per cent by weight.

Moisture content

It is advisable, during quality concreting, to check moisture contents of aggregates prior to batching, so that accurate adjustment of batch weights can be made as necessary; batch quantities of aggregates must be increased if free water is present and the amount of free water in the aggregates should be deducted from the water to be added. (A further possibility, though this is not very common with natural aggregates in the UK, is that extra water may be required if aggregates are dry, such that they *absorb* water on wetting. The latter situation is quite common with lightweight aggregates which absorb substantial quantities of water.) Fine aggregates normally contain more water per unit weight than coarse aggregates, since there are more points of contact between particles.

The principles of three types of test are given below and in each case the aim will be to obtain the *free* water content of aggregates, since no adjustment is necessary in mixing water for moisture which is absorbed *within* aggregate particles.

Drying methods

In these a sample of the damp aggregate is carefully weighed (Mw) and then dried until it reaches a saturated surface dry condition. A suitable method is by hairdryer, fine aggregate being dried uniformly until it is just free-flowing. Coarse aggregate should be dried until all traces of surface moisture have just disappeared. (A frying pan on a gas or electric ring may alternatively be used, though care is necessary to ensure uniform heating of the sample.) The aggregate is then weighed again (Md). The free moisture content (based on wet weight) is then given by

$$\text{free moisture content (wet weight)} = \frac{M_w - M_d}{M_w} \times 100 \text{ (per cent)}$$

Siphon can (see experiment 1.4)

This relies on the fact that the volume of an accurately-stated mass of aggregate of given density depends on the amount of moisture in it, moisture having a density of only approximately 40 per cent that of most natural dense aggregates. Hence the greater the moisture content, the greater the volume of a given mass (normally 2 kg). A sample of dried aggregate is necessary for the test and, to give free water content, this should be in the saturated surface dry condition. Accurate weighing of dry and damp samples is necessary in this method, which is suitable for both coarse and fine aggregates.

Calcium carbide method (see experiment 1.5)

A rapid estimate of the moisture content of fine aggregate can be made by mixing a standard quantity of aggregate with an excess of calcium carbide in a pressure vessel. The latter reacts with moisture, producing a gas whose pressure is measured. The pressure scale is calibrated to read moisture content based on wet weight directly. This method would normally measure the *free* water contents of hard materials such as aggregate, since the calcium carbide cannot easily penetrate pores in the stones. The sample size for this test is normally very small so that careful sampling is necessary.

Correction for moisture content

A method of collection of batch quantities for a given volume of concrete will be illustrated by means of a worked example.

Determine the correct batch quantities for 1 cubic metre of concrete if the quantities based on saturated surface dry aggregates are:

Cement	310 kg
Fine aggregate	650 kg
Coarse aggregate	1190 kg
Water	180 litres

Moisture contents of fine and coarse aggregates are 4.5 per cent and 1.5 per cent respectively, based on wet weight.

Answer

The moisture in 650 kg of fine aggregate equals

$$\frac{4.5}{100} \times 650 = 29.25 \text{ kg}$$

Hence *add* this amount extra to the quantity of fine aggregate giving

650 + 29.25 = 679.25 (say 680) kg

as the correct batch mass of fine aggregate.

The moisture in 1190 kg of coarse aggregate equals

$$\frac{1.5}{100} \times 1190 = 17.85 \text{ kg}$$

Again this amount must be added to the quantity of coarse aggregate, giving

1190 + 17.85 = 1207.85 (say 1208) kg

as the correct batch mass of coarse aggregate. To obtain the correct batch quantity of water, the water contents above are subtracted from the given batch content:

180 − (29.25 + 17.85) = 132.9 (say 133) kg, or litres

It may be argued that the above method is inaccurate, since the extra material added to fine and coarse aggregates to compensate for their water content also contains water, which should be allowed for. Strictly speaking, this is the case but the errors in percentage terms are small enough to be ignored and the actual errors would normally be smaller than tolerances in batching equipment. The above method is given on account of its simplicity.

The design of concrete mixes

The object of mix design is, by systematic analysis of materials properties and knowledge of how they affect concrete properties, to produce, as economically as possible, batch quantities for a given volume of concrete such that the properties of both the fresh and hardened materials are as required for the specific purpose.

Consideration has already been given to properties of cements and aggregates and it is now necessary to identify the important properties of the concrete itself in the fresh and hardened states and to examine the effect of material types and proportions on them.

Two important terms – water/cement ratio and aggregate/cement ratio – are often used in the context of mix design and are therefore now defined:

$$\text{Water/cement ratio} = \frac{\text{Mass of water in a concrete sample}}{\text{Mass of concrete sample}}$$

Note that *free* water/cement ratio is generally regarded as most important since it is this ratio that affects strengthened durability. Free water/cement ratio would be based on the free water content of the mix – that is, water absorbed by the aggregates is disregarded

$$\text{Aggregate/cement ratio} = \frac{\text{Mass of aggregate in concrete sample}}{\text{Mass of cement in that sample}}$$

Properties of fresh concrete

Workability

This is the most important term relating to fresh (plastic) concrete. Workability may be defined as that property of the concrete which determines its ability to be placed, compacted and finished. Of these three operations, the greatest emphasis should be placed on compaction, since the consequences of inadequate compaction are serious. Workability may be measured by means of the slump test, compacting factor test and (V-B) test (BS 1881: Part 2), brief details of each now being given. For each test, it is essential that a representative sample of concrete be obtained. Details of how to obtain such samples are given in BS 1881 Part 1.

In the slump test (experiment 1.6), concrete is placed into a special inverted cone in four layers of equal height, each layer being compacted in a standard manner. On removing the cone the concrete, 'slumps', the slump being equal to the difference between the height of the cone and the highest point of the concrete (Fig. 1.10). When the concrete slumps evenly, a 'true' slump is said to occur. In less cohesive concretes, collapse may occur on an inclined shear plane, producing a 'shear' slump. A wet mix of low cohesion may result in a 'collapse' slump. Slumps may vary from zero for dry concrete mixes, through 50 to 75 mm for medium workability concretes to 150 mm or more for wet or harsh mixes. The slump test does not give an absolute indication of workability – it measures 'consistence'. However this correlates well with workability for a given type of concrete and the test is widely used as an on-site check. The slump test is not suited to dry mixes, since it is not sensitive to small water content changes in such mixes.

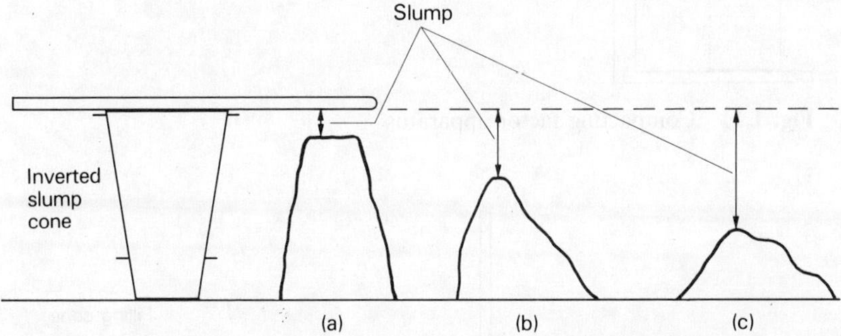

Fig. 1.10 Method of measuring slump in slump test together with types of slump (a) true slump (b) shear slump (c) collapse slump

In the compacting factor test (experiment 1.7) concrete is gently loaded into a hopper (Fig. 1.11) and then allowed to fall vertically, first into a similar lower hopper and then into a cylinder, producing a given degree of compaction by gravity. The concrete in the cylinder is struck off level and then weighed. The cylinder is then emptied and refilled, this time fully compacting the concrete. The ratio

$$\frac{\text{Mass of partially compacted concrete}}{\text{Mass of fully compacted concrete}}$$

is known as 'the compacting factor'. The value will approach unity for very wet mixes (for which the test is not suitable) and may be as low as 0.65 for very dry mixes.

The third test, the V-B test (experiment 1.8) utilises a slump

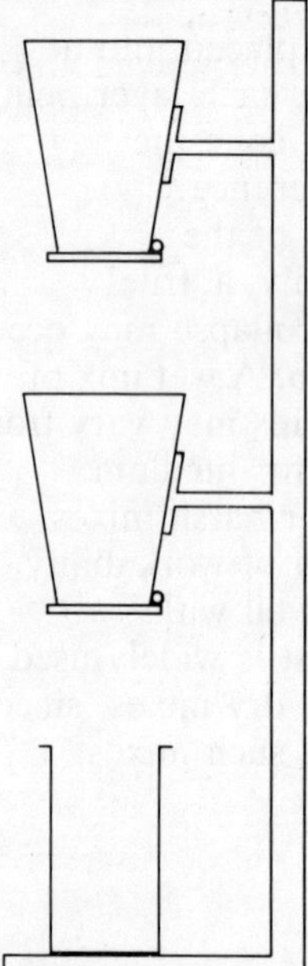

Fig. 1.11 Compacting factor apparatus

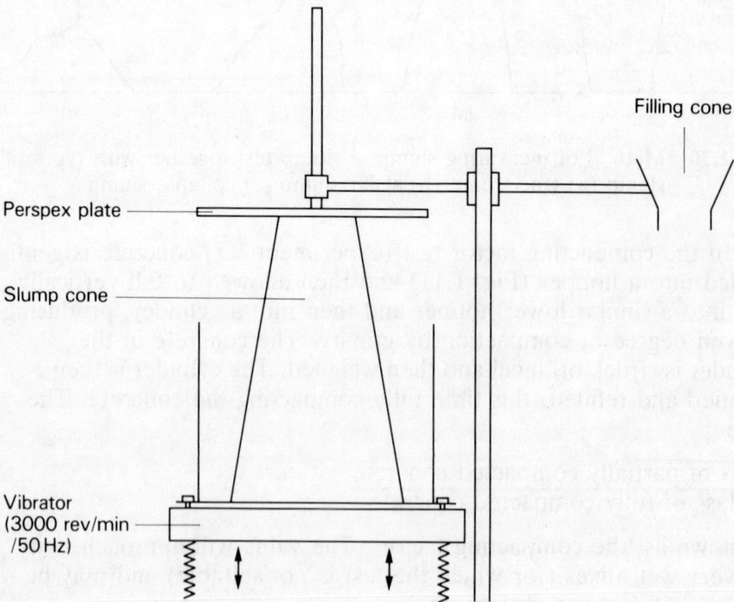

Fig. 1.12 V-B consistometer

cone in a cylindrical container fixed to a small vibrating table (Fig. 1.12). A slump test is first carried out and then a perspex disc attached to a vertical guide is allowed to rest gently on the concrete. The table is made to vibrate and the time taken for the underside of the perspex disc to become completely covered with concrete is measured in seconds. This is then the workability of the concrete in 'V-B degrees'. The time may vary from a few seconds for wet concretes (for which the test is not suitable) to over 20 seconds for dry concrete mixes.

Comments on workability tests

From the descriptions of the three tests given above, it will be evident that the slump test is the most suitable test for the measurement of medium to high workabilities. This test has the added advantage that the equipment needed is simple, portable and does not require an electricity supply.

The compacting factor test is sensitive to medium and low workabilities, though its use is not included in the current DoE design document 'Design of normal concrete mixes' since 'it is not possible to establish consistent relationships between it and the slump or V-B tests.' The compacting factor test may nevertheless be useful as a control test.

The V-B test has the disadvantage of requiring mains electricity, though it is very sensitive to changes in the water content of drier mixes, this providing the main basis of use.

Workability Requirements

The workability of concrete for a given situation should be the minimum value which will ensure adequate compaction with the plant available, due consideration being given to difficulties which may arise resulting from problems of access, congested reinforcement and so on. Table 1.6 gives the main workability categories and applications.

Factors affecting workability

The chief factor affecting workability is water content (usually expressed as volume in litres per cubic metre of concrete). For a given aggregate size and type workability is highly sensitive to changes of water content – for example, in the case of 20 mm irregular aggregate, a water content of 160 litres per cubic metre would result in low workability, while a water content of 190 litres would result in high workability.

Also affecting workability are maximum aggregate size and shape. Since a smaller maximum aggregate size results in a higher specific surface (surface area per unit mass) of the mix overall, more water is required to 'wet' the larger surface areas involved. For a given aggregate type, decreasing the maximum size from 20 mm to

Table 1.6 Workability categories and applications

Workability category	Slump (mm)	Compacting factor	V-B time	Applications
Extremely low	0	0.65–0.7	Over 20	Lean mix concrete for roads (compacted by vibrating roller) Precast paving slabs
Very low	0–10	0.7–0.75	12–20	Roads compacted by power-operated machines
Low	10–30	0.75–0.85	6–12	High quality structural concrete mass concrete compacted by vibration
Medium	30–60	0.85–0.95	3–6	Normal purposes – reinforced concrete compacted by vibrating poker or manually
High	60–180	0.95–1.0	0–3	Areas with congested reinforcement, concrete for placing under water

10 mm would increase the water requirement by approximately 10 per cent. Increasing the maximum aggregate size from 20 mm to 40 mm would naturally have the reverse effect. Crushed (angular) aggregates similarly result in a larger specific surface than uncrushed (irregular) aggregates and therefore increase the water requirement by 15 to 20 per cent. Aggregates having coarse surface textures will also increase water requirements, though it should perhaps be added that, for high-strength concrete, angular shapes combined with a rough surface texture allow fuller exploitation of the strength properties of strong, hard aggregates.

It is not considered appropriate to use the terms 'water/cement ratio' and 'aggregate/cement ratio' in the context of workability, though it may be stated that:

(a) if the water content of a mix is increased, other quantities remaining constant, both water/cement ratio and workability would increase – hence an indirect relationship exists between water/cement ratio and workability;
(b) if the water content of a mix is increased, keeping water/cement ratio constant, more cement and hence less aggregate would be present in a given volume. Hence, increasing the water in this way would increase the workability and decrease the aggregate/cement ratio and, again, an indirect relationship is seen to exist between aggregate/cement ratio and workability.

Cohesion

Though, perhaps, not of such critical importance as workability, the choice of concrete of correct cohesion is an essential part of the design process. Cohesion (or cohesiveness) may be defined as the ability of the fresh concrete to resist segregation, though a cohesive concrete will also be easier to finish than a relatively harsh mix. The cohesion of a concrete mix is provided by the fine material content – that is, the finer fractions of fine aggregate and the cement. It follows that richer mixes which have a higher cement content will, in general, have a reduced fine aggregate requirement and this is obtained when concrete is designed by the DoE method of mix design. It should, perhaps, also be stated that cohesion should be the minimum required for the purpose, since if, in common with workability, cohesion is higher than necessary, the water content of the mix will also be unnecessarily high, leading to the disadvantages described earlier.

Properties of hardened concrete

Strength

This is normally considered to be the most important property in relation to mature concrete. In the UK, 'strength' most commonly means compressive strength as measured by cubes manufactured, cured and tested according to BS 1881 (see experiment 1.9). The strength of concrete is affected by the following aspects of mix materials and proportions:

1. *Free water/cement ratio*. As the quantity of free water in a mix increases in relation to the quantity of cement, the density and, consequently, the strength of the concrete decrease. At very low water/cement ratios (e.g. below 0.4) a significant part of the cement never hydrates, due to inadequate space and/or

inadequate water. Since unhydrated cement is of high strength, the resulting product will also be of high strength, provided full compaction is achieved. As water/cement ratios increase above about 0.4, the cement is unable to expand sufficiently to occupy the space previously filled by water. Hence porosity increases and strength decreases. Figure 1.13 shows how the compressive strength of concrete of various ages is related to free water/cement ratio when OPC and RHPC are used. Note that there is a smooth, continuous relationship between strength and water/cement ratio throughout the range.

2. *Aggregate properties*. Crushed aggregates generally result in higher strength than uncrushed aggregates, since they form a better key with the hydrated cement. To obtain very high strength concretes, the use of crushed aggregates may be essential.
3. *Cement type*. Where high early strength is required, the use of rapid-hardening Portland cement may be considered.

Durability

The durability of normal concrete depends mainly on the permeability, and hence the porosity, of the hydrated cement. Hence the arguments are similar to those given under strength, low water/cement ratios resulting in greatest durability. To illustrate this, free water/cement ratios of 0.4, 0.6 and 0.8 would result in very good, moderate and low durability respectively in concrete subject to average exposure. It is not always easy to measure free water/cement ratio during concrete production, so that durability is sometimes specified alternatively by means of minimum cement content on the basis that, for a given workability, the water content would be approximately constant; hence, by specifying cement, one is effectively specifying a water/cement ratio. Another way of specifying durability indirectly is by specifying strength.

Department of Environment method of mix design

The description given here is intended to illustrate the principles of the method; the student would be well advised to carry out a number of design examples in order to become familiar with the detailed procedure. The DoE publication also includes information necessary to design concretes for indirect tensile strength and concretes containing entrained air. These are not given here, since they are easily followed by reference to the DoE publication once the basic method of design is understood.

The method is divided into sections, which will be taken in turn. (The section numbers refer to the sections in the standard mix

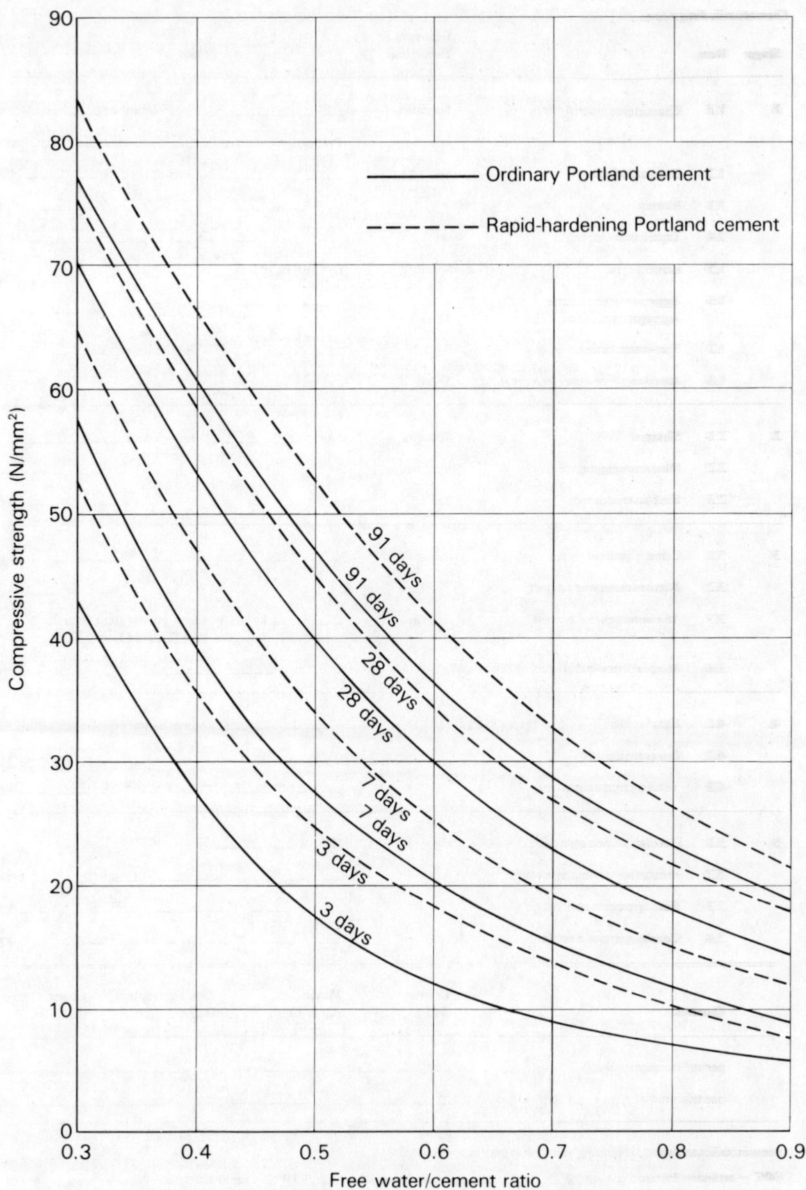

Fig. 1.13 The relationship between the compressive strength of concrete and free water/cement ratio (uncrushed aggregates). Based on DoE method of mix design (Crown copyright material from the Building Establishment 'Design of normal concrete mixes' by permission of the Controller, HMSO)

Concrete mix design form

Stage	Item		Reference or calculation	Values
1	1.1	Characteristic strength	Specified	______ N/mm² at ______ days Proportion defective ______ per cent
	1.2	Standard deviation	Fig. 1.15	______ N/mm² or no data ______ N/mm²
	1.3	Margin		(k = ______) ______ × ______ = ______ N/mm²
	1.4	Target mean strength		______ + ______ = ______ N/mm²
	1.5	Cement type	Specified	OPC/SRPC/RHPC
	1.6	Aggregate type: coarse Aggregate type: fine	Table 1.8	______ ______
	1.7	Free-water/cement ratio	Fig 1.16	______ } Use the lower value
	1.8	*Maximum free-water/cement ratio*	*Specified*	______ }
2	2.1	Slump or V-B	Specified	Slump ______ mm or V-B ______ s
	2.2	Maximum aggregate size	Specified	______ mm
	2.3	Free-water content	Table 1.9	______ kg/m³
3	3.1	Cement content		______ ÷ ______ = ______ kg/m³
	3.2	*Maximum cement content*	*Specified*	______ kg/m³
	3.3	*Minimum cement content*	*Specified*	______ kg/m³ — Use if greater than Item 3.1 and calculate Item 3.4
	3.4	Modified free-water/cement ratio		______
4	4.1	Relative density of aggregate (SSD)	Fig 1.17	______ known/assumed
	4.2	Concrete density		______ kg/m³
	4.3	Total aggregate content		______ − ______ − ______ = ______ kg/m³
5	5.1	Grading of fine aggregate	Fig 1.18	Zone ______
	5.2	Proportion of fine aggregate		______ per cent
	5.3	Fine aggregate content	}	______ × ______ = ______ kg/m³
	5.4	Coarse aggregate content	}	______ − ______ = ______ kg/m³

Quantities	Cement (kg)	Water (kg or l)	Fine aggregate (kg)	Coarse aggregate (kg)
per m³ (to nearest 5 kg)	______	______	______	______
per trial mix of ______ m³	______	______	______	______

Items in italics are optional limiting values that may be specified.

OPC = ordinary Portland cement; SRPC = sulphate-resisting Portland cement; RHPC = rapid-hardening Portland cement.

Fig. 1.14 Concrete mix design form

design form, Fig. 1.14. A worked example is described at the end of the method.) Subsection numbers in Fig. 1.14 are given in the margin.

Section 1. Strength considerations

1.1 Before describing the method of designing for strength, it is necessary to understand the meaning of the term 'characteristic strength' (f_c), which is normally used in strength specifications. Concrete, in common with other materials, is inherently variable, due to within-batch variations of materials, between-batch variations, tolerances and possibly errors in batching, mixing, compaction, testing and so on. Hence, statistical terminology must be used and the term 'characteristic strength' implies a strength with a permissible percentage of failures. For example, a characteristic 28-day compressive strength of 20 N/mm^2 with 5 per cent failures would imply that 95 per cent of results need to be at or higher than the strength level of 20 N/mm^2. The first step in mix design is to obtain a *target mean strength* f_m, which is the mean strength that would be required for the stated characteristic strength, f_c. Clearly the target mean strength will need to be higher than the characteristic strength, since *half* of the results would be expected to fall below the former. The increment which must be added to characteristic strength to obtain target mean strength depends on two factors:

(a) The percentage failures allowable. If, for example, only 1 per cent failures were permitted at a stated characteristic strength, the target mean strength would need to be higher than if 5 per cent failures were allowed. These percentage failure rates are taken account of by '*k*' factors. Table 1.7 gives common values.

1.2 (b) The variability of the concrete. If, due to say poor quality control, the concrete is more variable, an

Table 1.7 k factors used in statistical control

Percent failures	K
16	1.00
10	1.28
5	1.64
2	2.05
1	2.33

extra margin will need to be built into the design to compensate. The variability of concrete strength is represented by its standard deviation (s), which will be defined later. To allow for concrete variability, the s value should be known and this, of course, requires that some cube test results be available (usually at least 40 for the s value to be reliable). Where concrete production is starting for the first time or a new type of mix is to be used, standard deviations cannot be known, since no results will be available; hence in these circumstances an 's' value must be assumed and this is taken to be relatively high in order to 'play safe'. Figure 1.15 gives initial values suggested by the DoE method (graph A), together with minimum s values (graph B) in order to guard against the dangers of taking too small a value of s, once results are available. Note that, to some extent, s values reduce as characteristic strength decreases, since the variability of weaker concrete would be expected to reduce (negative strengths are impossible).

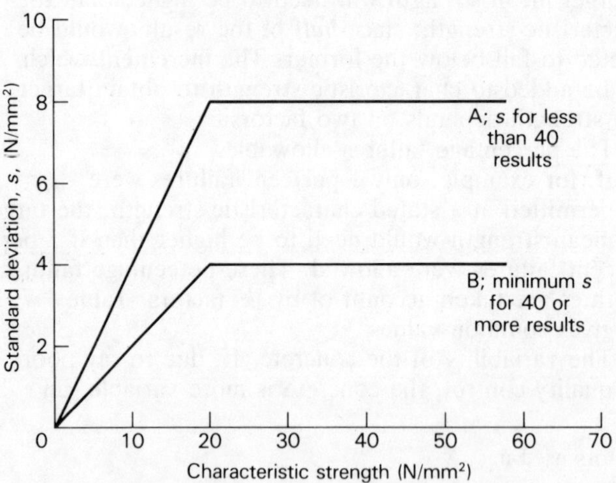

Fig. 1.15 DoE method of mix design: suggested standard deviations as a function of characteristic strength

1.3 The increment to be added to the characteristic strength f_c is the product of the two terms described – k factor and standard deviation s. Hence

1.4 $f_m = f_c + ks$

(target mean strength) f_m = (characteristic strength) f_c + ks

The product ks is often referred to as the current margin.

1.5; 1.6 It has already been explained that the strength of concrete is affected by free water/cement ratio, aggregate type and cement type (as well as age). Hence, the remaining part of this section involves determining the free water/cement ratio.

1.7 First, the strength appropriate to a free water/cement ratio of 0.5 and the materials specified is obtained from Table 1.8. This strength is then located on the graph of Fig. 1.16, using the 0.5 water/cement ratio starting line. Note that, since curves in this figure are separated by strength increments of 5 N/mm^2 or 10 N/mm^2 at the 0.5 free water/cement ratio line, they will not generally correspond exactly to strengths given in Table 1.8. To find the free water/cement ratio corresponding to the *required* target mean strength, move *parallel* to the nearest two lines on Fig. 1.16 (unless the strength located happens to fall on a line) from the point located towards higher or lower strength, as required, until the required target mean strength is obtained (reading horizontally). At this point, the correct free water/cement ratio is obtained by reading *vertically downwards*. Since this procedure may require some practice, it is worth checking the result for accuracy.

Table 1.8 Approximate compressive strengths (N/mm^2) of concrete mixes made with a free-water/cement ratio of 0.5

Type of cement	Type of coarse aggregate	Compressive strengths (N/mm^2) Age (days) 3	7	28	91
Ordinary Portland (OPC) or sulphate-resisting Portland (SRPC)	Uncrushed	18	27	40	48
	Crushed	23	33	47	55
Rapid-hardening Portland (RHPC)	Uncrushed	25	34	46	53
	Crushed	30	40	53	60

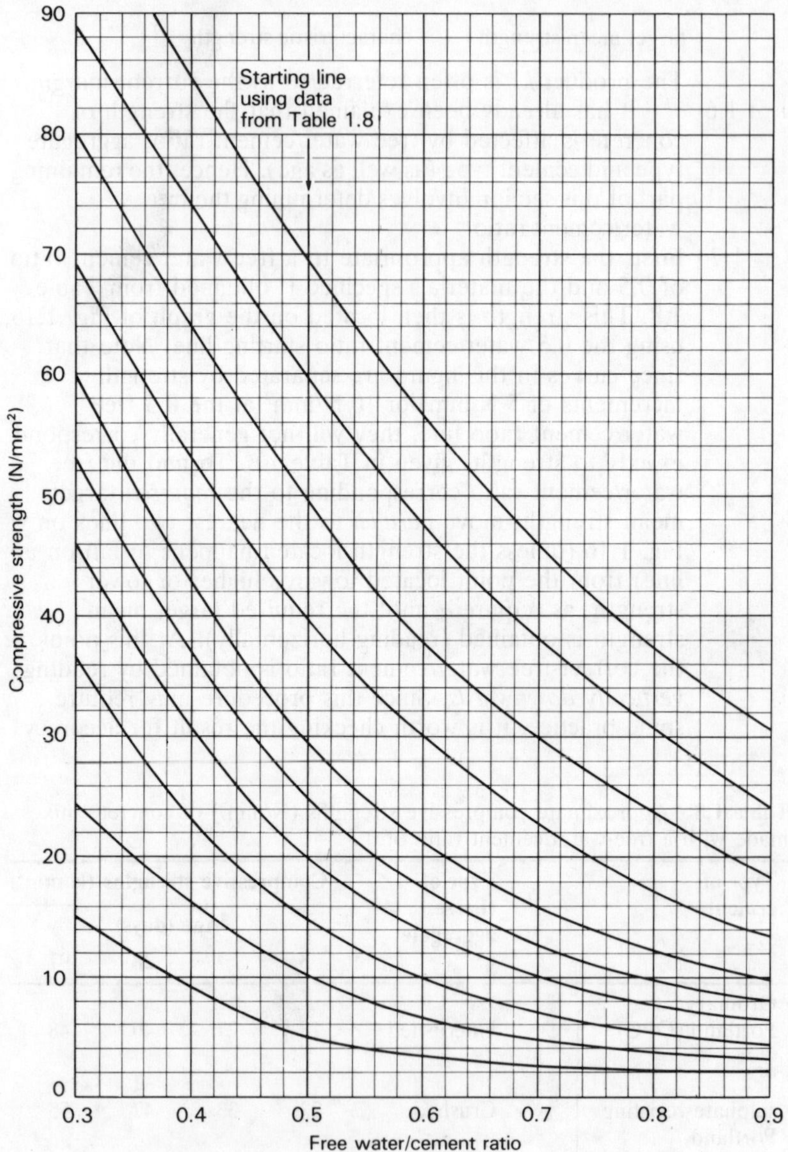

Fig. 1.16 DoE method of mix design: relationship between compressive strength and free water/cement ratio

The water/cement ratio obtained should be checked against any maximum value required for durability and the lower of the two values taken.

Section 2. Workability

2.1 Workability is specified by the slump or V-B time of the fresh concrete.

2.2 From the value required and the aggregate shape and size, the water content per cubic metre of concrete is obtained. (Table 1.9)

Table 1.9 Approximate free-water contents (kg/m³) required to give various levels of workability

Slump (mm) **V-B(s)**		**0–10** **>12**	**10–30** **6–12**	**30–60** **3–6**	**60–180** **0–3**
Maximum size of aggregate (mm)	Type of aggregate				
10	Uncrushed	150	180	205	225
	Crushed	180	205	230	250
20	Uncrushed	135	160	180	195
	Crushed	170	190	210	225
40	Uncrushed	115	140	160	175
	Crushed	155	175	190	205

Section 3. Cement content

3.1 It will be evident that, since free water/cement ratio and water content per cubic metre are now known and

$$\text{Cement content per cubic metre} = \frac{\text{Water content per cubic metre}}{\text{Free water/cement ratio}}$$

the cement content is easily calculated.

3.2 A maximum cement content may be specified (say to limit heat of hydration) in which case the cement content from 3.1 will need to be checked that it is not in excess of this value.

3.3 Similarly, a minimum cement content may be specified (say for durability), so the figure from 3.1 must be in excess of any such value. If it is not, the value specified must be used and the modified free water/cement ratio calculated.

Section 4. Fresh concrete density

This is important as a part of the design process because it affects the yield of the concrete. The DoE method uses a graphical technique for calculating fresh density; an alternative means is given after this explanation of the DoE method.

4.1 If the relative density of the aggregate (usually based on the saturated surface dry, SSD, condition) and the relative density of the cement is assumed, then the fresh concrete density can be related to the water content of the mix, as in Fig. 1.17

4.3 The aggregate content per cubic metre of concrete is then

Fresh density − (cement content + water content)

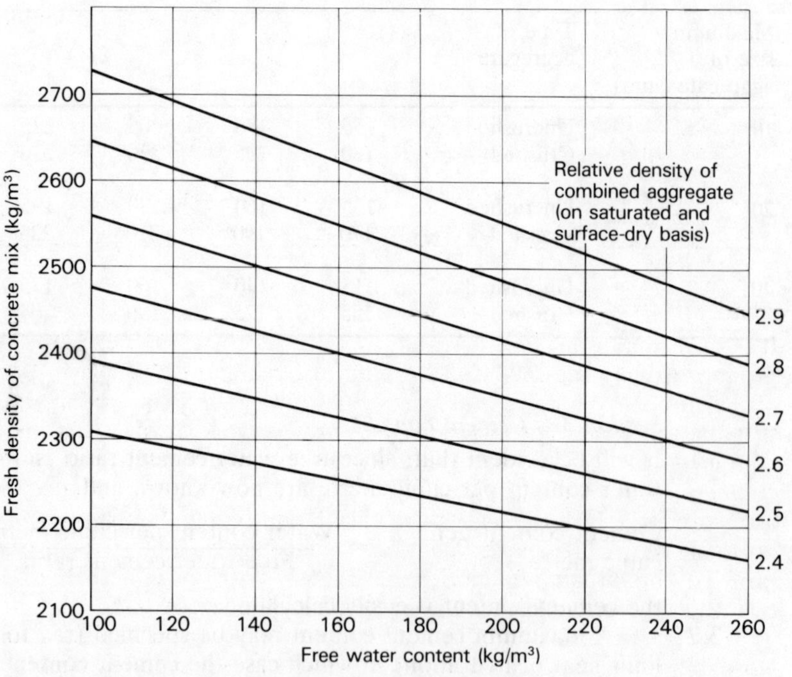

Fig. 1.17 Estimated fresh density of concrete

Section 5. Proportion of fine aggregate

5.1, 5.2 The proportion of fine aggregate to total aggregate depends on the grading zone of the fine aggregate, on the maximum aggregate size, the workability and the free water/cement ratio. (Smaller maximum aggregate size, higher workability and higher water/cement ratio each increases the fine aggregate requirement.) The DoE method gives a band of percentages for each case and the percentage corresponding to the centre of each band would normally be used, unless high cohesion (use higher percentage) or low cohesion (use lower percentage) are required (Fig. 1.18). Note that there are 12 sets of graphs in Fig. 1.18 – it is important to use the one appropriate to the aggregate size and workability chosen.

5.3 Fine aggregate content = percentage of fine aggregate × total aggregate content

5.4 Finally, the coarse aggregate content is found by subtraction of fine aggregate from total aggregate.

Worked example

Produce batch quantities for 1 m^3 of concrete to have a slump of 30 to 60 mm and characteristic 28-day compressive strength of 25 N/mm^2 (5% failures permitted). No previous results are available. The following materials are to be used:

Cement	Ordinary Portland
Fine aggregate	Crushed, zone 3, relative density 2.7
Coarse aggregate	Crushed, max. size 20 mm, relative density 2.7

This example has been worked on the standard design form in Fig. 1.19.

Trial mixes

It is most important to appreciate that no design method can produce exactly the right combination of fresh and hardened properties every time; a trial mix should always be made to ensure that the properties are as required with the particular materials and equipment used. The figures used in the design are based on 1 m^3 of concrete, which would be excessively large for a trial mix. Hence the form of Fig. 1.14 provides for the calculation of what would normally be smaller batch quantities, for example 50 litres for a trial mix. To obtain batch quantities for 50 litres (0.05 m^3), the batch quantities for one cubic metre would be multiplied by 0.05.

Concrete which is produced by the trial mix would be tested for workability and fresh density and cubes would be made to check strength. If (a) workability or (b) strength are slightly in error, corrections can be made as follows:

(a) The correct water content for workability can often be judged by experience. If, for instance, in the worked example given, the actual water per cubic metre is found to be 220 kg/m^3, the cement content must be increased to keep the water/cement ratio and hence the strength constant. Hence the new cement content would be

(continued on page 40)

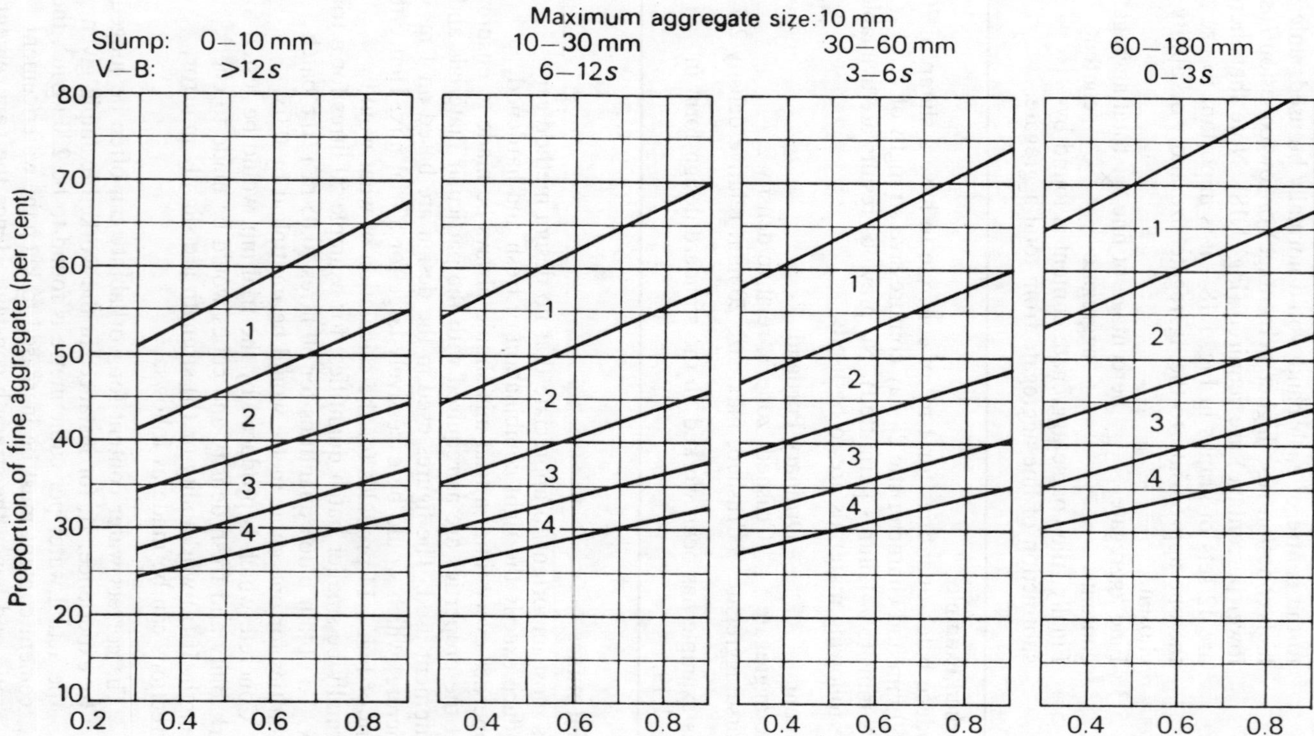

Fig. 1.18 Proportion of fine aggregate as function of grading zone of fine aggregate

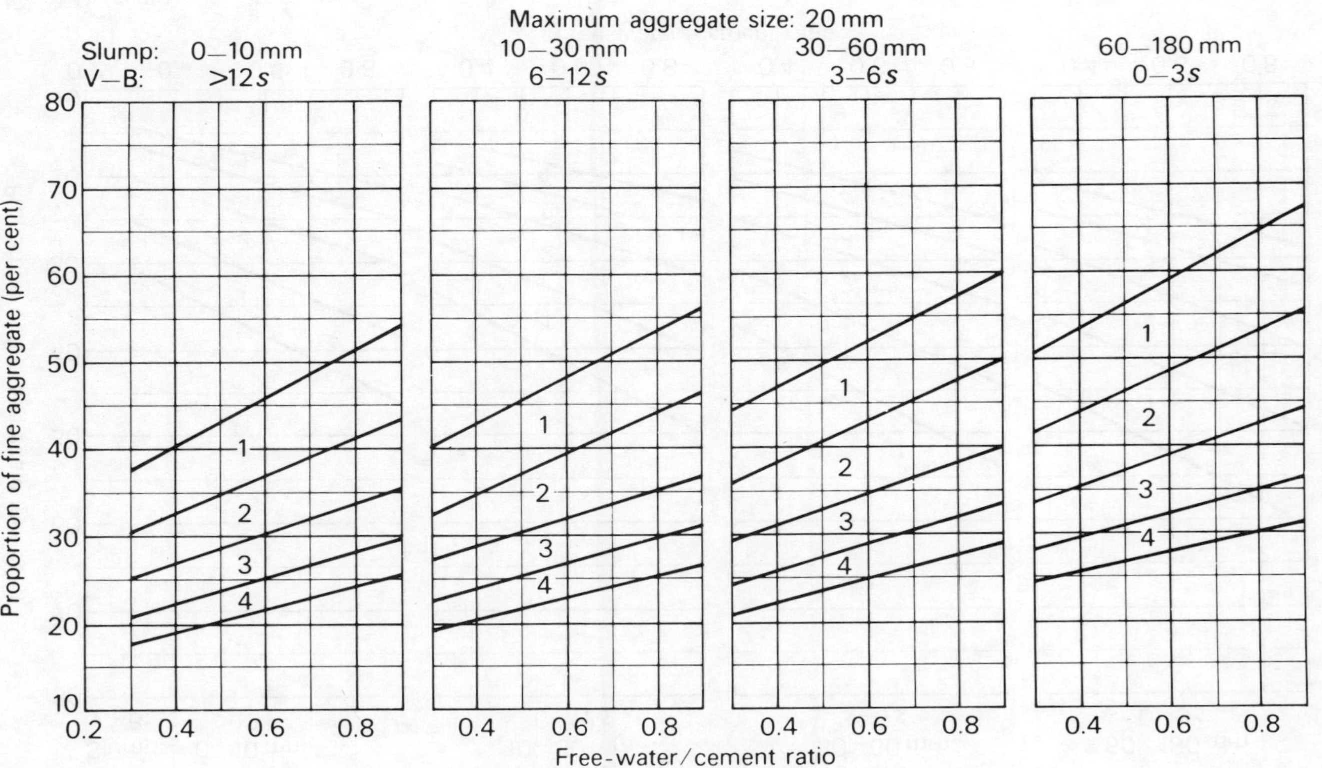

Fig. 1.18 (contd)

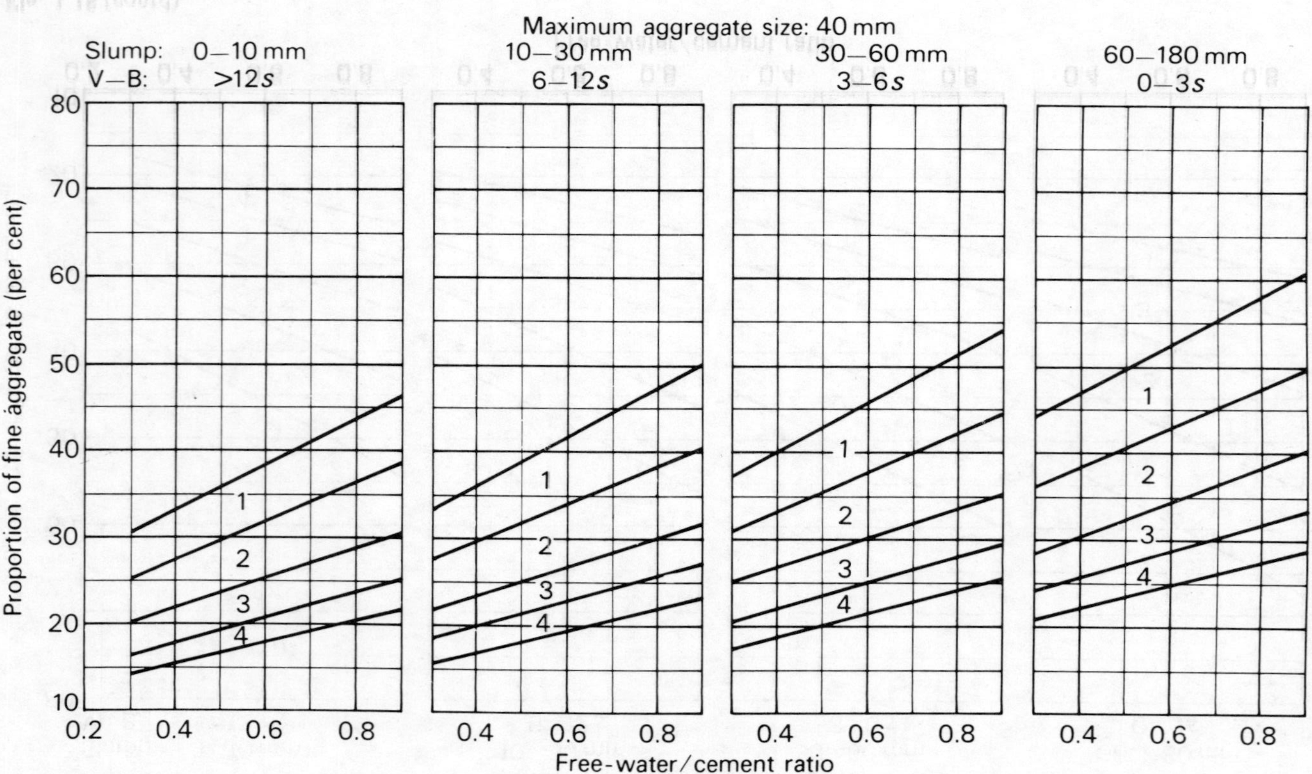

Fig. 1.18 (contd)

Concrete mix design form (WORKED EXAMPLE)

Stage	Item		Reference or calculation	Values
1	1.1	Characteristic strength	Specified	25 N/mm² at 28 days; Proportion defective 5 per cent
	1.2	Standard deviation	Fig 1.15	N/mm² or no data 8 N/mm²
	1.3	Margin		(k = 1.64) 1.64 × 8 = 13 N/mm²
	1.4	Target mean strength		25 + 13 = 38 N/mm²
	1.5	Cement type	Specified	OPC/~~SRPC~~/~~RHPC~~
	1.6	Aggregate type: coarse Aggregate type: fine		Crushed Crushed
	1.7	Free-water/cement ratio	Table 1.8 Fig 1.16	0.57 — Use the lower value
	1.8	*Maximum free-water/cement ratio*	*Specified*	—
2	2.1	Slump or V-B	Specified	Slump 30-60 mm or V-B —
	2.2	Maximum aggregate size	Specified	20
	2.3	Free-water content	Table 1.9	210
3	3.1	Cement content		210 ÷ 0.57 = 368
	3.2	*Maximum cement content*	*Specified*	—
	3.3	*Minimum cement content*	*Specified*	— kg/m³ — Use if greater than Item 3. and calculate Item 3.4
	3.4	Modified free-water/cement ratio		—
4	4.1	Relative density of aggregate (SSD)		2.7 known/~~assumed~~
	4.2	Concrete density	Fig 1.17	24
	4.3	Total aggregate content		2400 − 210 − 368 = 182
5	5.1	Grading of fine aggregate		Zone 3
	5.2	Proportion of fine aggregate	Fig 1.18	28-34 say 3
	5.3	Fine aggregate content		31% × 1822 = 5
	5.4	Coarse aggregate content		1822 − 565 = 1

Quantities	Cement (kg)	Water (kg or l)	Fine aggregate (kg)
per m³ (to nearest 5 kg)	370	210	565
per trial mix of ______ m³			

Items in italics are optional limiting values that may be specified.
OPC = ordinary Portland cement; SRPC = sulphate-resisting Portland cement; RHPC = rapid-hardening Portlar

Fig. 1.19 Concrete mix design form (worked example)

$$\frac{220}{0.57} = 386 \text{ kg}$$

The fresh density (if not measured) would also be expected to reduce slightly – Fig. 1.17 indicates that the correct value would be approx. 2390 kg/m³. The new total aggregate content is therefore

$$2390 - (220 + 386) = 1784 \text{ kg}$$

The fine aggregate would be found as previously.

(b) The point on Fig. 1.16 corresponding to the strength *obtained* and the water/cement ratio used should be located. Then proceed parallel to the curved lines until the desired strength is obtained and read the new water/cement ratio. If, for instance in the worked example, a strength of 35 N/mm² was obtained instead of 38 N/mm², find the point corresponding to 35 N/mm² and 0.57 water/cement ratio. Moving upwards parallel to the curved lines and then reading vertically produces a water/cement ratio of 0.54. The remaining mix details are now recalculated.

Where both workability and strength are incorrect, then both a new water content and new water/cement ratio would be obtained and then the method completed as before.

Second trial mixes should only be necessary where substantial errors are involved, though a final full-scale trial mix is advisable before going into production. Adjustments for moisture in aggregates are, of course, essential if trial mixes are to fulfil their function.

Calculation of concrete fresh density

It is only from an accurate knowledge of concrete density that batch masses of cement and aggregates for a given volume of concrete can be reliably predicted. The following technique is therefore given and serves as an alternative to the method used in the DoE method of mix design.

Suppose, for example, 400 m³ of concrete are to be produced to the specification given on page 39. The batch quantities per cubic metre are:

Water 210 litres; Cement 368 kg; Fine aggregate 565 kg; Coarse aggregate 1257 kg.

The relative density of cement is required and this is assumed to be 3.15.

The figures are tabulated as in Table 1.10 and, to simplify them, all figures are divided by the mass of cement, giving masses which would correspond to 1 kg of cement.

The volumes of each component in *litres* are easily obtained by dividing the reduced *mass* of the component by its *relative density*.

Table 1.10 Illustrating the method for calculating fresh concrete density

Material	Water	Cement	Fine aggregate	Coarse aggregate	Total
Mass (kg)	210	368	565	1257	2400
Mass ratio (per kg cement)	0.571	1	1535	3.416	6.522
Rel. density (SSD)	1.00	3.15	2.70	2.70	
Volume (litres)	0.571	0.317	0.569	1.265	2.722

$$\text{Then concrete density} = \frac{\text{total mass}}{\text{total volume}}$$

$$= \frac{6.522}{2.722} \text{ kg/litre}$$

$$= 2.396 \text{ kg/litre}$$

$$\text{or, to nearest 10 kg/m}^3 \quad 2400 \text{ kg/m}^3$$

(This figure agrees with the value obtained from Fig. 1.17.) To obtain the batch quantities for 400 m^3 of concrete, the batch quantities per m^3 are simply multiplied by 400. If, as may be the case, mass ratios only are given, the ratios are multiplied by the appropriate factor $\left[\frac{2400}{6.522}\right.$ in this case$\left.\right]$ to give batch quantities per cubic metre. The procedure is then as before.

If the presence of air is to be allowed for in calculating density, this is easily done by increasing the total volume of concrete but not the mass by the percentage of air which is expected.

Statistical interpretation of cube results

In concluding the section on the design of concrete, we return to the subject of variability. The reasons for strength variations have already been given and it will be evident that the extent of variations will depend to a large degree on the quality control procedures carried out on any one site. Figure 1.20 shows, for example, two histograms relating to 50 cube tests on two sites A and B. It will be evident that the curve A, although of lower mean strength, is much narrower than that of curve B and that, with site A, unlike site B, there are no cube results below 30 N/mm^2. Both curves have, in fact, been drawn such that characteristic strengths based on 8 per cent failures are the same, though site A satisfies this requirement with a lower mean strength (hence a more economical concrete) and fewer very low cube results. The standard deviation (s) of a set of n results, values $x_1, x_2 \ldots x_i \ldots x_n$ of average value x is given by

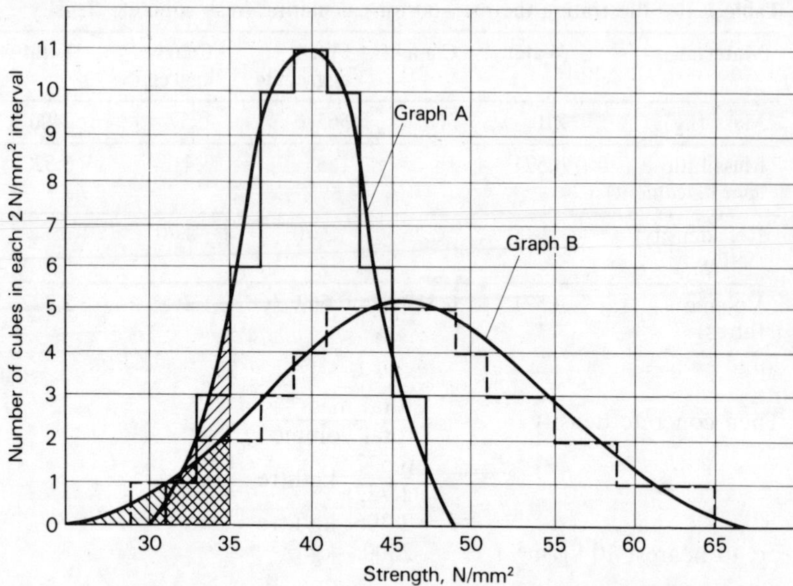

Fig. 1.20 Histograms drawn from the results of two sets of fifty concrete cube tests. Graph A represents good quality control and Graph B poor quality control. The total area under each graph is the same. Also, the area under each curve to the left of the 35 N/mm² line is the same, implying equal numbers of results beneath this strength. Curve B is, however, indicative of a greater probability of very low cube results than curve A.

$$s = \frac{\sqrt{\Sigma(x_i - x)^2}}{n - 1}$$

or, to put it alternatively

$$s = \frac{\sqrt{\text{sum of squares of (each individual result minus mean strength)}}}{n - 1}$$

The value of s obtained in practice for ordinary concrete of mean strength, say, 40 N/mm² might vary from 4 N/mm², which represents good quality control, to 8 N/mm², which represents poor quality control.

Perhaps the most direct way of checking that the characteristic strength is satisfactory is to keep calculating the mean strength (f_m) and standard deviation (s) using, say, the most recent 50 results and then to calculate characteristic strength (f_c) by the equation.

$f_c = f_m - ks$

k being the factor appropriate to the permissible number of failures, as given in Table 1.7. Such a method would, however, be mathematically quite arduous and would indicate rather slowly any change in quality control. It is especially important that any adverse change in strength be readily detectable as soon as possible and one convenient technique is the use of simple quality control charts in which strengths of consecutive cubes are represented as points. It is often found more convenient in practice to take means of four cubes and to plot the means, since this reduces the variability of results about the mean strength.

Suppose, for example, the required characteristic strength is 30 N/mm^2 with 5 per cent failures allowed and standard deviation equal to 6 N/mm^2. The target mean strength would then be

$$\begin{aligned} f_m &= f_c + ks \\ &= 30 + 1.64 \times 6 \\ &= 39.84 \text{ (say 40) N/mm}^2 \end{aligned}$$

If means of 4 are plotted, the standard deviation of the *means* should be

$$\frac{\text{standard deviation of individual results}}{\sqrt{\text{number in group}}}$$

$$= \frac{6}{\sqrt{4}} = 3 \text{ N/mm}^2$$

Hence not more than 5 per cent of means of 4 should be below

$$\begin{aligned} &40 - 1.64 \times 3 \\ &= 35.08 \text{ (say 35) N/mm}^2 \end{aligned}$$

A chart could then be constructed, as in Fig. 1.21, with mean strength 40 N/mm^2 and 'action lines' at 35 and 45 N/mm^2. If there is a definite trend towards, say, the 35 N/mm^2 line, then action, in the form of increasing the mean strength of the concrete must be taken, since the points should be evenly spaced about the mean with no more than one result in twenty (5 per cent) below the lower line if concreting is proceeding satisfactorily. 'Warning' lincs may also be included corresponding to, say, 10 per cent limits. Since, for 10 per cent failures, k is 1.28 (Table 1.7), the lines would be at strengths of

$$\begin{aligned} &40 \pm 1.28 \times 3 \\ &= 43.8 \text{ or } 36.2 \text{ N/mm}^2 \text{ approx.} \end{aligned}$$

The warning lines would serve to indicate that the concrete quality is varying. Increases in mean strength should also be checked, since unnecessarily high mean strengths (or reductions in standard deviation) may allow a reduction in cement content of the concrete, hence saving cost. Small corrections to strength are, in

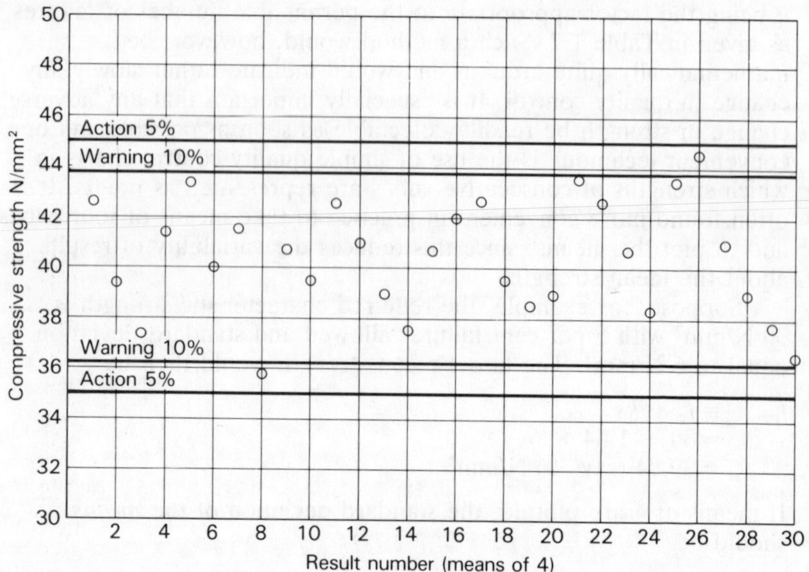

Fig. 1:21 Simple control chart for monitoring progress during production of concrete. In this case progress is satisfactory since there are no results outside 'Action' limits and results are equally distributed about the mean

fact, most commonly made by small alterations to cement content; a commonly used guide is that, to increase mean strength by 0.8 N/mm², the cement content should be increased by 5 kg/m³ concrete and vice versa. The aim, in all concrete testing, is to obtain results as soon as possible – accelerated curing may be used to predict 28-day strength as early as one day after placing provided reliable correlations have been produced. Hence faulty concrete can be identified and removed before it is fully mature or further lifts have been cast. More elaborate charts may be used alternatively; for instance, a second chart plotting variability within groups of 4 cube results, compared to a 'target mean variability' might be used. This would reveal any change in quality control (represented by standard deviation) as work proceeds.

Admixtures

Admixtures are materials other than cement, water or aggregates added at the mixer. Their use has increased greatly in recent years but, although there are many instances in which marked improvements in properties for specific applications are obtainable, careful precautions regarding their use are advised for the following reasons:

1. Dosages are usually very small – often less than 1 per cent by weight of cement, hence careful batching is necessary, the use of special dispensers being recommended.
2. Effects are sometimes very sensitive to variations in dose, hence good supervision is essential.
3. Side effects are often present, especially if overdoses occur.
4. To ensure effective dispersion, liquid admixtures should be added to the mixing water rather than to the mixer and water-soluble solid admixtures should be dissolved in the mixing water before use.

There are four main categories of admixture.

Water reducers (plasticisers)

These are perhaps the most widely-used admixture in the concrete industry, their use in ready-mixed concrete being especially common.

The main water-reducing compounds are lignosulphonates and hydrocarboxylic acids and they operate by attaching themselves to cement grains and imparting a negative charge, which causes grains to disperse more effectively. Hence the formation of 'flocs', (groups of cement particles), which tend to trap mixing water, is avoided. Water-reducing admixtures may be used either to:

1. allow a water reduction, hence reducing water/cement ratio and increasing strength; or
2. produce an increase in workability at given water and cement contents; or
3. allow a reduction in water and cement contents in concrete of a given strength, hence reducing cost.

Typical water reductions are in the region of 5 to 15 per cent when used as in (1) or (3) above. Side effects include air entrainment and retardation of set, though these are only slight at normal doses.

More recently a number of 'super plasticisers', based on compounds such as sulphonated melamine formaldehyde have been introduced. These can be used at higher dosages than ordinary water reducers without the same side effects. Since they are quite expensive, they are used mainly for applications (1) and (2) above. In the latter, the concrete, which has a slump of over 150 mm, is often referred to as 'flowing concrete', since it is more or less self-levelling and self-compacting, reducing labour costs in applications such as large floor slabs. The effect of super-plasticisers is short lived – only 30 to 45 min, hence they are usually added to the concrete just before placing. Care is necessary to avoid segregation but hardened properties, such as strength, shrinkage and creep, do not appear to be adversely affected.

Retarders

The object of these would normally be to retard the set (rather than the strength development) of concrete. Hence their effect should last for a few hours only.

They are usually based on lignosulphonates, hydrocarboxylic acids or sugars. They act mainly on those compounds in the cement which are responsible for early setting and early strength – that is the C_3A and C_3S respectively. Uses include the following:

1. To reduce the setting rate when concreting in hot weather. In many cases the retarder can improve long-term strength when used in this way, since slower hydration of cement leads to an improved 'gel' structure.
2. In very large pours, as, for example, in mass concrete foundations in order to produce monolithic (structurally continuous) concrete in spite of a prolonged placing period.
3. Since an overdose (which may still only be 0.5 per cent by weight of cement) will 'kill' the set, retarders can be used for example, to avoid hardening of concrete in the drum of a ready-mix agitator truck which has broken down.

Accelerators

These are designed to accelerate the early strength development of concrete. They are traditionally based on calcium chloride, which increases the hydration rate of the calcium silicates and, to some extent, the C_3A in the cement. Substantial improvements can be obtained between the ages of 1 day and 7 days, especially in cold weather – for example, the 3-day strength of concrete may be doubled at a temperature of 2 °C. Long-term strength is unaffected by the use of calcium chloride. Most important are the side effects of the material – the susceptibility of steel in structural concrete to corrosion is greatly increased by the presence of chlorides, such that CP 110 now limits chloride ion contents to 0.06 per cent by weight of cement in prestressed concrete, steam-cured concrete or when sulphate-resisting cement is employed. The maximum permitted chloride content in other steel-containing concretes is 0.35 per cent. (These chloride ion percentages are equivalent to approximately 50 per cent greater percentages of anhydrous calcium chloride by weight.) The shrinkage of concrete is also increased by the presence of chlorides. Other chloride-free accelerators are now available but these are more expensive than chloride-based accelerators.

Air-entraining agents

These are based on substances such as vinsol resins, which reduce the surface tension of water, allowing stable air bubbles to be introduced by mixing. These air bubbles are much smaller than pockets of entrapped air; most are less than 1 mm in diameter. The uses of air-entraining agents are based on the following properties of air-entrained concrete:

1. Resistance of hardened concrete to frost and de-icing salts is greatly improved, hence current specifications for concrete roads in the UK stipulate an air content of 4.5 per cent in the top 50 mm of the concrete.
2. Resistance to segregation or bleeding are improved, together with concrete workability, hence air-entrained concrete might be used to improve harsh mixes or to permit placing in conditions where segregation might otherwise be a problem. The air present reduces the concrete strength, though at least part of this shortfall can be avoided by the use of lower water contents for a given workability.

Lightweight concretes

These may offer the following advantages over ordinary dense concrete.

1. Since less raw material is involved, it may be argued that lightweight concretes help conserve materials resources.
2. A number of lightweight aggregates are produced from what may otherwise be waste materials – for example, pulverised fuel ash and blast furnace slag.
3. Foundation loads are reduced, hence foundation size can be decreased.
4. Higher lifts can be cast for a given formwork system, since formwork pressures are lower. Hence, the number of construction joints can be reduced.
5. Some lightweight concretes, such as precast aerated blocks and no-fines concrete produce an excellent key for rendering or plaster.
6. Fixings are often more easily made than with dense concretes. Some types can be nailed (using cut nails).
7. Thermal insulation is improved compared to dense aggregate concrete.
8. Fire resistance of lightweight concretes is superior to that of most dense concretes.
9. High frequency sound absorption is better than that of dense concrete.
10. Lightweight precast blocks are much easier to handle and cut than dense concrete equivalents.

There are three main methods of producing lightweight concretes, each method producing concrete with characteristic properties and applications.

No-fines concrete

As the name implies, this concrete is produced from cement and coarse aggregate only, the latter usually being graded between 20 mm and 10 mm. The aggregate may be ordinary dense aggregate, which would result in the concrete having a density in the region of 1800 kg/m^3, or lightweight aggregate, resulting in a concrete density as low as 500 kg/m^3. Dense aggregates would produce strengths of up to 15 N/mm^2, according to cement content, while the ceiling strength for lightweight aggregates would be around 10 N/mm^2.

In producing no-fines concrete, great care should be taken to obtain the correct water content, since a low value would result in uneven distribution of cement, while a high value would cause settlement of the cement paste fraction to the base of the concrete. Only minimal vibration should be used for compaction.

Shrinkage of no-fines concrete is low, since the cement paste is discontinuous, though shrinkage occurs quickly due to the high air permeability of the material. No-fines concrete is resistant to frost, though rendering of exposed surfaces is normally carried out to prevent water penetration.

No-fines concrete is widely used as an *in-situ* walling material for low-rise dwellings. It is also manufactured in the form of lightweight precast blocks.

Lightweight aggregate concrete

A large range of concrete densities can be obtained using lightweight aggregates – from as low as 500 kg/m^3 to 2000 kg/m^3. The thermal conductivity of concrete decreases as density decreases, values ranging from about 1.0 W/m °C for the higher densities to under 0.2 W/m °C for concrete of very low density. Strengths decrease similarly with density, though certain aggregates may give higher strength than others at a given density. An aggregate would normally be chosen according to the density and strength required, subject also, of course, to local availability. Lower density concretes would be used in situations where, perhaps, thermal insulation properties rather than strength are important – for example, as insulating layers in floors or roofs. Concretes having densities of over 1000 kg/m^3 can, however, be used 'structurally' and there are now many structures incorporating reinforced and prestressed lightweight aggregate concrete. By choice of suitable aggregates, such as foamed slag or sintered pulverised fuel ash, concrete strengths of over 40 N/mm^2 are obtainable with densities in the range 1500 to 2000 kg/m^3. The substitution of natural fine aggregate for lightweight fine aggregate can be used to increase strength (and density) still further. In designing lightweight concrete structures, allowance must be made for the lower elastic modulus and higher shrinkage and creep of lightweight aggregate concretes.

The design and production of lightweight aggregate concretes requires care because:

1. Design is best tackled from volume considerations in conjunction with trial mixes. Hence, bulk densities must be known if, as is normally the case, weight batching is used.
2. Aggregates absorb a great deal of moisture – 15 per cent or more by weight. Hence, the effective free water/cement ratio, an important factor in controlling strength, is often difficult to predict.

Aerated concrete

Aerated concrete comprises a cement/sand mortar into which gas is introduced. This may be obtained chemically – for example by the use of aluminium powder, which produces hydrogen in the presence of alkalis released by the cement, or by the use of foaming agents. Careful control of plastic properties is essential in order that the gas aerates the mortar without escaping, hence these concretes are mainly produced in the form of manufactured precast blocks. Densities in the range 400 to 800 kg/m^3 are obtained, corresponding to compressive strengths of 2 to 5 N/mm^2.

Conventionally cured aerated concretes would have high shrinkage but this can be reduced by high-pressure steam curing (autoclaving). Hence many commercial precast blocks are autoclaved and these would also normally contain a pozzolanic material, such as pulverised fuel ash, which contributes to strength.

With increased standards of thermal insulation now being enforced, the use of aerated concretes, which have very low thermal conductivity (in the region of 0.2 W/m °C) has increased greatly. Products are available for walling of low to medium strength requirement. Aerated blocks are reasonably frost-resistant, though they would normally be protected from the weather, if used externally, by cladding or rendering.

Experiments

Experiment 1.1 Grading of aggregates (BS 812: Part 1, BS 882)

Apparatus

BS sieves; weighing balance accurate to 1 g.

Sample preparation

A main sample is first obtained from the stockpile by the procedure outlined in BS 812: Part 1. The essential requirement is that this sample should consist of at least 10 increments, obtained from different parts of the stockpile and mixed thoroughly. The main sample should be of not less than 13 kg for fine aggregate and not less than 25 kg for aggregates of nominal size between 5 and 28 mm.

The main sample is reduced in size to a quantity suitable for sieving, using a riffle box (Fig. 1.22), or by quartering. It is recommended that division be continued until the minimum mass in excess of the requirements of Table 1.11 is obtained; larger masses, particularly of fine aggregates, tend to lead to blinding of sievc apertures. Note, however, that shaking a divided sample from a scoop to obtain the exact minimum mass of Table 1.11 is incorrect – it leads to particle segregation. The prepared sample must then be dried either in an oven or by leaving spread for some time on a flat sheet.

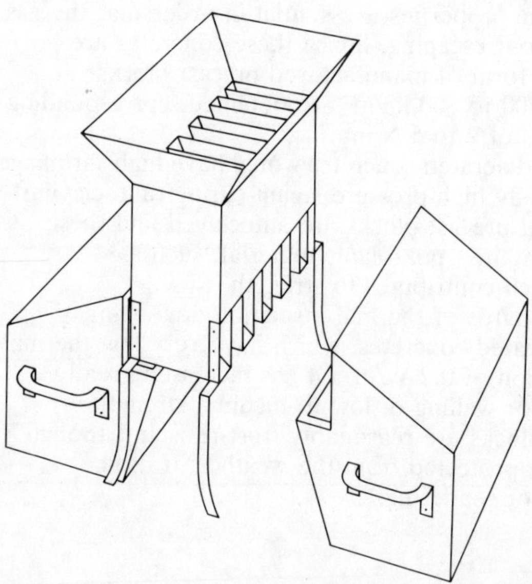

Fig. 1.22 Riffle box for reduction of aggregate sample size. Three receiving boxes are normally supplied

Procedure

Select the sieves appropriate to the nominal size of material being used by reference to Tables 1.12 and 1.13. Examples are:

20 mm graded coarse aggregate	37.5	20	10	5 mm
20 mm single size coarse aggregate	37.5	20	10	5 mm
10 mm single size coarse aggregate	14	10	5	2.36 mm
Fine aggregate	10	5	2.36	1.18 mm
	600	300	150 μm	

Table 1.11 Minimum mass of sample for sieve analysis

Nominal size of material (mm)	**Minimum mass of sample (kg)**
63	50
50	35
40	15
28	5
20	2
14	1
10	0.5
6	0.2
5	0.2
3	0.2
<3	0.1

Table 1.12 Grading zones for fine aggregate

BS 410 test sieve (mm/μm)	**Percentage by weight passing BS sieves**			
	Grading Zone 1	Grading Zone 2	Grading Zone 3	Grading Zone 4
mm 10.0	**100**	**100**	**100**	**100**
5.00	**90–100**	**90–100**	**90–100**	95–**100**
2.36	**60**–95	75–**100**	85–100	95–**100**
1.18	**30**–70	55–90	75–**100**	90–**100**
μm				
600	**15–34**	**35–59**	**60–79**	**80–100**
300	**5**–20	8–30	12–40	15–**50**
150	**0**–10*	**0**–10*	**0**–10*	**0–15***

* For crushed stone sands, the permissible limit is increased to 20%. 5% tolerance may be applied to the percentages in light type.

Shake the material through each sieve individually into a collecting tray starting with the largest, using a varied motion, backwards and forwards, clockwise and anti-clockwise and with frequent jarring. (Alternatively, sieves may be assembled into a sieve shaker.) In order to prevent blinding of sieve apertures, the quantity of material retained on sieves should not exceed the values given in Table 1.14. Smaller fine aggregate sieves are often a problem in this respect and one way of solving this is to use additional sieves – for example a 425 μm sieve prior to the 300 μm sieve. The quantities retained on these sieves are then *added*. Weigh quantities retained on each sieve and check that the total is approximately equal to the original sample size. If it is not, repeat the procedure with a new sample.

Table 1.13 Grading limits for coarse aggregates

BS sieve (mm)	Percentage by weight passing BS sieves							
	Nominal size of graded aggregate		Nominal size of single-sized aggregates					
	40 mm to 5 mm	20 mm to 5 mm	14 mm to 5 mm	63 mm	40 mm	20 mm	14 mm	10 mm
75.0	100	–	–	100	–	–	–	–
63.0	–	–	–	85–100	100	–	–	–
37.5	95–100	100	–	0–30	85–100	100	–	–
20.0	35–70	95–100	100	0–5	0–25	85–100	100	–
14.0	–	–	90–100	–	–	–	85–100	100
10.0	10–40	30–60	50–85	–	0–5	0–25	0–25	85–100
5.00	0–5	0–10	0–10	–	–	0–5	0–10	0–25
2.36	–	–	–	–	–	–	–	0–5

Table 1.14 Maximum amount to be retained on each sieve after sieving (to avoid 'blinding' of apertures)

	Maximum mass				**Maximum mass**
BS test sieve nominal aperture size (mm)	450 mm diameter sieves (kg)	300 mm diameter sieves (kg)	**BS test nominal aperture size (mm)**	**(μm)**	200 mm diameter sieves (g)
50.0	10	4.5	3.35	–	200
37.5	8	3.5	2.36	–	200
			1.70	–	100
28.0	6	2.5	1.18	–	100
				850	75
20.0	4	2.0	–	600	75
14.0	3	1.5	–	425	75
10.0	2	1.0			
			–	300	50
6.30	1.5	0.75	–	212	50
5.00	1.0	0.5	–	150	40
3.35	–	0.3	–	75	25

Complete a table similar to that of Table 1.4, using appropriate sieve sizes. Plot the percentage passing each sieve using percentage passing as *y* axis and sieve sizes increasing *equally spaced* as the *x* axis.

Join each point by a straight line. Classify fine aggregates into zone 1 to 4 by reference to Table 1.12. Fine aggregate may be regarded as within a given zone if it does not fall outside by more than a total of 5 per cent on all sieves. There is no tolerance on underlined percentages given in heavy type. Table 1.13 shows limits for coarse aggregates.

Experiment 1.2 Determination of bulking of fine aggregate

Apparatus

250 ml measuring cylinder; 5 ml measuring cylinder; large beaker; wide funnel; spatula; dry fine aggregate.

Procedure

Weigh out 250 g of dry fine aggregate and transfer to the 250 ml measuring cylinder using the funnel. Tap gently to level the sand and note the volume. Transfer the sand to the beaker and add 5 ml (2%) of water. Mix and again transfer to the measuring cylinder, noting the new volume after tapping. Repeat using 2 per cent increments of water until free moisture begins to separate from the sand – usually at about 20 per cent moisture content. Note that, to achieve consistent results, a standardised tapping (levelling) technique is necessary.

Results

Measure each volume as a percentage of the original dry volume and plot graphically against moisture content.

Note that even the dry fine aggregate contains substantial quantities of air.

Experiment 1.3 Determination of the volume of silt and clay in a sample of fine aggregate using the field settling test

Apparatus

A 250 ml measuring cylinder; common salt; sample of fine aggregate (not crushed stone sand).

Procedure

Prepare a 1 per cent solution of sodium chloride (common salt) in water. Two teaspoonsful of salt to 1 litre of water will suffice.

Pour 50 ml of this solution into the 250 ml measuring cylinder. Gradually add the sand until the volume of the sand is 100 ml. Make up the volume of solution to 150 ml by adding more solution. Shake vigorously until the clayey particles are dispersed and then place on a level bench and tap gently until the surface of the sand is level. After three hours, measure the volume of silt above the sand-silt interface and express as a percentage of the volume of sand (Fig. 1.9). Refer to the text of this chapter for the acceptable limits.

Experiment 1.4 Measurement of the moisture content of aggregates using the siphon can

Apparatus

Siphon can (Fig. 1.23); weighing balance of 3 kg capacity, capable of weighing to 1 g accuracy; 500 ml measuring cylinder.

Procedure

After ensuring that the siphon can is clean and empty, close both siphon tubes and fill until the water is above the highest point on the upper tube. Open the upper tube and discharge the water to waste. Open the lower tube and collect the water in the measuring cylinder. The volume V ml is the calibration volume for the can. Repeat and obtain an average value for V.

To find the moisture content of an aggregate, fill the siphon can with water and discharge using the lower siphon tube (this condition is attained after the calibration test). Close the lower siphon tube. Weigh 2 kg of dry aggregate to 1 g accuracy and add carefully to the

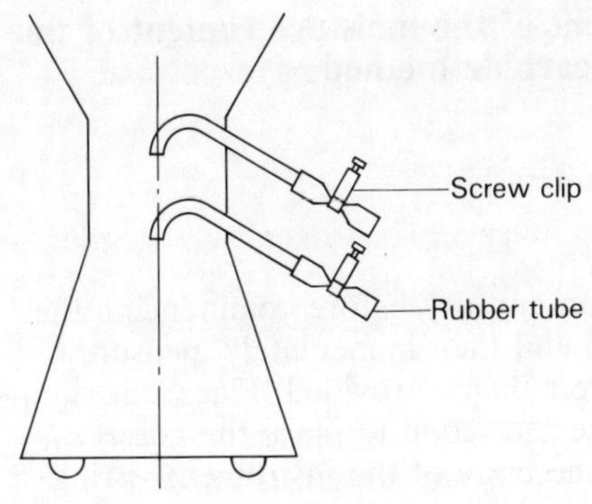

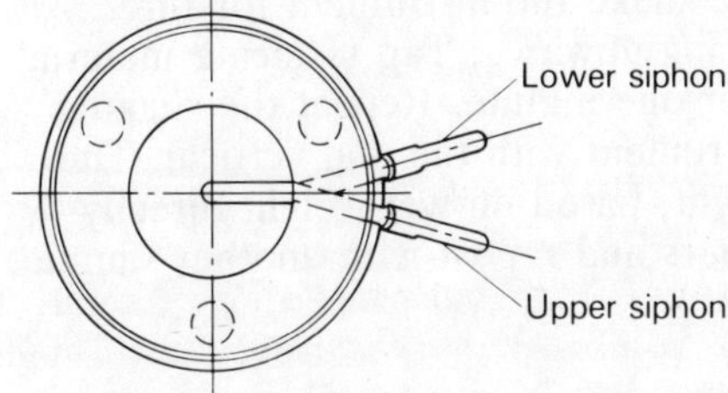

Fig. 1.23 Siphon can

siphon can, stirring to remove air bubbles. Allow the stirring rod to drain and then remove it. Open the upper siphon tube and collect the water in the measuring cylinder (volume v_b ml). Open the lower siphon tube and, after draining, close both tubes. Repeat using 2 kg of the damp aggregate whose moisture content is required, obtaining the volume v_b ml.

Results

Calculate the moisture content of the aggregate using the equations:

$$\text{Moisture content (per cent by dry mass)} = \left[\frac{v_w - v_b}{1000 - V - v_b}\right] \times 100$$

$$\text{Moisture content (per cent by wet mass)} = \left[\frac{v_w - v_b}{1000 - V - v_w}\right] \times 100$$

Note These equations are based on the assumption that no water is absorbed by the aggregates, hence that the 'dry' sample is saturated surface dry and that free moisture is present in the damp sample. These should apply in most cases but, where aggregates absorb water, the procedure in BS 812: Part 2 should be followed.

Experiment 1.5 Measurement of the moisture content of fine aggregate using the calcium carbide method

Apparatus

'Speedy' moisture meter; calcium carbide.

Procedure

Make sure the apparatus is clean and dry before commencing the test. Mix the main sand sample and then immediately measure out the sample for testing, using the balance provided. Place this sample in the cap of thc apparatus. Use the scoop to place the correct quantity of calcium carbide in the body of the instrument. Bring both parts together, keeping them horizontal to avoid mixing and tighten the cap, ensuring that the clamp screw is correctly located. With the dial facing downwards, shake the instrument for three seconds and then stand, dial facing upwards. Tap to locate material in the cap and allow to stand for one minute. Repeat the shaking operation. Finally, read the instrument with the dial vertical. The reading gives the moisture content, based on wet weight directly. Empty the instrument out of doors and repeat with another sample, obtaining the average reading.

Experiment 1.6 Determination of the slump of a concrete mix

Apparatus

Slump cone; hard, level, vibration-free, non-absorbent base; tamping rod; rule; trowel.

Procedure

Ideally the concrete should be sampled from a large batch and prepared in accordance with BS 1881: Part 1.

Alternatively, 8 litres of concrete to the specification of the worked example on Page 39 may be produced, assuming aggregates of this specification are available.

If neither of the above is convenient, a sample of about 8 litres may be made up using masses as follows: 3 kg cement; 5 kg fine aggregate; 8 kg coarse aggregate.

The materials are mixed dry and then sufficient water (about 1.5 litres) added to produce a workable concrete.

Place the clean slump cone on the base and hold firmly in position throughout the filling operation. Load concrete gently into the cone until a depth of about 75 mm is obtained. Rod 25 times with the round edge of the tamping rod. Add another 75 mm layer and repeat, rodding through to the underlying layer. Repeat until four compacted layers are obtained and strike the top layer off level with the trowel. While still holding the cone, clean away excess concrete from around the base. Then remove the slump cone by lifting carefully in the vertical direction. Invert the cone, place next to the concrete and, using the tamping rod as a reference height, measure the slump (to the highest part of the slumped concrete) (Fig. 1.10). Record the slump in mm.

Experiment 1.7 Determination of the workability of concrete using the compacting factor apparatus

Apparatus

Compacting factor apparatus (Fig. 1.11); 2 metal floats; vibrating table or 25 mm square tamping rod for compaction; weighing balance capable of weighing up to 25 kg to 0.1 kg accuracy; trowel; slump test tamping rod.

Procedure

Either obtain a sample of concrete or prepare a sample, as described in experiment 1.6. Very wet mixes should not be used.

Weigh the collection cylinder and then place in position and cover with the two metal floats. Close both trap doors. Load the concrete gently into the upper hopper until it is well heaped. Open the upper trap door and allow the concrete to fall through into the lower hopper. If the concrete 'hangs up' in the hopper, it may be rodded through gently with the slump test tamping rod. Remove the floats from the receiving cylinder and open the lower trap door, allowing concrete to fill the cylinder. Cut away excess concrete by sliding the metal floats across the top of the receiving cylinder. Wipe the outside of the cylinder clean and weigh to the nearest 0.1 kg. Subtract the weight of the container to obtain the mass of *partially compacted concrete*. Empty the cylinder and then refill in 50 mm layers, tamping each layer or compacting using a vibrating table to obtain *full compaction*. Weigh again and hence obtain the mass of fully compacted concrete. The compaction factor is then the ratio of these two masses:

$$\frac{\text{Mass of partially compacted concrete}}{\text{Mass of fully compacted concrete}}$$

Experiment 1.8 Measurement of the workability of a concrete, using the V-B consistometer

Apparatus

V-B consistometer and vibrating table (Fig. 1.12) trowel; stopwatch.

Procedure

Either obtain a suitable sample of concrete or prepare a sample, as described in experiment 1.6.

This method is most suited to dry mixes – the concrete should be barely plastic and should exhibit very little or no slump.

Fix the slump cone and outer container in position and attach the filling cone. Compact concrete into the cone as in the slump test (experiment 1.6). Remove the filling cone and then the slump cone and swing the perspex disc into position, making sure the disc is free to move vertically in its guide. Rest the disc gently on the concrete. Switch on the vibrator and measure the time taken for the disc to sink, so that the concrete wets it uniformly all round. The time in seconds is then the consistency of the concrete in 'V-B degrees'. It will be clear that stiffer mixes produce a higher result (Table 1.6).

Experiment 1.9 Measurement of the compressive strength of concrete, using the cube test

It is suggested that the greatest value will be obtained from this experiment if the concrete for cube tests is produced as a series of trial mixes which will enable the effect of mix proportions on strength to be investigated.

Apparatus

Compression machine of 1000 kN or greater capacity; 100 mm or 150 mm cube moulds, preferably steel; vibrating table or tamping rod for compaction.

Procedure

First ensure that the moulds are in good condition and that all clamps or bolts are tight. Coat all internal surfaces with a *thin* film of mould oil. Mix the concrete sample thoroughly and then place in the cube moulds to a depth of approximately 50 mm. At least five cubes per concrete sample are recommended. Compact this layer, either using a vibrating table or by hand and then add another 50 mm layer, repeating the procedure. When the moulds are full, trowel smooth and cover with an impermeable mat. Cubes must be identified, the most effective way initially being to use numbers painted on the moulds.

Leave undisturbed for 16 to 24 h at a temperature of 20 ± 2 °C and then demould, identifying each cube with waterproof ink. Transfer to a curing tank containing clean water and cure at 20 ± 1 °C until testing.

At the required age, (usually 7 or 28 days), remove the cubes from the tank and wipe away excess water and any grit. Place cubes, trowelled face sideways, centrally in the testing machine and load at the BS rate appropriate to that cube size until failure. Note the maximum load and the mode of failure, which should be one of those indicated in Fig. 1.24(a). If there are horizontal cracks in the concrete (Fig. 1.24(b)), a tensile failure had occurred and this must be reported. Calculate the stress in N/mm^2 by dividing the load in N by the cross-sectional area in mm^2.

Suitability of testing machine. Some machines in current use have

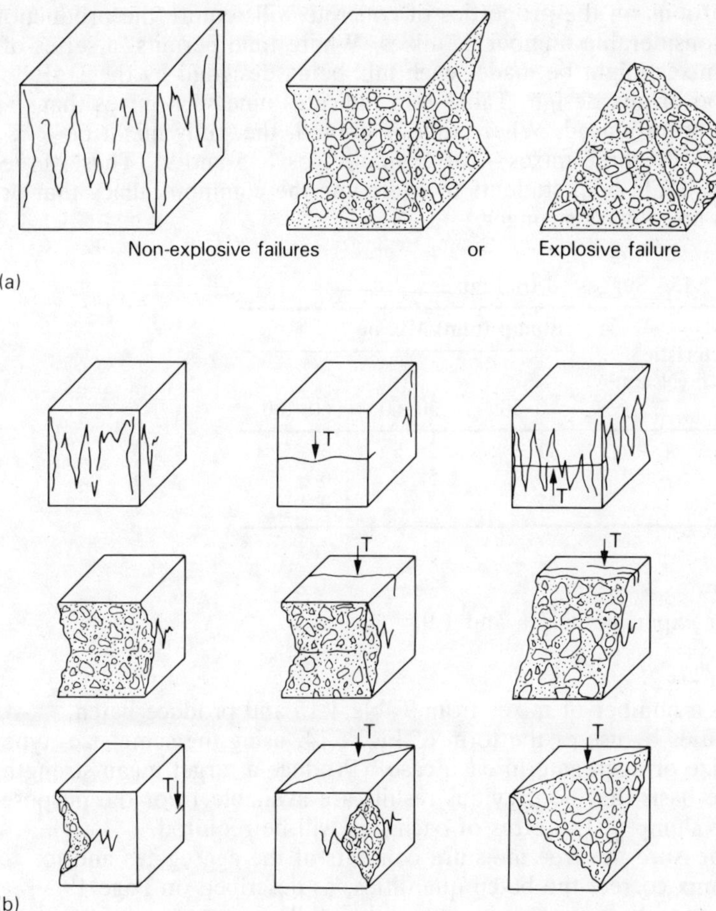

Fig. 1.24 Modes of failure of concrete cubes (a) normal (b) abnormal – tensile cracks marked T are indicative of incorrect testing or faulty machine

been found to be unsatisfactory for cube testing. Machines should comply with BS 1610 for accuracy of calibration and periodic checks are necessary to ensure that the upper ball seating functions correctly. These seatings are designed to lock under load. Where failures of the form given in Fig. 1.24(b) occur, the ball seating may be the cause (assuming testing technique is correct) and it should therefore be checked.

Experiment 1.10 The effect of mix proportions on the properties of fresh and hardened concrete

Note. A comprehensive investigation into the effect of mix proportions on the properties of concrete will require the production of a considerable number of mixes. Where time permits, a series of nine mixes might be made, each mix being designed by the DoE method of mix design. Table 1.15 indicates nine such mixes that might be produced. Where time is limited, the study might be confined to three mixes – for example Nos 1, 5 and 9. (These three mixes should help students to overcome the common fallacy that dry mixes are always stronger.)

Table 1.15 Suggested trial mixes

28 day characteristic strength (N/mm^2)	**Slump (mm)/Mix no**		
	0–30	30–60	60–180
15	1	2	3
25	4	5	6
40	7	8	9

Apparatus

As for experiments 1.6 and 1.9.

Procedure

Select a number of mixes from Table 1.15 and produce batch quantities by use of the form of Fig. 1.14, using the same size, type and size or aggregate in each case. (Produce a target mean strength on the basis that no previous results are available.) For the purpose of the slump test, 8 litres of each mix will be required.

Measure the free moisture contents of the aggregates and for each mix correct the batch quantities, as described on Page 19.

For each concrete mix, proceed as follows:

Mix the materials dry and then add a quantity of water something less than the required batch quantity. Try to estimate the likely slump and then continue to add water until what is judged to be the correct slump is obtained. Then carry out the slump test. Note that workability tests should, if possible, be carried out at a standard time (usually 6 min) after adding the mixing water. If the workability is outside the acceptable range, another mix should, strictly speaking, be produced.

The cohesiveness of the concrete should also be measured – produce a small heap of the concrete and trowel to a thickness of about 50 mm. A mix of normal cohesion should trowel to a smooth finish fairly easily. Mixes of high or low cohesion will be very easy or very difficult, respectively to trowel to a smooth finish.

Make up at least five cubes from the batch, curing and testing as described in experiment 1.9. All results should be recorded and compared with the original specification. The variability within each set of five cubes should also be measured by calculation of the standard deviation and comparison with values indicated on Page 42. (Note that five results are not really sufficient for a full analysis and that laboratory-produced concrete should have a relatively low standard deviation.) The cost of the concrete varies directly with the cement content; note which mix is the most expensive on this basis.

Questions

1. List the four chief components in Portland cements. State which of these:
   (a) gives off most heat during hydration;
   (b) is present in the largest quantity in OPC;
   (c) is vulnerable to sulphates;
   (d) is responsible for the grey colour of OPC.
2. State what is meant by a hydraulic cement.
3. Indicate two ways in which the manufacturer of a cement could increase its rate of hardening using given raw materials. Give typical applications of rapid hardening cements.
4. State the cause of sulphate attack in concrete. Indicate two ways in which the likelihood of this attack can be reduced.
5. Name the two principal compounds produced on hydration of ordinary Portland cement. Give one characteristic property of reinforced concrete which depends on each.
6. Explain the purpose of the following tests for cement:
   (a) setting time;
   (b) soundness;
   (c) mortar cube strength.
7. Explain the factors which affect the choice of the maximum size of aggregate for concrete and indicate what maximum size of aggregate would be suitable for the following purposes:
   (a) a normally reinforced concrete column of section 600 mm × 400 mm;
   (b) a 40 mm floor screed;
   (c) a concrete road base of thickness 200 mm.
8. A sieve analysis of 250 g of fine aggregate gives the following results:

Sieve size (mm/μm)	Mass retained (g)
10 mm	0
5	5
2.36	31
1.18	38
600 μm	38
300	79
150	51
Passing 150 μm	8

Classify the fine aggregate by means of Table 1.12.

9. Explain what is meant by 'bulking' of aggregates. Indicate why the extent of bulking of fine aggregates depends on moisture content.

10. A sample of damp aggregate weighing 2.35 kg. is dried by hair dryer until it just reaches the free-running (saturated surface dry) condition. It is then found to weigh 2.24 kg. After then drying in the oven to constant mass, it is found to weigh 2.15 kg.
Calculate:
(a) the free water content;
(b) the total water content;
based on dry mass.

11. Compare the following tests for the measurement of the workability of concrete:
(a) slump test;
(b) compacting factor test;
(c) V-B test.

A sample of concrete was divided into three and results for slump, compacting factor and V-B tests obtained. They were as follows: slump 5 mm; compacting factor 0.93; V-B time 18 s. Assuming that only one measurement was in error, which result is incorrect?

12. Explain what is meant by the term 'cohesion' in relation to fresh concrete. Indicate the problems that might arise in concretes of
(a) very low cohesion;
(b) very high cohesion.

13. Use Table 1.8 and Fig. 1.16 to determine the water/cement ratios required in mixes to the following specifications:

Cement/aggregate	**Target mean strength at stated age (N/mm²)**		
	3 days	7 days	28 days
1 OPC/uncrushed	(a) 25	(b) 22	(c) 40
2 OPC/crushed	(a) 20	(b) 40	(c) 60
3 RHPC/crushed	(a) 30	(b) 35	(c) 60

14. Use the DoE method of mix design in conjunction with Fig. 1.14 to produce batch quantities for 50 litres of concrete to the following specification:

Cement	Ordinary Portland
Aggregates	Fine – zone 2 uncrushed, relative density 2.6
	Coarse – 20 mm uncrushed, relative density 2.6

Compressive strength	35 N/mm² at 28 days (5 per cent defectives), no previous results available
Workability	30 to 60 mm slump

15. Use the DoE method of mix design in conjunction with Fig. 1.14 to produce batch quantities for 10 litres of concrete to the following specification:

Cement	Rapid-hardening Portland
Aggregates	Fine – zone 3 uncrushed, relative density 2.7 Coarse – uncrushed, relative density 2.7 maximum size 40 mm
Minimum cement content	350 kg/m³ concrete
Compressive strength	35 N/mm² at 28 days (5 per cent defectives. Standard deviation 5 N/mm²
Workability	10 to 30 mm slump

16. Concrete is required to be produced with a characteristic strength of 25 N/mm² with 2 per cent failures allowed. The first 20 cube results are as follows:

24.2	23.9	28.1	20.2	29.4
32.5	19.8	24.2	26.5	23.2
30.5	27.5	24.1	26.5	29.1
20.1	24.5	25.1	22.9	21.2

Calculate the standard deviation using the formula given on Page 42 and hence indicate whether the required characteristic strength is being reached.

17. Concrete for a particular contract is to be produced with a target mean strength of 33 N/mm² and the assumed standard deviation is 4.5 N/mm². The first 50 results are as follows (in N/mm²):

26.2	28.0	34.8	39.0	40.0	28.2	30.0	38.6	37.0	33.0
34.6	33.6	35.0	29.6	28.8	30.0	26.0	24.4	29.2	36.0
40.0	30.2	33.4	36.8	34.9	26.0	26.8	30.6	37.6	31.6
30.2	28.4	37.2	35.6	30.6	40.6	37.2	30.4	33.4	34.8
38.6	33.8	33.6	28.8	32.8	34.8	39.0	28.4	34.6	32.8

Draw a control chart of the type shown in Fig. 1.21, including the target mean strength and upper and lower control lines for 5 per cent and 10 per cent of *individual* results. Hence suggest whether the characteristic strength requirement of 25 N/mm² with 5 per cent permissible failures is being satisfied.

18. Concrete is required to have a characteristic strength of 30 N/mm² at 28 days of age with 5 per cent permissible failures. Calculate the water/cement ratio which will be needed if OPC and uncrushed aggregates are used. Assume a standard deviation of 5.5 N/mm².

19. Indicate three alternative reasons for using
(a) plasticisers;
(b) retarders;
in concrete.

References

Design of Normal Concrete Mixes, Department of the Environment, HMSO 1975.

British Standards

BS 12: 1978, *Portland Cement* (ordinary and rapid-hardening).
BS 146: 1973, *Portland Blast Furnace Cement.*
BS 812: *Methods for Sampling and Testing of Mineral Aggregates, Sands and Fillers.*
BS 877: Part 2: 1973 (1977), *Foamed or Expanded Blast Furnace Slag Lightweight Aggregate for Concrete.*
BS 882 and 1201: 1973, *Aggregates from Natural Sources for Concrete (including Granolithic).*
BS 1047: 1974 (1977), *Specification for Air-cooled Blast Furnace Slag Coarse Aggregate for Concrete.*
BS 1165: 1966 (1977), *Clinker Aggregate for Concrete.*
BS 1370: 1979, *Low-heat Portland Cement.*
BS 1881: *Methods of Testing Concrete.*
BS 3148: 1980, *Tests for Water for Making Concrete.*
BS 3681: 1973 (1977), *Methods for Sampling and Testing of Lightweight Aggregates for Concrete.*
BS 3797: 1976 (1982), *Lightweight Aggregates for Concrete.*
BS 4027: 1980, *Sulphate Resisting Portland Cement.*
BS 5075: Part 1:1982, *Accelerating Admixtures, Retarding Admixtures and water-reducing admixtures. Part 2: 1982. Air Entraining Admixtures.*

Chapter 2

Bricks and Building Blocks

Bricks

Bricks may broadly be described as building units which are easily handled with one hand, though BS 3921 defines bricks as units not exceeding 337.5 mm in length, 225 mm in width or 112.5 mm in height. (Units which exceed any of these dimensions are referred to as blocks.) By far the most widely used size at present is the single standard metric brick of actual size 215 × 102.5 × 65 mm.

For the past 100 years, clay bricks have dominated the UK market as building units but more recently concrete blocks have provided strong competition, especially since thermal insulation regulations were tightened and lightweight concrete blocks became available. The development of coloured calcium silicate bricks has provided further competition but clay bricks continue to be a most important building unit, combining excellent durability (when they are selected and used correctly) with, in the case of facing bricks, lasting aesthetic properties.

Clay bricks

These are made by pressing a prepared clay sample into a mould, extracting the formed unit immediately and then heating it in order to sinter (partially vitrify) the clay.

Many different types of brick may be produced, depending on the type of clay used, the moulding process and the firing process.

There are three basic subdivisions of type.

1. *Common bricks*. These are ordinary bricks which are not designed to provide good finished appearance or high strength. They are therefore in general the cheapest bricks available.
2. *Facing bricks*. These are designed to give attractive appearance, hence they are free from imperfections such as cracks.

   Facing bricks may be derived from common bricks to which a sand facing and/or pigment has been applied prior to firing.
3. *Engineering bricks*. These are designed primarily for strength and durability. They are usually of high density and well fired.

Bricks may also be classified in other ways, e.g. by *quality*, of which there are three classifications: internal quality bricks being suitable for internal use only; ordinary quality being satisfactory for moderate exposure externally; and special quality bricks being satisfactory in conditions of extreme exposure.

Many clay bricks are designated by their place of manufacture, colour or surface texture. Examples:

Fletton – a common brick manufactured from Oxford clay, originally in Fletton, near Peterborough.

Staffordshire blue – an Engineering quality brick produced from clay which results in a characteristic blue colour.

Dorking stock – The term 'stock', originally a piece of wood used in the moulding process, now denotes a brick characteristic of a certain region.

Indentations and perforations in bricks

Indentations (frogs) and perforations (cylindrical holes passing through the thickness of the brick) may be provided for one or more of the following reasons:

(a) They assist in forming a strong bond between the brick and the remainder of the structure;
(b) they reduce the effective thickness of the brick and hence reduce firing time;
(c) they reduce the material cost and hence the overall cost of the brick without serious *in-situ* strength loss.

For greatest strength, bricks with a single frog should be laid frog-up, since this ensures that the frog is filled with mortar.

According to BS 3921, bricks are not strictly 'perforated' unless the perforations occupy at least 25 per cent of the total volume. The term is nevertheless widely used to describe bricks containing less than this percentage of voids.

Manufacture of clay bricks

There are four basic stages in brick manufacture, though many of the operations are interdependent – a particular brick will follow through these stages in a way designed specifically to suit the raw material used and the final product.

Clay preparation

After digging out, the clay is prepared by crushing and/or grinding and mixing until it is of a uniform consistence. Water may be added to increase plasticity (a process known as 'tempering') and in some cases chemicals may be added for specific purposes – for example, barium carbonate which reacts with soluble salts producing an insoluble product.

Moulding

The moulding technique is designed to suit the moisture content of the clay, the following methods being described in order of increasing moisture content.

Semi-dry process

This process, which is used for the manufacture of Fletton bricks, utilises a moisture content in the region of 10 per cent. The ground and screened material has a granular consistence which is still evident in fractured surfaces of the fired brick. The material is pressed into the mould in up to four stages. The faces of the brick may, after pressing, be textured or sandfaced.

Stiff plastic process

This utilises clays which are tempered to a moisture content of about 15 per cent. A stiff plastic consistence is obtained, the clay being extruded and then compacted into a mould under high pressure. Many Engineering bricks are made in this way, the clay for these containing a relatively large quantity of iron oxide which helps promote fusion during firing.

The wire-cut process

The clay is tempered to about 20 per cent moisture content and must be processed to form a homogeneous material. This is extruded to a size which allows for drying and firing shrinkage and units are cut to the correct thickness by tensioned wires. Perforated bricks are made in this way, the perforations being formed during the extrusion process. Wire cut bricks are easily recognised by the perforations or the 'drag marks', caused by the dragging of small clay particles under the wire.

Soft mud process

As the name suggests, this process utilises a clay, normally from shallow surface deposits, in a very soft condition, the moisture content being as high as 30 per cent. Breeze or town ash may be added to provide combustible material to assist firing or improve appearance. The clay is pressed into moulds which are sanded to prevent sticking. The green bricks are very soft and must be handled carefully prior to drying.

Hand-made bricks are produced by a similar process, except that 'clots' of clay are thrown by hand into sanded moulds. This produces a characteristic surface texture (Fig. 2.1), which has great aesthetic appeal and is the reason for the continued production, on a limited scale, of hand-made bricks.

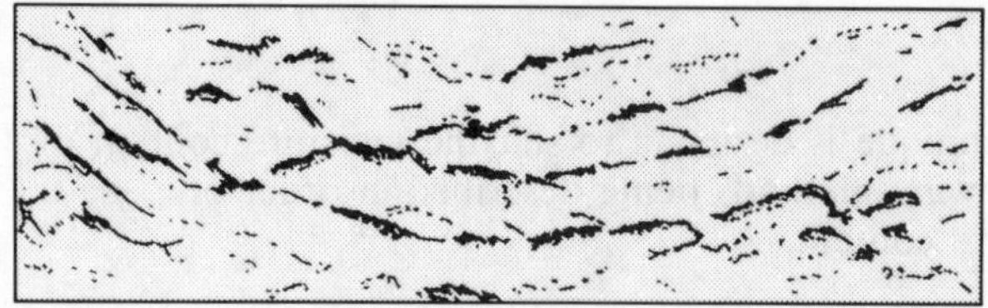

Fig. 2.1 Characteristic surface texture of a handmade clay brick. Each brick is slightly different

Drying

This must be carried out prior to firing when bricks are made from clay of relatively high moisture content. Drying enables such bricks to be stacked higher in the kiln without lower bricks becoming distorted by the weight of bricks above them. Drying also enables the firing temperature to be increased more rapidly without problems such as bloating, which may result when gases or vapour are trapped within the brick. Drying is carried out in chambers, the temperature being increased and the relative humidity progressively decreased as bricks lose moisture. The process normally takes a number of days, higher moisture content bricks requiring a greater time. Wire-cut bricks and those produced by the soft mud process must be dried prior to firing.

Firing

The object of firing is to cause localised melting (sintering) of the clay, which increases strength and decreases the soluble salt content without loss of shape of the clay unit. The main constituents of the clay – silica and alumina, do not melt, since their melting points are very high; they are merely fused together by the lower melting point minerals such as metallic oxides and lime. The main stages of firing are:

100 °C	evaporation of free water
400 °C	burning of carbonaceous matter
900–1000 °C	sintering of clay.

The latter stages of firing may be assisted by fuels either present naturally in the clay or those added during processing – one of the factors contributing to the low cost of Fletton bricks is the presence of carbonaceous material, which is largely responsible for the heat supplied in the later stages of firing.

The control of the rate of increase of temperature and the maximum temperature is most important in order to produce bricks having satisfactory strength and quality; in particular, too-rapid firing will cause bloating and overburning of external layers, while too-low a temperature seriously impairs strength and durability. Stronger bricks, such as engineering bricks, are normally fired at higher temperatures.

The following are the main processes:

Clamps

Bricks are stacked in large special formations on a layer of breeze, though the bricks also contain some fuel. The breeze base is ignited and the fire spreads slowly through the stack, which contracts as the bricks shrink on firing. The process may take up to one month to complete and the fired product is very variable, many underburnt and overburnt bricks being obtained. After firing, the bricks are sorted and marketed for various applications. Well-fired bricks are extremely attractive with local colour variations being caused by temperature differences and points where fuel ignition occurred. The use of clamps has now decreased, owing to the difficulty in controlling these kilns and the high wastage involved.

Continuous kilns

These are based on the Hoffman kiln and comprise a closed circuit of about 14 chambers arranged in two parallel rows with curved ends (Fig. 2.2). Divisions between the chambers are made from strong

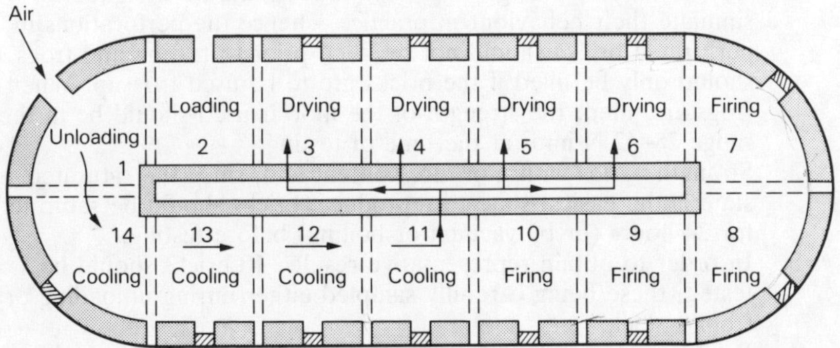

Fig. 2.2 Continuous kiln showing sequence of zones and movement of air for drying purposes

paper sealed with clay and, by means of flues, the fire is directed to each chamber in turn. Drying is carried out prior to the main firing process and is achieved by warm air obtained from fired bricks during cooling. The kilns are described as continuous, since the fire is not extinguished – it is simply diverted from one kiln to the next the cycle taking about one week. Coal was traditionally used but firing now may be by oil or gas. These kilns are very widely used for brick production.

Tunnel kilns

These are the most recently introduced kilns and they can reduce firing time to little over one day. Units are specially stacked onto large trolleys incorporating a heat-resistant loading platform. The trolleys are then pushed end-to-end into a straight tunnel with a waist that fits the loading platform closely. The bricks pass successively through drying, firing and cooling zones, firing normally being by oil or gas. The process provides a high degree of control over temperature, so that the process is suited to the production of high-strength, dimensionally accurate bricks. Perforated bricks are often fired in this way.

Properties of Clay Bricks and Their Measurement (BS 3921)

Strength

Since bricks are invariably used in compression, the standard method of test for strength involves crushing the bricks, the direction of loading being the same as that which is to be applied in practice – normally perpendicular to their largest face. Attention is drawn to the following aspects of the BS test (See experiment 2.1).

1. The treatment of frogs or perforations should be designed to simulate their behaviour in practice – hence the perforations in perforated bricks should not be filled prior to testing and frogs should only be filled if the bricks are to be used frog up. When frogs are filled, the strength of the mortar used should be in the range 28–42 N/mm^2 at the time of testing.
2. Strength varies with moisture content and, since the saturated state is the easiest state to reproduce, bricks should be saturated for 24 hours (or by vacuum or boiling) before testing.
3. In order to obtain representative results, 10 bricks should be tested, these being carefully sampled either during unloading or from a stack.
4. Bricks are tested between 3 mm thick plywood sheets which reduce stress concentrations resulting from irregularities in the brick surfaces.

5. The strength of the brick is

$$\frac{\text{Maximum load}}{\text{Area of smaller bed face}}$$

   (the two bed faces may not always be identical in size).
6. Bricks are designated as Class 1, 2, 3, 4, 5, 7, 10 or 15, according to their average compressive strength. These classes derive from formerly-used Imperial units, the numbers being multiplied by 6.9 to give minimum crushing strength in N/mm^2. Hence, a class 10 brick has a minimum compressive strength of 69 N/mm^2.
   There is normally good correlation between density and strength, though the precise relationship depends on the method of forming and firing the brick. Underfired bricks would have much reduced strength for a given density, as would bricks which are damaged by firing too rapidly.
7. The strength of *brickwork* is usually quite different from that of the brick, as measured according to BS 3921. It depends on the mortar used (though this would not normally need to be stronger than 10–20 per cent of brickwork strength) and in particular on the shape of the masonry unit. A very common mode of failure in walls is by buckling, especially when they are tall and slender with little lateral restraint.

Water absorption

Water absorption may be an important property of clay bricks, since bricks having very low absorption are invariably of high durability (though the converse is not always true).

In the BS water absorption test, (experiment 2.2) oven-dried bricks are either boiled for 5 h or subjected to a vacuum test in order to ensure maximum possible penetration of water (even in these tests there will normally be some voids which remain unfilled). An alternative method for control purposes only is to soak the brick in water for 24 h, though this gives a lower result that the first two tests.

The water absorption is

$$\frac{\text{Mass of water absorbed}}{\text{Mass of oven dried brick}} \times 100 \text{ (per cent).}$$

Efflorescence

This is the name given to the build-up of white surface deposits on drying out. It results from dissolved salts in the brick and quite commonly spoils the appearance of new brickwork.

In the test for efflorescence bricks are saturated with distilled water in order to dissolve any salts present and then allowed to dry such that salts are carried to one exposed face (experiment 2.3). The

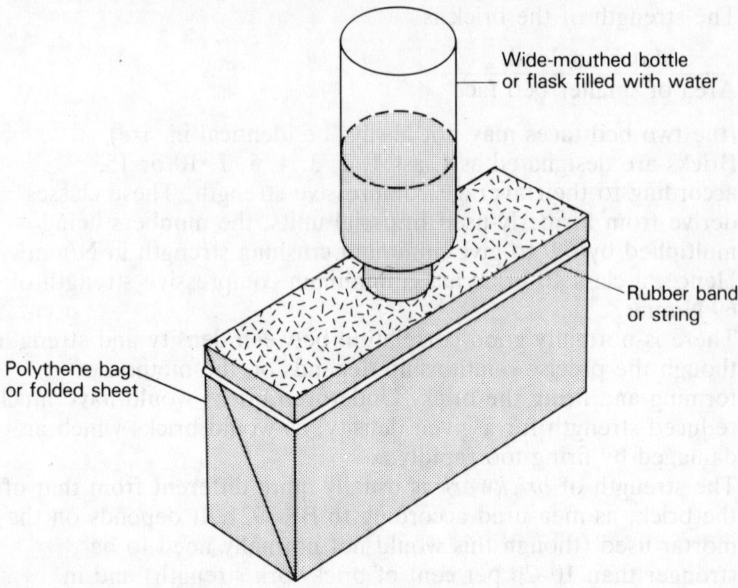

Fig. 2.3 Apparatus for efflorescence test

apparatus is shown in Fig. 2.3.

The efflorescence is assessed as follows:

No perceptible deposit of efflorescence	Nil
Not more than 10 per cent of area covered with thin deposit of salts	Slight
A heavier deposit than slight covering up to 50 per cent of the area of the face but unaccompanied by powdering or flaking of the surface	Moderate
A heavy deposit of salts covering more than 50 per cent of the area of the face but unaccompanied by powdering or flaking of the face	Heavy
A heavy deposit of salts accompanied by powdering and/or flaking of the surface and tending to increase with repeated wettings of the specimen	Serious

British Standard requirements for Engineering and special quality bricks

Engineering bricks

Bricks have specific requirements relating to absorption and strength in addition to those such as dimensional tolerances and efflorescence requirements which apply to ordinary quality bricks. Table 2.1 indicates these requirements for Engineering class A and class B bricks.

Table 2.1 BS 3921 requirements for Engineering bricks

Type	Average compressive strength not less than (N/mm²)	Average absorption not more than (%)
Engineering Class A	69.0	4.5
Engineering Class B	48.5	7.0

Special quality bricks

In addition to the requirements of ordinary quality bricks, special quality bricks should be 'hardfired' and should satisfy the following:

1. When a cut surface is examined, it should reveal a reasonably uniform texture with no very coarse particles.
2. Contents by weight of the following soluble radicals should not exceed the percentages given:
   Sulphate 0.5%
   Calcium 0.3%
   Magnesium 0.03%
   Potassium 0.03%
   Sodium 0.03%.

   The sulphate content is restricted in order to reduce the risk of sulphate attack in the cement mortar, while the other radical contents are restricted to reduce crystallisation damage and efflorescence. The permitted proportion of the calcium radical is much higher than that of the magnesium, potassium and sodium because the latter cause the most difficulty.
3. Evidence of frost-resistance should be provided by one of the following means:
   (a) Satisfactory performance of the bricks in a situation of similar exposure to that required in the same locality for at least three years.
   (b) Satisfactory performance of brickwork panels in an exposed situation for at least three years.
   (c) Where (a) or (b) are not feasible, bricks which satisfy the engineering class B standard in respect of strength *or* absorption are deemed frost-resistant.

It should be noted that Engineering bricks satisfy special quality requirements, though many non-Engineering bricks also satisfy these requirements. Conversely, a number of failures have been observed in clay bricks which are deemed frost resistant according to the third clause. In the next edition of BS 3921 this clause may therefore be amended.

Durability of clay brickwork

The durability of clay brickwork is much more likely to be a problem than its strength, since in most situations clay bricks are very much stronger than is required structurally.

Virtually all durability problems are associated with moisture penetration and it is therefore of paramount importance that bricks be suited to the degree of moisture likely to be found in any one position and that exposure to moisture in this position does not exceed the intended value. Examples of three broad exposure categories to which the internal, ordinary and special quality bricks are suited are given in Table 2.2.

It will be noticed that bricks other than special or engineering quality bricks should not be fully exposed to weather, except in mild climates, if eventual deterioration is to be avoided. The causes and mechanism of the three main modes of deterioration are now considered.

Table 2.2 Exposure capabilities of clay bricks

Degree of exposure	Quality of brick	Examples of use
Mild	Internal	Internal walls, partitions, any walls completely protected from rising damp or rain. May need protection on site during winter
Normal	Ordinary	External walls in most buildings
Severe	Special (or Engineering)	Parapet walls. External walls of buildings subject to extreme exposure, paved areas. Brickwork below d.p.c.

Frost damage (see experiment 2.4)

This is associated with the crystallisation (freezing) of water below the surface of the bricks. Hence, for this to occur the bricks must be fairly porous in order to admit water. There is strong evidence to suggest that water contained in bricks moves into cracks or large voids or towards the surface as the temperature is lowered, damage occurring as ice crystals grow in any enclosed positions.

Fig. 2.4 shows ice crystals being extruded from pores and cracks in the brickwork. Damage is progressive, a few freezing cycles rarely causing visible damage – it will normally take several years for frost damage to become apparent. The susceptibility of bricks to frost damage clearly increases as their water content rises, though some highly porous bricks are found to be frost-resistant even when saturated. Investigations have shown that it is the size distribution of pores in a brick rather than total porosity which determines frost resistance; bricks containing a coarse pore structure are generally more frost-resistant than those with a fine pore structure.

Figure 2.5 shows fractured surfaces of a Fletton (ordinary quality) brick and an Otterham (special quality) brick magnified about 3000 times using a scanning electron microscope. Although the two brick types have similar absorption values of about 20 per cent, the degree of vitrification is seen to be larger in the case of the

Fig. 2.4 Ice extrusions formed when saturated brickwork is frozen (courtesy of BRE)

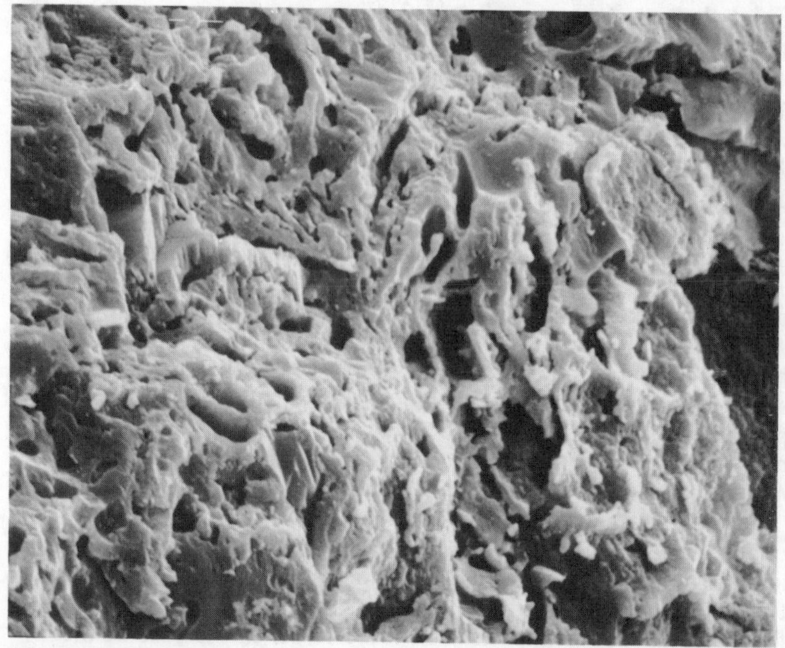

(a)

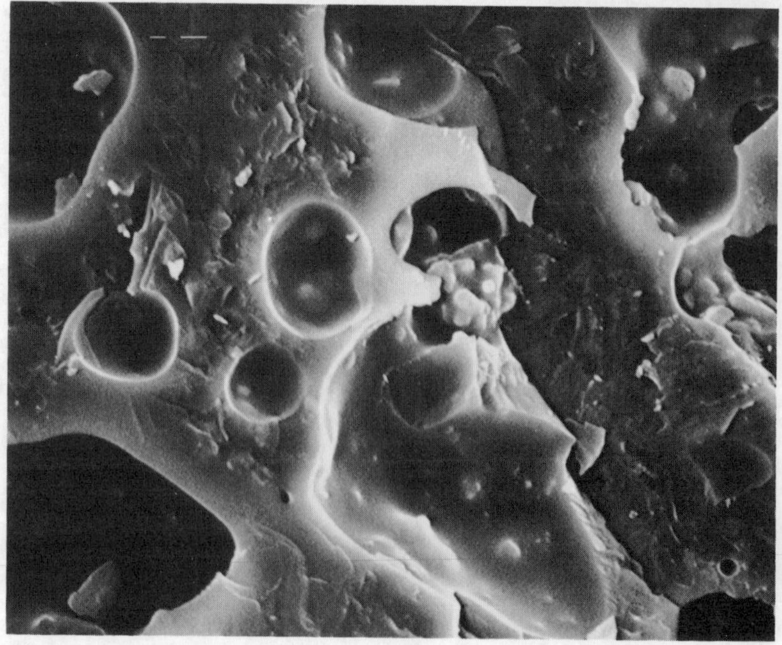

(b)

Otterham brick, resulting in fewer fine spaces within the brick and therefore a more frost-resistant product. However, since pore size distribution is difficult to measure, frost resistance is best assessed practically as explained above. Perhaps surprisingly, some stock bricks having quite low strength and high water absorption satisfy the 'special quality' criteria and are hence frost-resistant, presumably because they contain a coarse pore structure.

As a general rule, the resistance of brickwork to frost will be greatest when all possible means are taken to prevent moisture penetration wherever possible. In the case of internal quality and ordinary quality bricks, the highest risk may be present during construction; it is important to keep bricks dry and to avoid high moisture contents in partially complete structures which do not have the protection of a roof, especially during cold winter spells.

Crystallisation damage (see experiment 2.5)

This is associated with the crystallisation of salts beneath the brick surface. The extent of damage is directly related to the soluble salt content of bricks, hence the best way of avoiding damage is to use special quality bricks. Salts from other sources may also contaminate brickwork. Such sources include poor quality sand in the mortar, contaminated ground water and wind-borne spray from the sea. Nitrates or chlorides are more common than sulphates, though they all have largely the same effect. Some salts may even be released from the cement, though the effect of these should be short-lived.

One problem of salt crystallisation is that it tends to occur locally at boundaries between damp areas of brickwork, such as parapet walls and adjacent drier areas. Salts in solution are drawn to these drier areas and deposits therefore build up, causing local damage. Many salts are hygroscopic (they absorb water), so that they may tend to perpetuate dampness where they occur. Hence in order to avoid these problems:

1. Use well-fired bricks or, in situations where dampness is likely, special quality bricks.
2. Use clean materials and avoid contact between brickwork and ground-water or soil.
3. Design and detail brickwork in such a way as to minimise moisture penetration.

Fig. 2.5 (a) Scanning electron micrograph of fracture surface in Fletton brick, showing fine, lightly vitrified clay surface (magnification approximately 3000 times) (b) Scanning election micrograph of fracture surface in Otterham special quality stock brick showing smooth, well-vitrified surfaces (magnification approximately 3000 times)

Sulphate attack

This occurs in cement mortars – especially those in which the cement contains appreciable quantities of tricalcium aluminate, though the sulphates responsible often originate in the bricks. Sulphate attack will only occur in damp situations and it results in expansion and eventual disruption of the brickwork. Avoidance of sulphate attack is achieved by the same precautions as given under the section on crystallisation damage, though the use of sulphate-resisting cement in the mortar will reduce the severity of attack where these precautions cannot be met fully, such as in earth-retaining walls.

Clay building blocks

These may be defined as clay building units having at least one dimension in excess of the maximum value specified for bricks (see 'Bricks'). They are designed to be bedded in mortar to produce walling or to be used as filler blocks in reinforced concrete floors. Clay blocks are generally hollow units (formed by extrusion), since the voids result in:

1. reduced firing times;
2. reduced weight;
3. increased handleability;
4. increased thermal insulation.

Figure 2.6 shows various types of block available. Since blocks are made from well-sintered clay, the material is dense, brittle and difficult to cut. Some varieties, however, contain slots to assist in cutting.

Clay wall and partition blocks are keyed for rendering or plastering, as they are not intended to be used as finished facing materials.

Calcium silicate (sand lime) bricks BS 187

These are made by blending together finely-ground sand or flint and lime in the approximate ratio 10 : 1. The semi-dry mixture is compacted into moulds and then 'autoclaved', using high-pressure steam for several hours. A surface reaction occurs between the sand and lime, producing calcium silicate hydrates which 'glue' the sand particles into a solid mass. The main properties of calcium silicate bricks are:

1. A high degree of regularity, with smooth surface texture and sharp arrises.
2. Very low soluble salt content, so that efflorescence is not a problem.

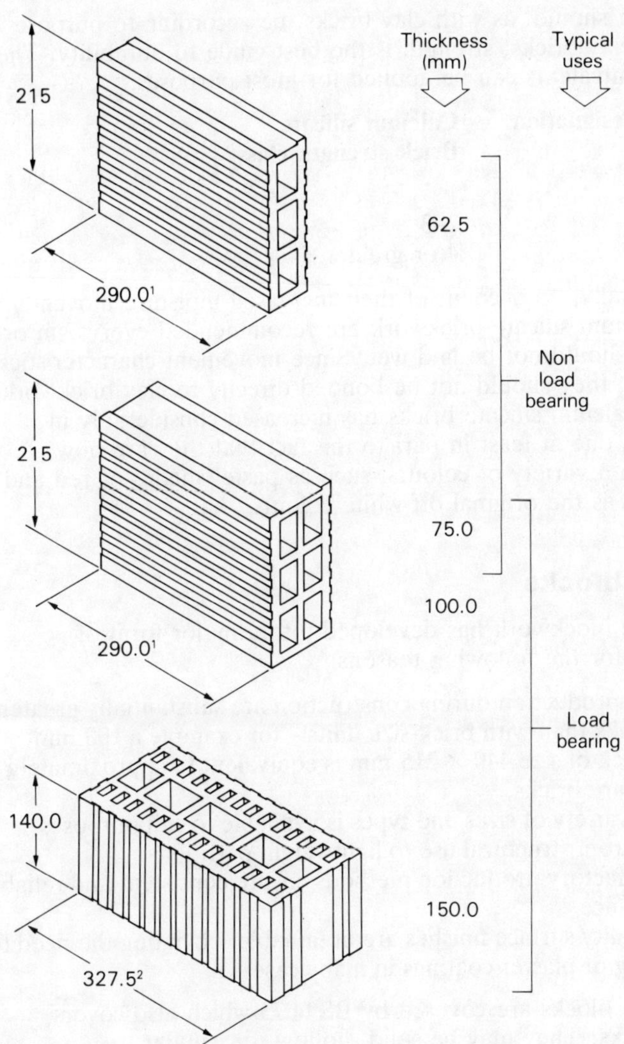

[1] Special bonding lengths are available.
[2] These blocks can be easily cut to length.

Fig. 2.6 Clay building blocks (Mitchells Building Construction: Components and Finishes)

3. Fairly high moisture movement.
4. Compressive strength in the range 7 to 50 N/mm². (Strength classes are employed by BS 187 as in BS 3921 for clay bricks.)
5. Good overall durability in clean atmospheres, though they may deteriorate slowly in polluted sulphur-containing atmospheres.

Selection should, as with clay bricks, be according to purpose but, unlike clay bricks, strength is the best guide to durability. The following equivalents can be applied for most purposes.

Clay brick designation	Calcium silicate Brick strength class
Internal	1
Ordinary	2–3
Special	4 or greater.

Additionally, on account of their increased moisture movement, joints in calcium silicate brickwork are recommended every 7 m or so and they should not be laid wet. Since movement characteristics are different, they should not be bonded directly to clay brickwork. The use of calcium silicate bricks has increased considerably in recent years, due at least in part to the fact that they are now obtainable in a variety of colours, such as pastel shades of red and blue, as well as the original off-white colour.

Concrete blocks

Concrete blockwork has developed into a major form of construction for the following reasons:

1. Rates of production during construction are substantially greater with blocks than with brick-size units – for example a 100 mm thick block of size 440 × 215 mm is equivalent to approximately six standard bricks.
2. A great variety of sizes and types is available to suit purposes ranging from structural use to lightweight partitions.
3. Modern factory production methods ensure consistent and reliable performance.
4. High-quality surface finishes are obtainable, obviating the need for rendering or plaster coatings in many cases.

Concrete blocks are covered by BS 6073 which also covers concrete bricks. They may be solid, hollow, or cellular.

Solid blocks are largely voidless but may have grooves or holes to reduce weight or facilitate handling. These must not exceed 25 per cent of the gross volume of the block.

Hollow blocks have voids passing right through. They can be 'shell-bedded' – that is, the mortar is laid in two strips adjacent to each face, so that there is no continuous capillary path for moisture through the bed. Loadbearing capacity is, or course, reduced when blocks are laid in this way. The strength of hollow blockwork can be increased by filling the cavities with concrete, especially if reinforcement is included. Sound insulation is also improved in this way.

Cellular blocks are a special type of hollow block in which the cavities are closed at one end. The solid edge would normally be laid upwards and, in the case of thin blocks, this makes it easier to produce an effective bed joint.

A great variety of aggregate types is used in the production of concrete blocks – these include natural aggregates, air cooled blast furnace slag, furnace clinker, foamed, expanded or granulated blast furnace slag, bottom ash from boilers and milled softwood chips. The density and strength of the resultant product vary accordingly and they are also influenced by the manufacturing technique.

Denser types of block can be used for loadbearing purposes and decorative or textured facings may be applied.

Lightweight types are now in particular demand, due to the need for high thermal insulation walling. Many types include pulverised fuel ash and may be aerated and/or autoclaved.

BS 6073 does not lay down strength classes but gives minimum strengths for all block types. These are:

Thickness not less than 75 mm	– Average strength of 10 blocks not less than 2.8 N/mm^2. No individual block less than 80 per cent of this value.
Thickness less than 75 mm	– Average transverse strength of 5 blocks not less than 0.65 N/mm^2.

BS 6073 also stipulates drying shrinkage – this should be:
not more than 0.06 per cent (except autoclaved aerated blocks);
not more than 0.09 per cent (autoclaved aerated blocks).
It is important, on account of their high shrinkage, that autoclaved aerated blocks are not saturated prior to laying, otherwise shrinkage cracking may result. Handlability is also much impaired when wet due to their greatly increased weight in this condition.

No guidance regarding durability of blocks is given in BS 6073. The principles as given in Chapter 1 on concrete, apply, though it may be added that some open-textured or autoclaved blocks are often more resistant to frost than their strength would suggest. This may be due to the type of void present and the fact that saturation is rare. Nevertheless, where severe exposure or pollution is likely, blocks of average compressive strength not less than 7 N/mm^2 should be specified. Other types can, of course, be protected by rendering.

Experiments

Experiment 2.1 Determination of the compressive strength of clay bricks

The experiment is much more valuable if 10 bricks of a given type are tested, since the variability of the bricks can then also be ascertained. If this is not possible, a smaller number, say, three bricks, might be tested to give some indication of the ranges.

Apparatus

Gauging trowel, four 75 mm cube moulds for mortar, curing tank; compression tester; plywood sheets of size 225 × 112 mm and thickness 3 mm – two per brick tested, assuming standard metric bricks.

Preparation of bricks

All bricks should first be soaked for 24 h and then removed and allowed to drain for 5 min.

If bricks have frogs which are to be laid frog-up, the frogs must be filled with mortar prior to testing.

The mortar should comprise a 1 : 1½ cement: sand mix with sufficient water for satisfactory workability. (To achieve the required 3 to 7-day strength with very fine sands, it may be necessary to use a 1 : 1 cement : sand mix.) Fill the frogs with mortar and, after allowing 2 to 4 h for stiffening, trowel as smooth and flat as possible. Make four 75 mm cubes from the mortar. Store the bricks and cubes under damp sacking for 24 h and then demould cubes and transfer both bricks and cubes to a curing tank. Bricks may be tested when the mortar strength is between 28 and 42 N/mm^2 (usually achieved in 3 to 7 days).

Procedure

Remove bricks from the water and wipe away excess water and any grit. Label the bricks and record the dimensions of the smaller bed face of each brick. Mount centrally in the compression machine with plywood sheets above and below. Bricks should be mounted in the same orientation as they are intended to be used in service (normally frog-up). Apply the load at 15 N/mm^2 per minute (approximately 33 kN per minute for standard bricks) until maximum load is reached. Record this load and calculate the stress at failure, using the dimensions of the smaller bed face. Repeat for the other bricks and find:

(a) the average strength;
(b) the range of strengths.

Hence classify the brick (see page 71).

Experiment 2.2 Determination of the water absorption of clay bricks

To obtain a meaningful result, the BS 3921 boiling or vacuum test should be carried out. The vacuum test is much quicker than the boiling test but requires additional apparatus so that the latter test will be described here for simplicity. It is suggested that two brick types should be investigated – for example, Flettons and Engineering bricks.

Apparatus

Weighing balance capable of 0.1 g accuracy; tank of capacity (ideally) sufficient to heat ten specimens; drying oven.

Procedure

Ten bricks should, ideally, be used, though they may be sawn into half or quarter sections to save space in the heating tank.

Dry the bricks for 2 days at 110 °C and then allow to cool to room temperature. Label and weigh the bricks and record the masses. Place in the water tank so that water can circulate freely. Heat to boiling and maintain the temperature of 100 °C for 5 h. Allow to cool *still submerged in the tank* for 16–19 h. Remove the bricks, wipe off surface moisture and weigh immediately.

Calculate the water absorption (see page 71) and compare with the limits for Engineering bricks (Table 2.1).

Experiment 2.3 Measurement of efflorescence in clay bricks

In common with other tests, 10 specimens should be used, since results often vary considerably from brick to brick.

Apparatus

Ten wide-mouthed bottles or flasks; large flat tray.

Procedure

The test should be carried out in a warm, well-ventilated room. Wrap the bricks in polyethylene sheet, leaving only the face which is to be exposed in the brickwork uncovered. Tie with a rubber band or string (Fig. 2.3). Fill the first bottle with distilled water and place a brick over the mouth so that it completely covers the opening. Invert both brick and bottle while maintaining them in close contact and stand in the tray. Repeat for the other bricks. Leave for a few days, replacing the distilled water if it is completely absorbed within 24 h. When the bricks have dried, add more water and repeat the process. After drying for the second time, examine the bricks for efflorescence and classify, using the criteria given on page 72.

Experiment 2.4 Measurement of frost damage to clay bricks

Frost usually takes a number of years to result in visible damage to brickwork in practice, so that a laboratory test must attempt to accelerate the process. A fully realistic test must include the effect of mortar joints also – panels comprising 30 or more bricks would be ideal but would require a very large refrigerated enclosure. This experiment is designed to give some indication of the likely properties of a brick, using only a small domestic freezer, though a period of some weeks will still be necessary for its execution.

Apparatus

Shallow containers, domestic freezer (upright type is more convenient), compression test machine.

Procedure

Ideally 10 or more bricks of each type should be subject to freeze/thaw cycles, otherwise variability between individual bricks may over-shadow the effects of frost, especially in naturally durable bricks.

Take a batch of 20 bricks of the type required and place half under water at room temperature for the duration of the test. Place the other 10 in shallow trays in the freezer. Subject to temperature cycles in the range 20 to −20 °C, keeping continuously saturated. With an upright freezer one cycle per day should be possible – for example switch on at 17.00 hours and by 09.00 hours the next day the temperature of −20 °C should have been reached. At this point, switch off the freezer and leave the door open so that the bricks thaw *fully* – a period of 8 h should suffice. (The thawing cycle may have to be lengthened for chest freezers, which are slower to thaw unless the bricks are removed.) Repeat the procedure, topping up trays with water as necessary.

Inspect every 10 cycles for signs of visible damage. After 50 cycles, thaw the bricks and test in a compression machine (see experiment 2.1). Measure the average strength of the bricks which were subject to freezing and express as a percentage of that of the remaining bricks.

This is a severe test and, although no clear criterion exists for frost-resistance, bricks might be assumed to have a high degree of frost-resistance if their strength after 50 cycles has not decreased by more than 10 per cent and there is no visible flaking.

Experiment 2.5 Measurement of crystallisation damage in clay bricks

Crystallisation damage, in common with frost damage, usually occurs progressively over a number of years and this simple test is therefore designed to accelerate the process, though it may still take several weeks to complete.

Apparatus

Large tray in which ten or more bricks can be immersed; plastic rack or grid on which bricks can be dried; compression machine; 5 per cent solution of magnesium sulphate.

Procedure

To accelerate drying, the test should be carried out in a warm, well-ventilated room. Place 10 bricks in the solution so that they are completely covered. Place another 10 bricks of the same type under water for the duration of the test. After a few hours, remove the bricks from the solution and place on a rack or stand which allows them to drain freely. Allow to dry completely – this should be easy to ascertain, since dry bricks are usually a lighter colour. The process may take several days, depending on the type of brick and drying conditions.

Repeat the procedure until at least 20 wetting and drying cycles have been applied, topping up the salt solution as necessary.

Finally, rinse in ordinary water and observe any visible effects on the bricks. Test the 10 bricks in a compression machine, as described in Experiment 2.1. Test also the 'control' bricks and express the average strength of the bricks subject to the salt solution as a percentage of that of the others.

Crystallisation may be assumed to have had a significant effect on the bricks if there is visible damage or if the strength has decreased by more than 10 per cent.

Questions

1. Describe the production of:
   (a) Fletton bricks;
   (b) Engineering bricks.
   Give characteristic properties of both types of brick and two common applications of each.
2. Explain the meaning of the term 'sintering' as applied to clay bricks. Indicate the effects on performance when bricks are:
   (a) overfired;
   (b) underfired.
3. Outline the essential requirements of a 'special quality' clay brick. Give typical applications of these bricks.
4. A clay brick of length 220 mm and width 106 mm failed in compression at a load of 1830 kN. After 5 h boiling in water, the mass increased from 2.94 to 3.05 kg. Use Table 2.2 to classify the brick, assuming it was typical of its type.
5. Outline the three ways by which a clay brick may be checked for frost resistance. State which of these has not proved completely reliable.
6. Explain what is meant by 'crystallisation damage' in clay brickwork. Give situations in which it is especially likely to occur. Give three steps which may be taken to minimise the risk of damage.

7. State the cause of sulphate attack in brickwork. Give three precautions by which the likelihood of such attack can be reduced.
8. State what is meant by 'efflorescence' and indicate when and where it is most likely to be seen. Explain why efflorescence is unlikely in sand–lime brickwork.
9. Give the main reasons for the current widespread use of autoclaved aerated concrete blocks. Indicate why it is important that these blocks are not saturated prior to use.

References

British Standards

BS 187: 1978, *Calcium Silicate* (*Sand Lime and Flint Lime Bricks*).
BS 3921: 1974, *Clay Bricks and Blocks*.
BS 6073: 1981, *Precast Concrete Masonry Units*.

Chapter 3

Dampness in buildings

A great many of the problems which commonly occur in buildings are associated with the penetration of moisture. Specific problems will be dealt with in more detail later but it may be worthwhile to indicate the range of difficulties which could arise. They include fungus attack, swelling/distortion, loss of strength, frost damage, sulphate attack, crystallisation, efflorescence, corrosion of metals and damage to finishes. It is for this reason that great care needs to be given to design, detailing and construction; those buildings which shed rain water (including wind-blown rain) effectively and prevent admission of ground moisture will be largely resistant to the problems listed.

The extent to which water is admitted and retained by the building fabric depends not only on the amount of water which is incident from the exterior of the building, (although obviously good design will minimise this) it depends on the surface characteristics of the materials used. The most common means of admittance of water is by capillarity.

Capillarity

In order to explain this term, it will be helpful to consider first the term 'surface tension'.

Surface tension is exhibited by virtually all materials by virtue of cohesive forces which exist within them. These are inter-molecular forces which arise naturally, due to the electronic nature of the outer shells of atoms. In a liquid, the forces are relatively small and hence they only exert a slight restriction on mobility. Liquids falling freely through space nevertheless take up a spherical shape, since molecules at the surface of the liquid experience a net inwards attraction (Fig. 3.1). The surface is said to be in 'tension' because the inward attraction results in the body of liquid trying to minimise its surface area, hence producing a sphere – the same shape that would be produced if the surface of the liquid were covered by a thin elastic membrane.

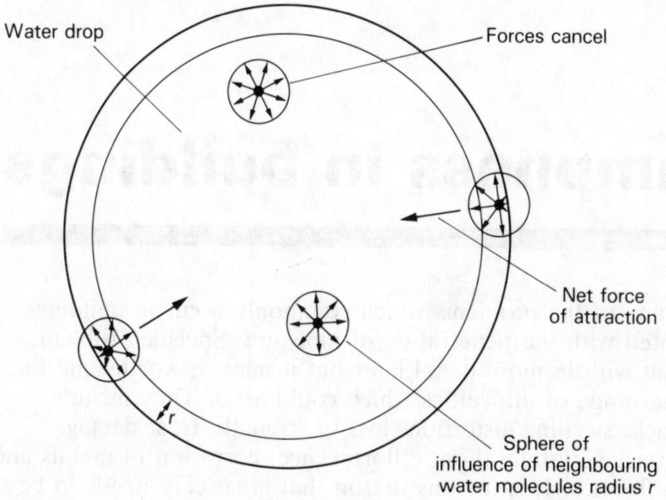

Fig. 3.1 Molecular cohesion – the origin of surface tension

Solids also exhibit surface tension – in fact the cohesive strength of solids can be likened to a sort of surface tension but without the flexibility which exists in liquids. In gases, surface tension effects are very small.

At an interface between a liquid and solid, liquid molecules will be under two influences.

1. Cohesion within the liquid tending to lead to surface tension.
2. Adhesion between the liquid molecules and the solid, caused by the same type of electronic attraction which results in surface tension.

The behaviour of the liquid will depend on the relative magnitude of these two effects. If cohesion within the liquid is greater, it will still tend to minimise its surface area. This occurs when, for example, mercury contacts most solids or when water rests on a greasy surface

(Fig. 3.2). When adhesion between the liquid and solid is greater than cohesion within the liquid, the liquid spreads out on ('wets') the surface, forming only a very thin layer. Reducing the surface tension (cohesion) of water – for example by adding detergent – increases the relative magnitude of the attraction. Water wets most building materials, including ceramics such as brick, stone and concrete, wood, metals and some plastics. This attraction is described as capillarity and it can theoretically occur in all these materials.

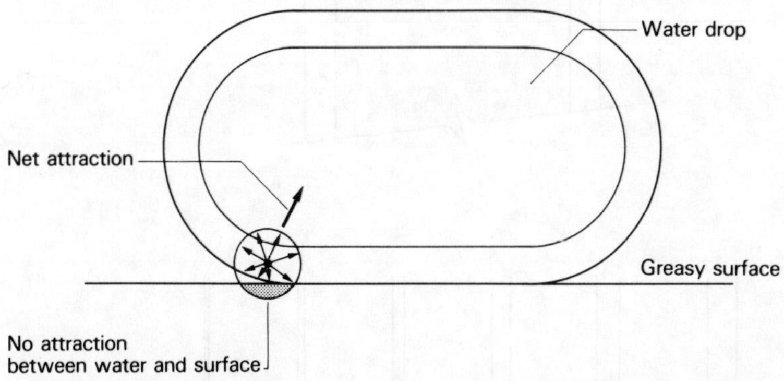

Fig. 3.2 Non-wetting properties resulting when cohesive forces exceed adhesive forces

An important factor affecting capillarity in practice is whether there are small spaces or pores associated with individual materials. The effect may be explained by consideration of the water rise up capillary tubes (hence the term 'capillarity') of various diameters. (Fig. 3.3(a), experiment 3.1). It is well known that the capillary rise in glass tubes increases as the tube diameter decreases (Fig. 3.3(b)). This is because the force exerted on the liquid at the interface increases in relation to its cross-sectional area as the tube diameter decreases. It is true that the total capillarity force involved reduces as the tube gets narrower, since the length of meniscus decreases but the area of the liquid supported decreases at a greater rate, so the result is an apparently higher attraction.

In summarising, it may be stated that, if water wets a solid surface, it will be drawn in any gaps or pores in that material, the attractive force increasing as the width of gaps or pores decreases. Water can in fact be drawn with some force into cracks or pores in materials which are too small to be seen with the naked eye. For the same reason, such water will also be slow to evaporate from such materials once the source of dampness is removed, since it is held in position by the same capillary forces which caused admission initially.

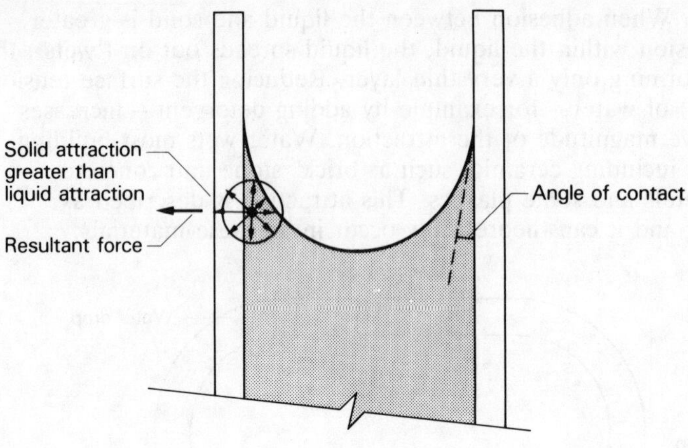

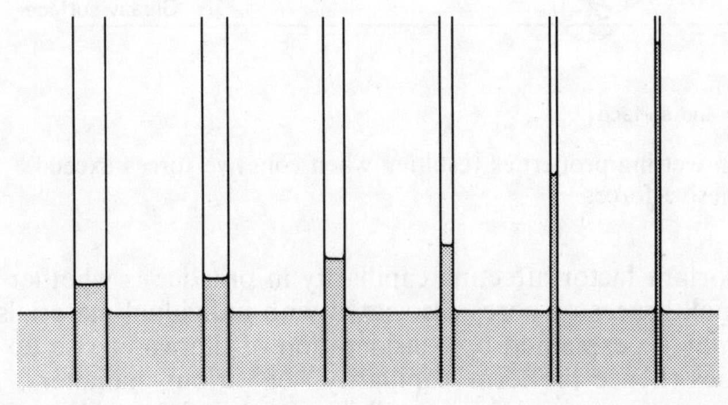

Fig. 3.3 Capillarity (a) attraction of water to the solid surface; the greater the attraction, the smaller is the angle of contact (b) effect of tube size on capillary rise

Porosity

This is one of the factors which affect capillarity, though it is not the only factor, as will be illustrated by reference to a number of materials later. Porosity can be defined as

$$\frac{\text{Volume of pores in a given sample}}{\text{Bulk volume of sample}} \times 100$$

or

$$\frac{\text{Bulk volume of sample} - \text{solid volume of sample}}{\text{Bulk volume of sample}} \times 100$$

Note also that 'pores' in a material do not have to take the form of small capillary tubes. They may include these but may also take the form of cracks or irregular-shaped voids (see Fig. 2.5).

Bulk density (D_B) and solid density (D_S) can be related as follows:

Bulk density $D_B = \frac{M}{V_B}$ — M = mass, V_B = bulk volume

Solid density $D_S = \frac{M}{V_S}$ — V_S = solid volume

Porosity $P = \frac{(V_B - V_S)\,100}{V_B} = \left(1 - \frac{V_S}{V_B}\right)100$

Hence $\frac{V_S}{V_B} = 1 - \frac{P}{100}$

Substituting

$$D_B = \frac{M}{V_B} = \frac{D_S V_S}{V_B} = D_S\left(1 - \frac{P}{100}\right) \text{ (see experiment 3.2)}$$

Interconnection of voids and pore structure

Capillarity can clearly only take place in materials which have interconnected voids. Some voids in most materials are not easily accessible to water and therefore cannot be easily saturated. Taking timber by way of example, the solid density of timber is quite high (approx. 1500 kg/m^3), so that, if voids filled readily with water, timber would sink quite quickly on immersion. In fact, even low-density timber such as balsa wood can float for some time, indicating that not all voids are readily saturated. Some aerated concrete blocks will float on water for some time, again indicating that voids are not easily filled. The voids in air-entrained concrete are formed within the cement mortar and are therefore highly resistant to water penetration.

The importance of pore size distribution has also been mentioned under 'Clay bricks' – it appears that coarse pores (say greater than 30 nm diameter; 1 nm = 10^{-9} m) although they may be readily saturated, do not constitute a frost hazard because, on freezing, water tends to flow out of them to surface regions. The main problem occurs with smaller pores from which water tends to flow, to 'feed' growing ice crystals.

At the present time, no simple way has been found of relating weathering resistance to pore structure and materials specifications for durability consequently must relate to other aspects of materials properties which control durability rather than to terms such as porosity. It was stated earlier that, in the case of clay bricks for example, some types of brick which are highly absorbent nevertheless satisfy the special quality requirement of BS 3921. In some cases, an absorbent brick can indeed increase the durability of the wall it is a part of – for example the resultant 'suction' of the brick can increase the cement mortar bond and thereby reduce the likelihood of capillarity at the brick/mortar interface. An absorbent brick will also tend to reduce the moisture content of the mortar joint – often the most vulnerable part of the wall (see experiment 3.3).

Table 3.1 summarises some of the problems which may arise in materials into which moisture has penetrated.

The prevention of moisture penetration in buildings

The following are intended to illustrate the various mechanisms by which moisture may penetrate buildings.

Cavity walls

There should be no path for moisture between the outer and inner skins. Hence cavities must be kept free of mortar droppings, vertical dpc's should be provided in reveals (Fig. 3.4) and wall ties should be designed to shed water (Fig. 3.5). Complete bridging of cavities with plastic foams or other materials for thermal insulation purposes will increase the risk of moisture penetration in exposed areas (see BS 5618). Preformed types which leave part of the cavity unfilled if used with special wall ties are to be preferred.

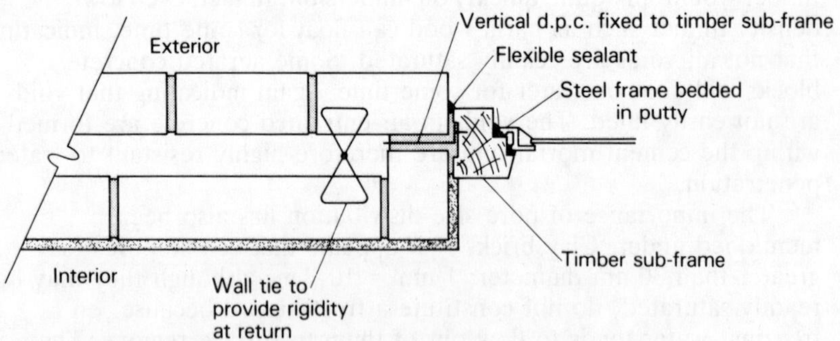

Fig. 3.4 Vertical dpc to prevent water penetration at window return (additional insulation would be required in practice)

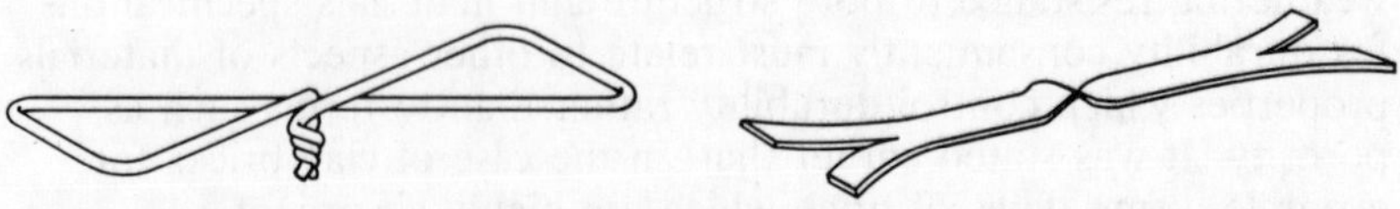

Fig. 3.5 Wall ties designed to prevent passage of water across cavity

Table 3.1 Effects of water admission in porous materials.

Effect of dampness	Materials involved	Result
Fungus attack	Timber	Softening, eventual failure
Swelling/ distortion	Timber	Distortion, poor fit of windows, doors etc.
	Brickwork	May cause buckling if inadequate movement joints.
Strength loss	Brickwork, concrete Timber	Not normally a direct cause of failure May cause premature failure or increased deflections
Frost damage	Brickwork, concrete, mortar Clay tiles	Spalling followed by crumbling and failure at later stage Delamination, eventual failure
Sulphate attack	Concrete, mortars	Disruption followed by failure
Crystallisation	Clay brickwork	Disruption followed by failure
Efflorescence	Brickwork, plaster and concrete	Unsightly appearance
Corrosion of embedded metals	Mainly steel (aluminium if in contact with cement). Examples – wall ties, steel reinforcement in poor quality concrete, screws, nails etc.	Impaired efficiency followed by failure
Damage to finishes	Wallpaper, emulsion paints, fabrics	Discoloration, mould growth, loss of adhesion
	Oil paints on cement substrate	Saponification (alkali attack)

Brickwork

Moisture can penetrate by capillarity into the mortar and the brick individually but also at the brick/mortar interface unless there is good bonding at this position. To reduce moisture penetration into brickwork:

1. Provide adequate eaves projection to shed water clear of brickwork.
2. Avoid recessed pointing which would provide horizontal surfaces to receive water.
3. Ensure adequate bond between bricks and mortar (the use of lime as the mortar plasticises may help).
4. Use dpc's, correctly positioned at low level and at high level for parapet walls (Fig. 3.6).
5. Use weathered (sloping) coping where tops of walls are exposed (Fig. 3.6).

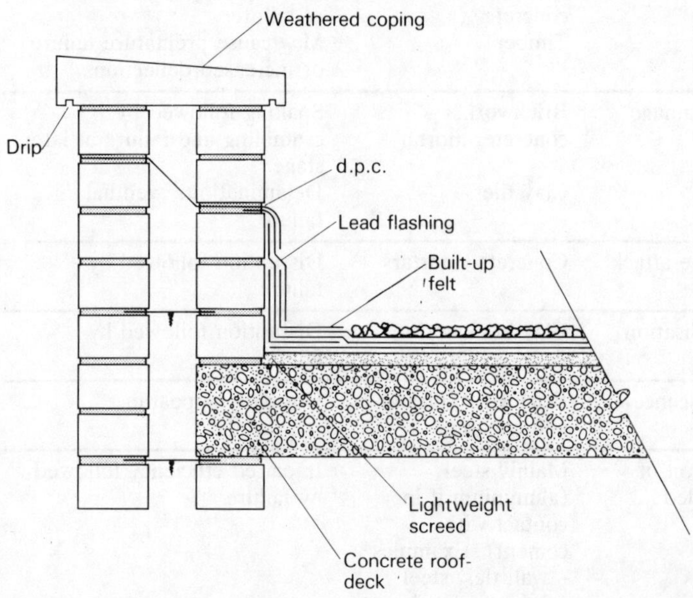

Fig. 3.6 Weatherproofing details in parapet wall (additional insulation may be required)

Windows and doors

Rotting of window and door frames is one of the most common problems in building. The likelihood of this can be reduced by:

1. Use of glued joints in joinery to prevent water access when paint cracks.
2. Use of anti-capillarity grooves (Fig. 3.7).
3. Recessing frames from wall surface.
4. Use of sealant around frame edges.
5. Inward opening of external doors – these are then less vulnerable.
6. Provision of weather bar to shed water clear of door bottoms.

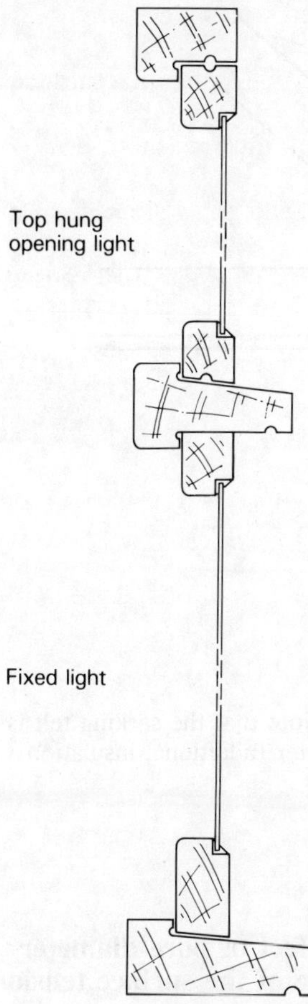

Fig. 3.7 Section through timber casement window showing anticapillary grooves and drips on weathered transom and sill

Roofs

The pitch of a roof must be related to the roof finish, the object always being to minimise water penetration into the surface material. Taking plain tiles (Fig. 3.8) as an example, important features are:

1. A minimum pitch, usually of 35° to reduce water absorption.
2. Tiles are curved to reduce capillarity between them.
3. No joints above one another (requires 'one and a half' width tiles at end of alternate courses.
4. Fascia board upstand to prevent capillarity between eaves course tile and first full tile course.
5. Roofing felt under tiles to shed wind-blown rain or snow.

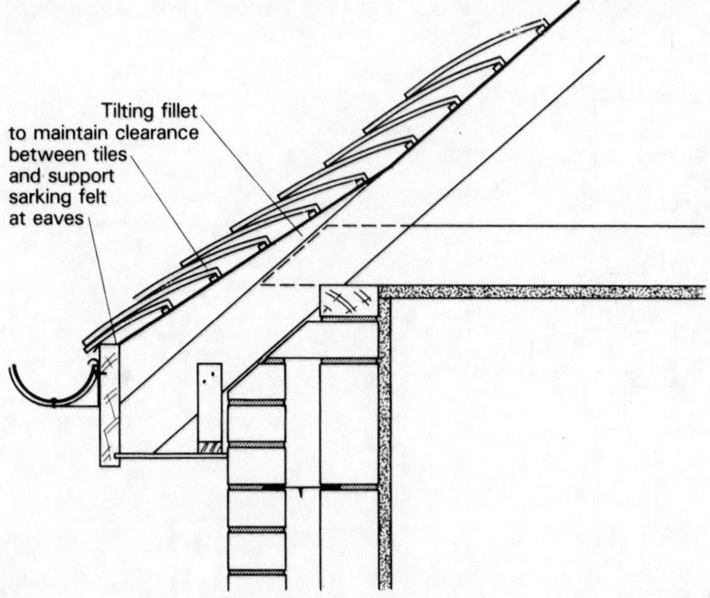

Fig. 3.8 Detail of plain tiling on pitched roof. Note that the sarking felt is fully supported and carried into the gutter (additional insulation may be required)

Experiments

Experiment 3.1 Determination of the effect of pore diameter on capillary attraction and the magnitude of the surface tension of water

Apparatus

Approx. 200 mm lengths of capillary tubes in a range of bore diameters, for example 0.2, 0.5, 1, 2 mm; beaker; clamp stand; acetone; distilled water; travelling microscope or accurate weighing balance.

Procedure

Clean the capillary tubes thoroughly with acetone, rinse with distilled water and dry. Do not touch either end of the tube once cleaned. Place each tube in turn in a beaker of distilled water filled to the brim and fix in a vertical position with a clamp stand. Measure the capillary rise to the nearest mm. Repeat for the other tubes. The capillary rise should increase progressively as the tube diameter decreases – if it does not, reclean the tubes and repeat.

Measure tube diameter with a travelling microscope (or by

accurately weighing the tube dry and then with the bore filled with water

$$\text{Diam (mm)} = 1000\sqrt{\frac{\text{Mass increase (g)} \times 4}{\pi \times \text{length of bore (mm)}}}$$

(Alternatively, bore diameters may be given.)

Plot the capillary rise graphically (y axis) against bore diameter (x axis). Notice the trend in the capillary rise for very small bore diameters – pores in building materials may be as small as 10 μm (= 0.01 μm = 10^{-8} m). The surface tension (T) of water can be calculated from the formula:

$$T = \frac{R\rho gh}{2}$$

R = radius of bore
ρ = density of water (1000 kg(m^3)
h = capillary rise

Experiment 3.2 Measurement of bulk density, solid density, porosity and degree of saturation of porous building materials

Apparatus

Oven; beaker; relative density bottle; balance accurate to 0.1 g and a further balance accurate to 0.000 01 g; clamp stand; cling-film; fine thread; mortar and pestle; 150 μm sieve; funnel.

Specimen preparation

Pieces of brick, concrete or insulation block of size about 50 × 50 × 50 mm are suitable. It is helpful if materials which float on water are cut accurately so that the bulk volume can be determined by dimensional measurement.

Procedure

Dry specimens thoroughly in an oven at 110 °C and allow to cool in air.

To measure bulk density (D_B)

Weigh specimen to 0.1 g accuracy. Find bulk volumes as follows:

(a) Specimens which float on water – for example aerated concrete blocks. Obtain the volume by dimensional measurement

$$\text{Vol. in litres} = \frac{\text{vol. in mm}^3}{10^6}$$

(b) Specimens which sink in water. Wrap carefully in cling-film. Fill a beaker with sufficient water to enable the specimen to be totally immersed in it without causing overflowing. Place this beaker on a top-loading balance and note the mass (0.1 g accuracy). Wrap the specimen carefully in cling-film, making sure there are no trapped air pockets and attach a thread. Suspend, using a clamp stand, in the beaker of water, avoiding contact with sides or base. Note the new balance reading.

Bulk volume in ml = (new reading − old reading)
Hence find bulk density (D_B)

$$= \frac{\text{mass (g)}}{\text{bulk volume } \textit{in litres}} \text{ g/l or kg/m}^3$$

To measure solid density (D_s)
Pulverise about 20 g of the material, using a mortar and pestle, until it passes a 150 μm sieve. Weigh out about 10 g of the material, using the sensitive balance (mass M_1 g) and transfer, using a funnel, to the relative density bottle, avoiding spillage. Add one or two drops of soap solution to a beaker of distilled water, stir and then half fill the relative density bottle, using the funnel. Swirl gently until *all* solid material has sunk and entrapped air is removed. Fill to overflowing, insert the stopper and dry the outside of the relative density bottle. Weigh (M_2 g).

Empty and clean the bottle, refill with distilled water, insert the stopper, dry and weigh (M_3 g).

The solid volume of the material is

$M_1 - (M_2 - M_3)$ (ml)

The solid density (D_s) of the material is

$$\frac{\text{mass}}{\text{solid volume}} = \frac{M_1}{M_1 - (M_2 - M_3)} \text{ g/ml}$$

(multiply by 1000 to change to kg/m³).

Use the following formula to calculate the porosity (p)

$$D_B = D_s\left(1 - \frac{p}{100}\right)$$

To find the water absorption and the percentage of pores filled on saturation

The sample used for the bulk density determination (oven dry mass W_1 g) can also be used for this determination. To obtain an indication of the degree of saturation obtained by short exposure (say to rain), immerse in water for a period of about 10 min. Weigh again (W_2 g).
The percentage water absorption is

$$\frac{W_2 - W_1}{W_1} \times 100$$

The degree of saturation is found as follows:

Bulk volume of this sample

$$= \frac{W_1}{D_B} \text{ litres } (D_B \text{ in g/l})$$

Solid volume of this sample

$$= \frac{W_1}{D_S} \text{ litres } (D_s \text{ in g/l})$$

Volume of pores equals bulk volume minus solid volume

$$= W_1 \left[\frac{1}{D_B} - \frac{1}{D_S} \right] \text{litres}$$

$$\text{or } 1000\, W_1 \left[\frac{1}{D_B} - \frac{1}{D_S} \right] \text{ml}$$

Volume of water absorbed = $(W_2 - W_1)$ ml

Hence percentage of pores filled (degree of saturation)

$$= \frac{W_2 - W_1}{1000\, W_1 \left[\frac{1}{D_B} - \frac{1}{D_S} \right]} \times 100$$

This experiment should be repeated, boiling the sample for some time to determine what total proportion of pores is accessible to water. The performance of different bricks or block types should also be compared.

Experiment 3.3 Measurement of the water absorption of different types of mortar

Apparatus

70 mm mortar cubes; gauging trowel; weighing balance; plasticiser; curing tank; oven.

Procedure

Make up samples of mortar using the following quantities of cement and builder's sand.

Ratio cement: sand	1 : 3	1 : 6	1 : 9	1 : 12
Cement (g)	250	150	100	80
Sand (g)	750	900	900	960

Mix each into a workable mortar with water which has been plasticised either with a mortar plasticiser or a few drops of washing-up liquid. The consistence of each should be the same.

Fill 70 mm mortar cubes with each, identify and cover.

Demould after one day and cure under water until one week old.

Oven-dry the cubes. Weigh each cube and record the masses. Immerse in water and leave for 5 min. Record masses again. Re-immerse and obtain masses after 10, 20 and 60 min. Calculate the water absorption of each, as a percentage, at each stage.

$$\text{Water absorption} = \frac{\text{Water absorbed}}{\text{Dry mass}} \times 100$$

Plot water absorption against time. Comment on the relation for the different mortar types and give implications regarding the use of these mortars.

Questions

1. State the meaning of the following terms:
   (a) cohesion;
   (b) adhesion.
   Hence explain the meaning of the terms 'surface tension' and 'capillarity'.
   Give simple illustrations of the behaviour of water which results from these two phenomena.
2. Describe how the degree of attraction of water into water pores varies with pore diameter. Hence indicate whether coarse or fine-pored materials tend to be quicker drying after being saturated.
3. A lightweight block is found to have a solid density of 2400 kg/m^3 and a bulk density of 800 kg/m^3. Calculate its porosity.
4. A common brick has a bulk density of 1300 kg/m^3. If the porosity is 45 per cent, calculate the solid density of the material.
5. Explain the meaning of the term 'suction' in bricks. Give two advantages that result from bricks having some suction.
6. Draw a section through a 1 m high, 215 mm free-standing boundary wall, indicating features designed to minimise water admission:
   (a) from above;
   (b) from wind-blown rain;
   (c) from the ground.
7. (a) Show by means of a sketch how plain roofing tiles resist capillarity.
   (b) Give two reasons why tiles on a more steeply-pitched roof are less likely to be damaged by frost.

Chapter 4

Metals

Metals are a most important group of structural materials because they are the only bulk materials which exhibit high strength in tension – even lead, the softest of the metals commonly used in building, has a tensile strength substantially in excess of that of ordinary concrete. Their high strength is also matched by high stiffness (modulus of elasticity). Table 4.1 gives ultimate tensile strengths (that is, breaking strengths) and elastic moduli of the most commonly used building metals, together with their relative densities. It will be noted that there is reasonable correlation between strength and stiffness, since both are related to metallic bond strength, values for iron being substantially in excess of those for the other metals. Density is not, however, so correlated to the

Table 4.1 Properties of chief building metals (commercially pure). Metals listed in order of increasing ultimate tensile strength

Metal	Relative density	Elastic modulus kN/mm^2	Ultimate tensile strength (N/mm^2)
Lead	11.3	16.2	18
Zinc	7.1	90	37
Aluminium	2.7	70.5	45
Copper	8.7	130	210
Iron	7.8	210	540

other properties. The following comments apply to the strength values in the table.

1. The tensile strength of metals may depend on the cooling regime – more rapid cooling generally produces a finer grain structure and hence higher strength.
2. Yield stresses, which determine how large a load can be supported in service, are usually substantially less than (approximately half) ultimate stresses.
3. Metals such as zinc and lead may, in the long term, 'creep' to failure at much lower stresses than those indicated.
4. The presence of impurities or alloying elements generally has a marked effect on strength. Most impurities increase strength up to a point but they also increase brittleness.

Steel

Steel, the most important ferrous metal in building construction, is an alloy of iron and carbon. The presence of carbon in iron leads to the formation of a non-metallic compound – iron carbide (cementite) – which is intensely hard and brittle, and exists as very fine sheets interwoven with iron sheets to form a compound called pearlite. The advantage of having some pearlite in steel is that plastic flow, or 'yield' occurs much less readily than in pure iron which contains no pearlite, though the presence of too much pearlite reduces ductility, toughness and weldability. The quantity of pearlite contained in a steel depends on its carbon content. The average carbon content of pearlite is 0.83 per cent (by weight), so that steels having this percentage of carbon would consist of 100 per cent pearlite. Steels containing less than 0.83 per cent carbon comprise a mixture of pearlite and iron crystals, the amount of pearlite increasing proportionately as the carbon content rises to 0.83 per cent. Steel may contain up to 1.7 per cent carbon, the carbon in excess of 0.83 per cent in steels of carbon content in the range 0.83 to 1.7 per cent existing in the form of thin cementite layers around pearlite 'crystals'. Figure 4.1 shows magnified photographs of polished, etched sections of steels having various carbon contents.

Low carbon steels

These may be defined as steels containing less than 0.25 per cent carbon and include steels referred to as mild steels and high yield steels. They form a very large proportion of the steels used in building, having moderate strength but good toughness, ductility and welding properties on account of the fairly low proportion of pearlite. Examples include weldable structural steels, cold rolled

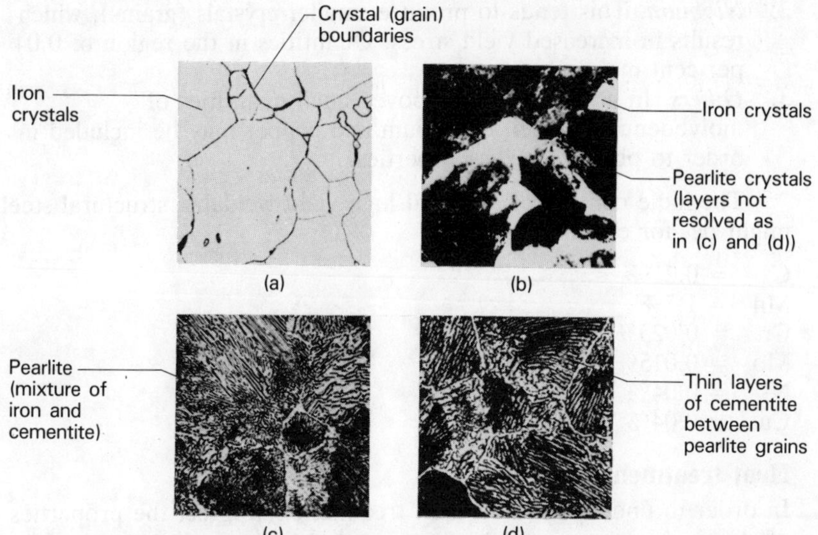

Fig. 4.1 Magnified photographs of polished etched sections of steel having various carbon contents (a) carbon content almost zero (b) carbon content 0.5 per cent (c) carbon content 0.83 per cent (d) carbon content 1.2 per cent

steel sections for lintels etc., window frames, reinforcing bars and mesh, expanded metal and wire for wall ties.

In addition to containing some carbon, low carbon steels contain a number of other elements, some present as a result of the steel manufacturing process and others included to benefit certain properties of the steel.

Common impurities are:

1. *Sulphur and phosphorous*. These form precipitates of iron sulphide (FeS) and iron phosphide (Fe_3P) respectively, which cause embrittlement. Hence contents of each are limited to 0.05 per cent in mild steel.
2. *Silicon*. When present in small quantities it dissolves in the iron, increasing strength. Larger quantities cause embrittlement, hence silicon is usually restricted to about 0.2 per cent.

Common alloying elements are:

1. *Manganese*. This is useful since it increases the yield strength and hardness of low carbon steels. It also increases hardenability and may combine with sulphur, reducing brittleness caused by the latter. Mild steel contains approximately 0.5 per cent manganese, while high yield steel contains about 1.5 per cent.

2. *Niobium*. This tends to produce smaller crystals (grains), which results in increased yield stress. Quantities in the region of 0.04 per cent may be present.
3. *Others*. In addition to the above, small quantities of molybdenum, nickel, chromium and copper may be included in order to obtain specific properties.

The ladle content of a typical high yield weldable structural steel might be, for example:

C = 0.21%
Mn = 1.5%
Cr = 0.025%
Mo = 0.015%
Ni = 0.04%
Cu = 0.04%

Heat treatment of steels

In order to understand how heat treatment can affect the properties of steels, it is necessary to appreciate that the crystalline form of iron alters each time it is heated or cooled through temperatures in the region of 900 °C. Above this temperature the iron crystals ('gamma', γ iron) can fully dissolve all the carbon present (up to 1.7%) forming a material called austenite. Below this temperature, low temperature ('alpha', α iron) crystals form as the carbon is rejected to produce a separate compound – iron carbide or cementite, whose physical form has been described. It will be obvious that the formation of new crystals involves the movement of carbon within a solid material and this requires a certain length of time to occur. Hence the properties of the resultant steel can be greatly affected by the rate of cooling. It will also be apparent that steel containing more carbon will be more sensitive to variations in cooling rate (see experiment 4.1). The main forms of heat treatment are:

Annealing

The steel is heated to about 900 °C so that all carbon dissolves in the high-temperature iron crystals. The steel is then cooled very slowly in the furnace, which results in a coarse crystal structure with relatively thick cementite and iron sheets forming in the pearlite. The result is a soft malleable steel of fairly low yield point (Fig. 4.2(a)).

Normalising

This involves heating the steel as in annealing and then allowing the metal to cool in still air rather than in the furnace. The grains so produced are smaller (Fig. 4.2(b)), as are the cementite layers in the pearlite, resulting in increased strength and impact resistance. Hot

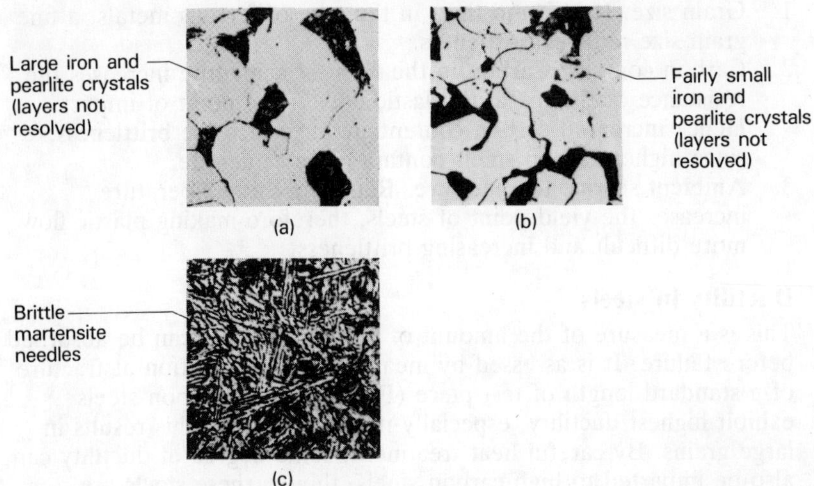

Fig. 4.2 The effect of cooling rate on a low-carbon steel (a) annealing – very slow cooling in the furnace (b) normalising – cooling in still air (c) quenching – rapid cooling in water

rolling of structural steel sections, followed by cooling in air may give properties similar to those obtained by normalising if the 'finishing' temperature is correct; this then avoids the expense of reheating the steel.

Quenching

This involves plunging the red hot metal into cold water, resulting in a very rapid cooling rate. The carbon in this case is unable to form cementite and so a fine, brittle crystalline structure called martensite forms instead. (Fig. 4.2(c)). This structure is highly stressed and, in the case of high carbon steels, cracking may occur in the metal. Quenching is, for this reason, followed by tempering – controlled heating to 200–400 °C to restore toughness to the steel without losing all the hardness imparted by quenching.

It should be emphasised that the effects of heat treatment are far greater when steels have higher carbon contents, since high carbon steels have, on cooling, more carbon to 'reject' from their high temperature crystal structure. Rapid cooling will also be more effective when applied to small components, since they have lower thermal inertia and therefore cool more quickly in given conditions.

Brittleness in steels

Brittleness implies the inability of the metal to absorb energy by impact (shock loading). Steels which are able to absorb energy in this way would be described as 'tough'. Brittleness depends on:

1. Grain size. It is found that, in the case of ferrous metals, a fine grain size reduces brittleness.
2. Carbon content. Carbon in the form of cementite increases the resistance of the metal to plastic flow at the point of impact. Hence increased carbon contents tend to increase brittleness, since higher carbon steels contain more cementite.
3. Ambient service temperature. Reducing the temperature increases the yield point of steels, therefore making plastic flow more difficult and increasing brittleness.

Ductility in steels

This is a measure of the amount of plastic flow that can be absorbed before failure. It is assessed by measuring the elongation at fracture of a standard length of test piece (Fig. 4.3). Low carbon steels exhibit highest ductility, especially if annealed since this results in large grains. By careful heat treatment, some degree of ductility can also be imparted to high carbon steels, though these steels are always more brittle than mild steels because they undergo less plastic flow prior to failure. High carbon steels do not exhibit a visible yield point. Figure 4.4 shows stress strain curves for mild steel, and a high carbon high tensile steel together with curves for copper and lead for comparison.

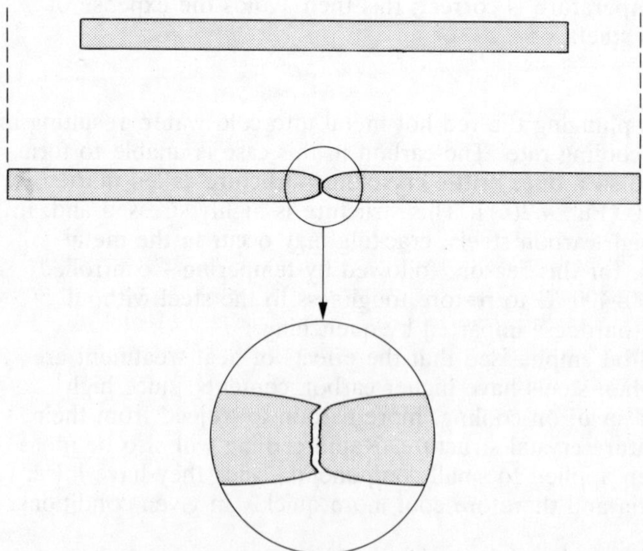

Fig. 4.3 Elongation at failure of a tensile specimen as an indication of ductility. Elongation around the point of fracture is very high in low-carbon steels

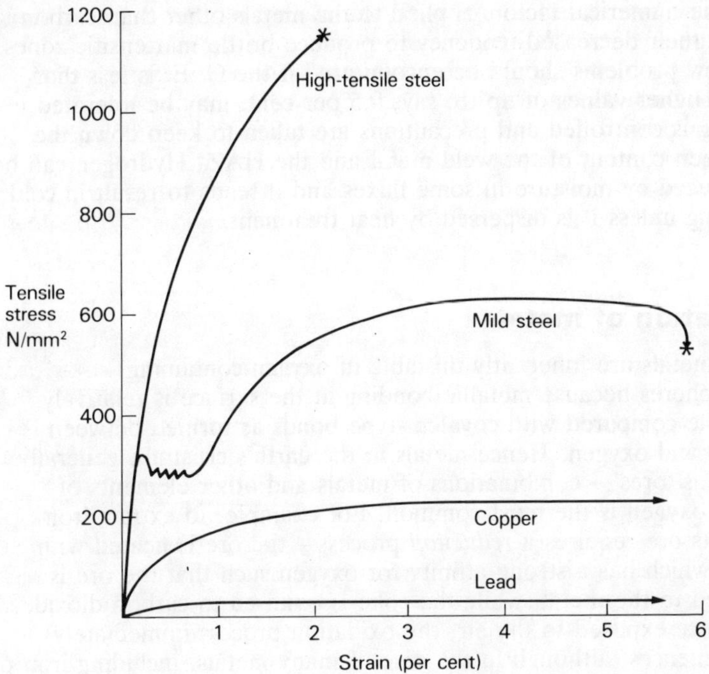

Fig. 4.4 Stress strain curves for mild steel, high-tensile steel, copper and lead. The last two reach very high strains before failure

Weldability in steels

This is the ability of two pieces of steel to be joined by fusion in a localised region at their boundary. The high temperatures involved in welding may result in fortuitous 'heat treatment' of an area of metal in the neighbourhood of the filler metal – the heat affected zone (HAZ). Where conditions are such that rapid cooling occurs (mainly in large sections) a brittle martensitic structure results, while slower cooling may cause an undesirably coarse grain structure. Since brittleness problems are most severe in steels having a high carbon or alloy content, steels which are designed to be welded would normally have a specified 'carbon equivalent' content. This is given by the formula:

$$\text{C. E.} = \%\text{C} + \frac{\%\text{Mn}}{6} + \frac{\%\,(\text{Cr} + \text{Mo} + \text{V})}{5} + \frac{\%(\text{Ni} + \text{Cu})}{15}$$

(C = carbon
Mn = manganese
Cr = chromium
Mo = molybdenum
V = vanadium
Ni = nickel
Cu = copper)

The numerical factors applied to the metals other than carbon reflect their decreased tendency to produce brittle martensitic zones.

Few problems should be encountered if the C. E. is less than 0.25. Higher values of up to, say, 0.5 per cent, may be tolerated if cooling is controlled and precautions are taken to keep down the hydrogen content of the weld metal and the HAZ. Hydrogen can be introduced by moisture in some fluxes and it tends to result in cold cracking unless it is dispersed by heat treatment.

Oxidation of metals

Most metals are inherently unstable in oxygen-containing atmospheres because metallic bonding at the surface is relatively unstable compared with covalent-type bonds as formed between metals and oxygen. Hence metals in the earth's crust are generally found as 'ores' – combinations of metals and other elements of which oxygen is the most common. For example, to extract iron from its ore requires a *reduction* process – the ore is heated with coke, which has a strong affinity for oxygen such that the ore is reduced to the metal, while the coke is oxidised to carbon dioxide.

Once exposed to the air, the oxidation process immediately recommences, although in the case of many metals, including iron or steel at ordinary temperatures, this fortunately occurs to a very limited extent. The restriction on the rate of oxidation of steel results from the difficulty of access of oxygen to the metal – as soon as an oxide layer forms, oxygen must diffuse through this layer in order to gain access to underlying metal atoms. There follows a progressive reduction in oxidation rate such that, after a time, destruction of the metal ceases. Hence in a dry atmosphere steel components will remain sensibly free of corrosion for many years.

The main problem with respect to oxidation occurs at high temperatures at which the oxide film grows much more quickly. Thicker films tend to crack, thereby exposing fresh metal, which continues to oxidise. Hence substantial oxide coatings (mill scale) can form on steel during hot working. This is recognisable as a thin grey coating on hot rolled steel beams or reinforcing bars. (In cold worked reinforcing bars, the mill scale falls off during the deformation process.) Similarly when steel is being welded, fluxes may be used to prevent oxygen access to the hot metal.

Corrosion of metals

This process is quite different from oxidation, although oxygen may assist the corrosion process as, for example, in the rusting of iron or steel. Corrosion may take two basic forms – acidic and electrolytic –

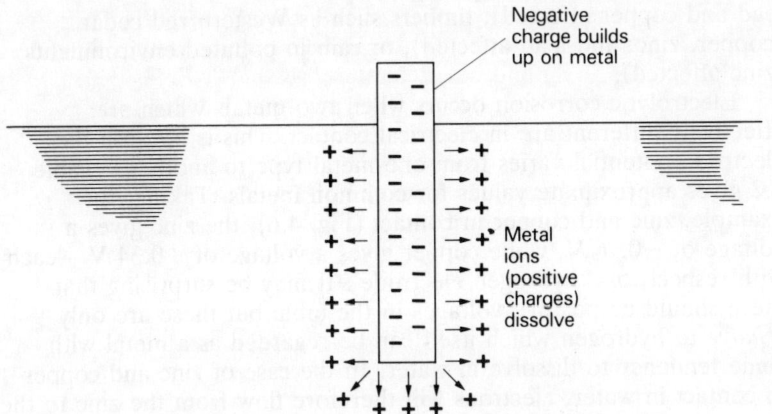

Fig. 4.5 Tendency for metals to dissolve when placed in water

and these both result from the tendency of metals to ionise (dissolve) when placed in water or aqueous solutions (Fig. 4.5). This ionisation is the result of interaction between the surface atoms of the metal (which, as has already been explained, are relatively unstable) and ions in the water. The basic process can be represented:

M	$\longrightarrow$	M^+	+	e^-
surface metal atom		positive metal ion		electron (remains on metal)

The electrons remaining on the metal cause it to become negatively charged, resulting in a negative voltage which increases as further metal dissolves. It eventually reaches a value, called the electrode potential of that metal, when the negative charge is sufficient to prevent further positive ions leaving the metal. Ionisation (corrosion) ceases at this point.

Continued corrosion, resulting in visible loss of metal, will only take place if, by some mechanism, the negative electric charge on the metal is reduced, thereby allowing more positive ions to 'escape'.

In acidic corrosion, the negative charge is removed by hydrogen ions in solution which then form hydrogen gas:

$2H^+$	+	$2e^-$	$\longrightarrow$	$H_2 \uparrow$
in solution		from the metal		hydrogen gas

Metals which, in clean damp conditions are normally protected by coatings of oxides or other compounds may nevertheless corrode in the presence of acids such as are obtained in peaty soils (zinc, lead and copper affected); timbers such as Western red cedar (copper, zinc, and lead affected), or rain in polluted environments (zinc affected).

Electrolytic corrosion occurs when two metals which are effectively different are in electrical contact. This is because the electrode potential varies from one metal type to another – Table 4.2 gives approximate values for common metals. Taking, for example, zinc and copper in contact (Fig. 4.6), the zinc gives a voltage of −0.76 V, while copper gives a voltage of +0.34 V – each with respect to a 'hydrogen electrode'. It may be surprising that there should be positive voltages in the table but these are only *relative* to hydrogen which itself can be regarded as a metal with some tendency to dissolve in water. In the case of zinc and copper in contact in water, electrons will therefore flow from the zinc to the copper at their point of contact (conventional current in the reverse direction) such that the negative voltage on the zinc is partially cancelled and the zinc continues to corrode. The zinc is called the *anode*. The copper, which cannot corrode, is called the *cathode*. Hence electrolytic corrosion will occur between any two metals in contact if moisture is present, the metal which is *higher* in Table 4.2 corroding. The corrosion will be more serious if the anode area is small and the cathode area large (e.g. galvanised nails in copper sheet), if salts are present to assist ion movement in solution or if the temperature is raised. Table 4.3 gives some common situations in which electrolytic corrosion can occur.

Very important also is the fact that corrosion can occur within a piece of a single metal type, since its structure and also possibly environmental variations may result in effectively different electrode potentials at different parts of the surface. Table 4.4 indicates a number of ways in which this may occur. Oxygen assists in the

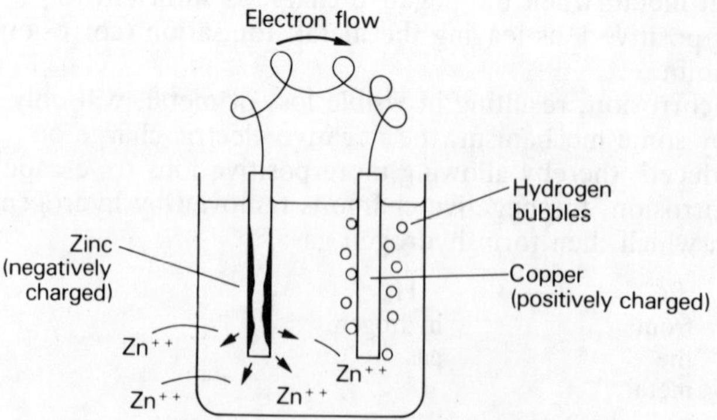

Fig. 4.6 Electrolytic corrosion resulting from zinc and copper rods immersed in aqueous solution while in electrical contact

Table 4.2 Standard electrode potentials of pure metals

Metal	Electrode potential (V)
Magnesium	−2.4
Aluminium	−1.7
Zinc	−0.76
Chromium	−0.65
Iron (ferrous)	−0.44
Nickel	−0.23
Tin	−0.14
Lead	−0.12
Hydrogen (reference)	0.00
Copper (cupric)	+0.34
Silver	+0.80
Gold	+1.4

Note that the most reactive metals are the alkali and alkaline earth metals which hold their electrons most loosely

Table 4.3 Some common situations in which electrolytic corrosion occurs

Situation	Metal which corrodes	Remedy
Galvanised water cistern or cylinder with copper pipes; traces of copper deposited due to water flow	Galvanised film corrodes electrolytically at point of contact with the copper particles. Film is destroyed, then steel corrodes similarly	Use a sacrificial anode in cistern. Otherwise use a plastic cistern or copper cylinder
Brass plumbing fittings in certain types of water	Zinc-dezincification	Use low zinc content brass or gunmetal fittings
Copper ballcock soldered to brass arm	Corrosion of solder occurs in the damp atmosphere resulting in fracture of joint	Use plastic ball on ballcock
Copper flashing secured by steel nails	Steel corrodes rapidly	Use copper tacks for securing copper sheeting
Iron or steel railings set in stone plinth using lead	Steel corrodes near the base	Ensure that steel is effectively protected by paint
Steel radiators with copper pipes	Steel radiators corrode	Corrosion can be reduced by means of inhibitors

Table 4.4 Situations in which electrolytic corrosion of a single metal may occur

Cause	Anode	Examples	Remedy
Grain structure of metals	Grain boundary	Any steel component subject to dampness	Keep steel dry
Variations in concentration of electrolyte	Low concentration areas	All types of soil	Cathodic protection
Differential aeration of a metal surface	Oxygen-remote area	Improperly protected underground steel pipes	Cathodic protection
Dirt or scale	Dirty area (oxygen remote)	Exposure of some types of stainless steel to atmospheric dirt	Use more resistant quality or keep the surface clean
Stressed areas	Most heavily stressed region	Steel rivets	Protect from dampness

corrosion of steel by combining with electrons from cathodes to form the hydroxyl ions necessary to produce rust (ferric hydroxide):

$$2H_2O \quad + \quad O_2 \quad + \underset{\text{from cathode}}{4e^-} \quad \longrightarrow \quad \underset{\text{hydroxyl ions}}{4\,(OH)^-}$$

Electrolytic corrosion is by far the most serious form of corrosion of metals in general building applications.

Prevention of corrosion

It will be apparent that, since both acidic and electrolytic corrosion involve ionisation, each can be prevented by keeping the metal dry, moisture being necessary for ionisation. Where dampness cannot be avoided, impermeable coatings will greatly reduce the likelihood of corrosion. However, no coating is absolutely waterproof. The resistance of a paint film, for example, increases with its thickness and defects such as cracks or chips can cause concentrated corrosion at these positions. Many metals, such as aluminium, zinc, lead and copper are protected by thin oxide or corrosion films, hence they may not need painting in clean environments. Corrosion may, however, be promoted by rain in polluted atmospheres or by contact with acid soils.

There are other means by which corrosion can be prevented or reduced – for example, galvanising of steel, in which a thin zinc coating is applied. The steel is protected for a time, even if exposed by scratches in the zinc. Thick coatings, as obtained by hot dip galvanising, are necessary if effective long-term protection is to be achieved without painting. The zinc corrodes in the region of scratches when damp is present and the exposed area of steel increases until it is too large for the zinc to give full protection (Fig. 4.7).

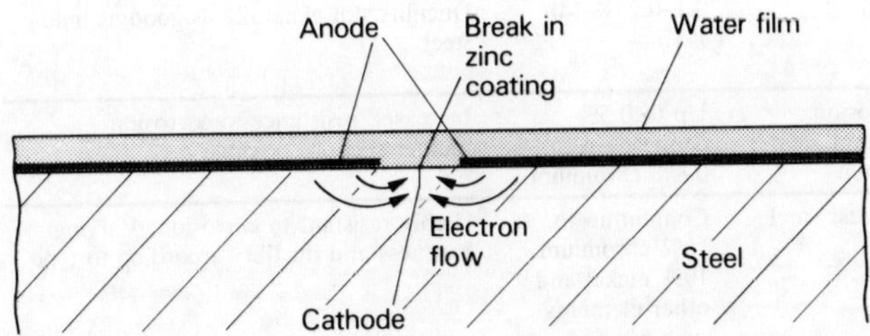

Fig. 4.7 Protection provided by galvanising at breaks in the zinc coating

A further possibility is to charge artificially the exposed metal negatively, using a direct current supply (Fig. 4.8). This method is used for the protection of underground steel pipelines, though it is designed to prevent corrosion occurring in defects in a protective coating rather than to obviate the need for a protective film.

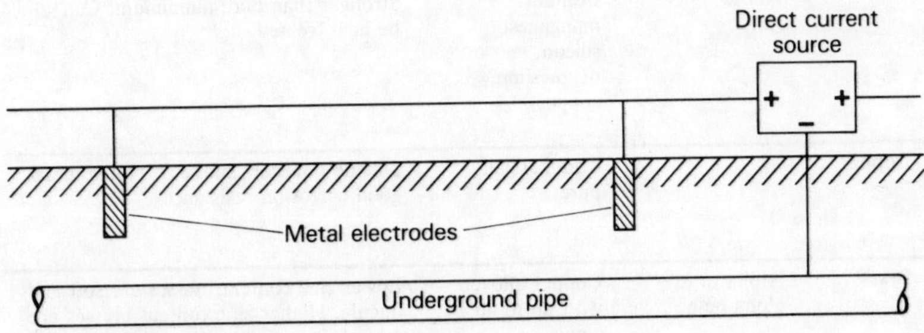

Fig. 4.8 Protection of an underground steel pipe by the impressed current method

Metals used in construction

Table 4.5 gives details of the composition, characteristic properties and applications in construction of a number of metals and alloys.

Table 4.5 Properties, recognition and applications of some common metals

Metal	Type	Composition	Special Properties
Low-carbon steel	Mild steel	Carbon 0.1–0.25% Mn 0.5%	Low cost, good machinability, ductility, weldability, toughness
	High yield steel	Carbon 0.1–0.25% Mn 1.5%	Greater yield strength than mild steel. Ductility not generally as good as mild steel
	Corrosion resistant steel (Corten)	Up to 0.5% copper. Up to 0.8% chromium	Increased resistance to corrosion – thinner sections possible
	Stainless steel	Contain up to 18% chromium, 10% nickel and other elements such as molybdenum	Highly resistant to corrosion. Varying hardness and ductility according to type
Cast iron	Grey	Up to 4% carbon, often high silica content	Low melting point – easily castable Hard, brittle
Aluminium	Pure	99.50–99.99 percent al.	Good corrosion resistance in clean atmospheres. (Protect from salt, cement mortar, contact with copper) Can be hand-formed
	Alloys	Contain manganese silicon, magnesium, copper	Stronger than pure aluminium. Can be heat treated
Copper	–	Commercially pure	Ductile but work hardens. Noble metal, good corrosion resistance
Brass	Alpha or alpha-beta	Copper alloyed with up to 46% zinc	Lower zinc content brasses are soft and ductile. Higher zinc content brasses are more brittle. Corrosion resistant
Phosphor-bronze	–	Copper; up to 13% tin; up to 1% phosphorus	High strength and corrosion resistance Can be hardened
Lead	–	Commercially pure	Eminently ductile, does not work harden. Very durable. (Protect from organic acids and cement mortar) Creeps. High thermal movement
Zinc	–	Commercially pure	Fairly ductile, moderate durability in clean atmospheres. Avoid contact with copper or copper alloys

Recognition	Application			
	Structural	Cladding/ Roofing	Aesthetic	Manu- factured
Easily identified by high density and high stiffness. Soon rusts in damp atmosphere. Mild steel reinforcing bars normally plain round	Steel sections. Reinforcing bars Wire.	Plastic coated steel sheet guttering	Wrought products	Window frames, office furniture, sundries.
As mild steel. High yield steel reinforcing bars are ribbed. More springy than mild steel	Steel Sections. Reinforcing bars	–	–	Nuts, bolts, springs
Orange/brown coating, darkening with age to purple/brown	Exposed sections			
Usually 'satin' finish. Some types may rust if dirty	Reinforcing bars	Sheet cladding.	Balustrades	Tubing, sanitary applications
High density, rough surface texture. Brittle fracture revealing grey granular surface	Compression members in older structures	Rainwater goods.	Ornamental work – staircases	Boilers, radiators, manhole covers, door furniture
Low density. Bright greyish metal surface when new, white deposit when corroded. Fairly soft metal	–	Flashings, weatherings. Guttering.	–	Aluminium foil for insulating boards
As above	Lightweight frames	Roofing, cladding, Rainwater goods according to type.	–	Door handles
Characteristic 'copper' colour, darkening to brown on ageing. Green 'patina' formed in dirty atmospheres	–	Sheet roofing, flashings, weatherings.	Household utensils.	Tubing
Yellow/gold colour, can be polished	–	–	Door furniture	Pipe fittings, hinges, screws etc.
Dark copper colour		Widely used for fixing of claddings.	–	Weather proofing strips
High density, dull grey finish, very easily distorted	–	Sheet roofing or cladding. Flashings, Weatherings.	Castings such as rainwater hoppers	Pipes
Higher density than aluminium, fairly soft, light grey finish, becoming powdery with age	–	Roofings, flashings, weatherings	–	Door handles (die cast alloy)

Experiments

Experiment 4.1 The effects of heat treatment on steels of differing carbon content

Apparatus

Samples of steel wire of low- and high-carbon content (diameters should be the same, values of 2 or 3 mm are suitable); Bunsen burners; large beaker; two pairs of pliers; tensometer (if available); small hacksaw and supply of new blades; wire cutters.

Procedure

1. *Untreated properties*. Cut suitable lengths of each type of wire and compare:
   (a) ductilities by attempting to bend and rebend wires until failure; the number of rebends to cause failure may be noted;
   (b) hardness by cutting through using a hacksaw with new blade; the number of strokes to cut through may be noted;
   (c) tensile properties. Ideally a tensometer should be used. A low carbon steel will show a definite yield point if a load extension graph is plotted (Fig. 4.4). High-carbon steel wire will show no such yield point and will sustain a much higher load for a given diameter before failure (Fig. 4.4). If tensile testing apparatus is not available, the difficulty of producing a permanent bend in the two types of wire, using pliers, can be compared.
2. *Properties of the quenched material*. Position a large beaker of cold water near to two or more Bunsen burners set up so that they can be used to heat a 150 mm length of wire. Hold the low-carbon steel wire in pliers and heat the end until it glows red hot. 'Soak' for about one minute and then plunge the sample immediately into cold water. Repeat for the high-carbon steel wire. Test both samples as described in (1) and compare properties.
3. *Properties of the annealed material*. Repeat (2) but, instead of plunging the red hot samples into cold water, withdraw them as slowly as possible from the bunsen flame by lifting them vertically upwards. Repeat the tests of (1) on these samples.
4. *The effect of quenching followed by annealing*. To demonstrate that quenching does not chemically alter the steels (though cracking may result in objects of large section) quench samples as in (2) and then anneal as in (3) before testing. Compare results with those for the samples previously subjected to operation (3) only.

Conclusion

Comment on the effects of each process on the properties of the low- and high-carbon steel. Note that most wires of this diameter are manufactured by drawing through a die. This produces *work hardening* so that annealing may result in reduced tensile performance compared to the untreated wire.

Questions

1. (a) Give characteristic properties of
  (i) iron;
  (ii) cementite.
(b) Describe the physical form of pearlite.
(c) State how the proportions of pearlite and cementite in steel depend on its carbon content.

2. Describe the essential properties of low-carbon (mild) steels. Explain why a high-carbon steel would not be suitable for reinforcement for concrete.

3. Describe the effects of the following elements on the properties of steel, giving typical percentages present in mild steel:
(a) sulphur;
(b) silicon;
(c) manganese;
(d) niobium.

4. (a) State, with reasons, which type of steel is more susceptible to heat treatment – low-carbon or high-carbon steel.
(b) Describe briefly the following heat treatment processes:
  (i) annealing;
  (ii) normalising;
  (iii) quenching.

5. (a) Explain how the cooling rate of a welded steel joint affects the performance of the weld.
(b) Indicate the importance of the 'carbon equivalent' of a steel in relation to welding.

6. A Grade 50C steel gives a ladle analysis as follows:

Carbon	0.21%
Manganese	1.5%
Chromium	0.025%
Molybdenum	0.015%
Nickel	0.04%
Copper	0.04%

Calculate the carbon equivalent of the steel and hence comment on its weldability.

7. State the three mechanisms by which metals may corrode.

Indicate which of these is responsible for most damage to metals used in buildings.

8. Give three examples of situations in buildings where electrolytic corrosion may result from the use of different metals in contact.

9. Give three mechanisms by which electrolytic corrosion can occur within a single piece of metal such as steel in a damp situation.

10. Explain the function of traditional oil paints in the protection of metals from corrosion. State precautions which should be taken to ensure that paint fulfils this function effectively in practice.

11. State characteristic properties or features of the following metals which would enable them to be identified:

(a) high-tensile steel;
(b) copper;
(c) brass;
(d) phosphor bronze;
(e) zinc.

Give applications of each in the building industry.

Chapter 5

Timber

Although one of the earliest materials to be used in building, timber is by no means outdated and continues to play a major part in general building, particularly in domestic dwellings and furniture. More recently, use in larger public, commercial and industrial buildings in the form of trussed rafters and laminated sections has increased. This is due to more efficient utilisation of timber resulting from stress grading techniques combined with much better methods of jointing, including mechanical joints and synthetic resin adhesives. Further important factors in the continued success of timber are its high strength-to-weight ratio, its ease of working with hand tools and, in many applications, its aesthetically pleasing appearance.

The structure of wood

Wood is a naturally occurring fibrous composite, the fibres consisting chiefly of crystalline cellulose $(C_6H_{10}O_5)_n$ chains of high molecular weight bonded by non-crystalline hemicellulose and lignin adhesives to form rigid, though largely hollow, cells.

These cells differ considerably from one another according to the classification of timber (whether softwood or hardwood), the particular species and their various functions within each tree.

Softwoods

Figure 5.1 shows radial, tangential and transverse sections of a

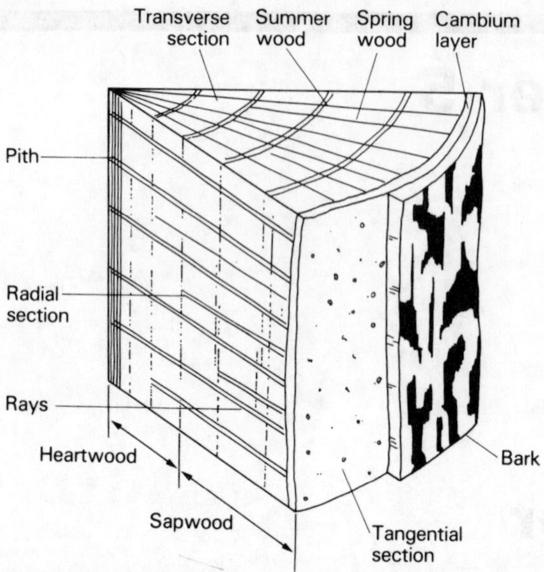

Fig. 5.1 Radial, tangential and transverse sections, through a five-year-old softwood log

5-year-old softwood log and it is evident that cells run chiefly in two directions – longitudinally and radially. There is a preponderance of cells running in the longitudinal direction in order to support the tree and to provide food conduction. Further food conduction and storage is provided by rays which run in the radial direction. Rays also increase the strength of the timber in this direction.

In softwoods the functions of both food conduction and support are mainly fulfilled by a single type of cell known as tracheids. Additionally in the rays there are hollow food storage cells known as parenchyma. Figure 5.2(a) shows a simplified radial section of the softwood cell structure. Adjacent cells are joined in all directions by pits which are responsible for transmission of food between them. The rays in softwoods are usually small and not visible to the naked eye. Figure 5.3 shows a scanning electron microscope photograph of cut transverse, radial and tangential surfaces of a sample of European Redwood (*Pinus sylvestris*). Note the resin ducts which are found in some softwoods and the variation in thickness of the tracheid cell walls between spring (rapid growth) and summer (slow growth).

Softwood timbers are coniferous (cone bearing) and have needle-shaped leaves which are retained in winter. They grow relatively quickly, the resultant wood generally being soft, of low density and easily worked. Softwoods are substantially more economical than

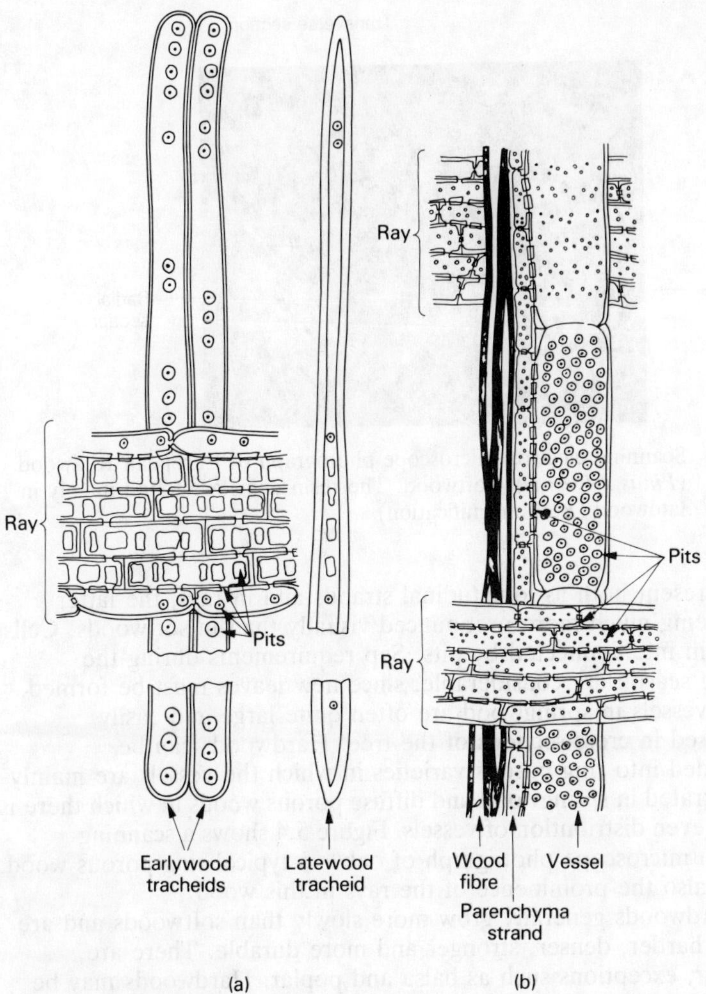

Fig. 5.2 Simplified radial sections of (a) softwood (b) hardwood

hardwoods. They are now the most widely used type of wood for general structural purposes. Commonly used species in the UK are Scots pine (redwood), European spruce (whitewood), Douglas fir and cedar.

Hardwoods

Hardwoods have a more complex cell structure than softwoods, structural support being provided by long, thick-walled cells known as fibres, while food conduction is by means of thin-walled tubular cells called vessels (Fig. 5.2(b)). Parenchyma (food storage cells) are

Fig. 5.3 Scanning electron microscope photograph of European Redwood (*Pinus sylvestris*). Softwood. The resin ducts are found mainly in latewood (× 10 magnification)

again present both as longitudinal strands and in rays, the latter often being much more pronounced visually than in softwoods. Cells are again interconnected by pits. Sap requirements during the growing season are considerable, since new leaves must be formed. Hence vessels in springwood are often quite large and easily recognised in cross-sections of the tree. Hardwoods can be subdivided into ring porous varieties in which the vessels are mainly concentrated in springwood and diffuse porous woods in which there is a more even distribution of vessels. Figure 5.4 shows a scanning electron microscope photograph of oak – a typical ring porous wood. Notice also the prominence of the rays in this wood.

Hardwoods generally grow more slowly than softwoods and are usually harder, denser, stronger and more durable. There are, however, exceptions such as balsa and poplar. Hardwoods may be used where their durability is beneficial – for example in window and door sills; or in high quality joinery. They are also extensively used in producing veneers for doors and furniture.

Heartwood and sapwood

The food conduction and storage functions of trees are fulfilled by the outer, more newly-grown layers of cells, referred to as sapwood. Sapwood usually comprises about one-third of the thickness of the trunk of a tree, the remainder being referred to as heartwood. The latter no longer stores food but is still important with regard to support of the tree, the cells in them tending to become acidic in order to assist preservation of the tree. Heartwood is normally darker in colour than sapwood and, on account of its acidity, tends

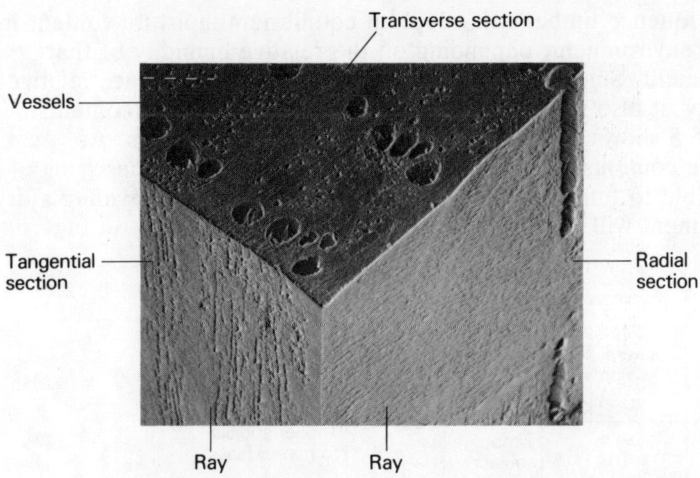

Fig. 5.4 Scanning electron microscope photograph of oak (*Quercus robus*). Ring porous hardwood. There are broad rays between each group of about four vessels in earlywood. Most of the radial section in this picture is occupied by a ray with a clear horizontal grain (× 10 magnification)

to be more resistant to fungi and insects in service.
(See experiment 5.1 for a detailed treatment of the identification of wood species.)

The effects of moisture in timber

The moisture content of timber is defined:

$$\text{Moisture content} = \frac{\text{Mass of water present in a sample}}{\text{Mass of that sample when dry}} \times 100$$

It will be noticed that, if the mass of water contained exceeds the mass of the dry timber, a moisture content of over 100 per cent is obtained and this is, in fact, not unusual in newly-felled (green) timber. The sapwood tends to contain more moisture at the time of felling, the average moisture content being about 130 per cent, though values of over 200 per cent are possible. In heartwood the moisture content is more likely to be around 50 per cent. The moisture content of green timber varies considerably with species – denser timbers, which include most hardwoods, have smaller cavities and larger cell walls, hence they can store less water.

The moisture content of timber in service is greatly influenced by the fact that wood is hygroscopic, that is, it tends to attract water from a damp atmosphere and to give up water to a dry atmosphere.

In consequence timber will adopt an equilibrium moisture content in a given environment, depending on the relative humidity of that environment. Since increase of temperature tends to reduce relative humidity, it also results in reduced equilibrium moisture contents. Figure 5.5 shows typical values for softwoods in buildings. At moisture contents in excess of 20 per cent, timber becomes susceptible to fungal attack, hence the importance of providing a dry environment will be appreciated.

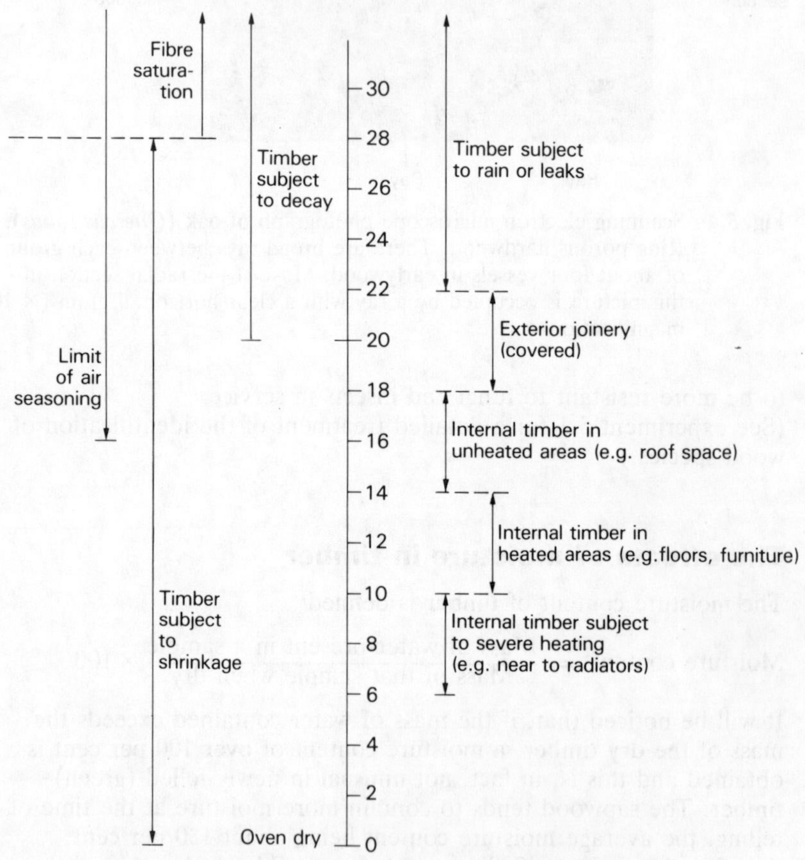

Fig. 5.5 Moisture contents of timber in various environments (per cent)

A further most important property of timber is that the cell walls become swollen on wetting, so that wet timber invariably occupies more space than dry timber. At moisture contents below fibre saturation value (approximately 28%) the volume of timber varies linearly with its moisture content. At moisture contents over saturation value there is no such variation, since additional water occupies cell cavities where there is no swelling effect. The amount of moisture movement depends on the direction considered, typical average shrinkages between the saturated state and 12 per cent moisture content being 4 to 10 per cent tangentially, about two-thirds of this radially and negligible (about 0.1%) longitudinally. These values reflect the fact that wood is most stable in the longitudinal direction, since most cells are aligned in this direction, while some stability in the radial direction is afforded by the rays. As would be expected, the moisture movement of timber varies considerably according to type. An important consequence of the variation of movement of timber with direction is that distortion occurs when green timber is dried. Since tangential shrinkage is greater, growth rings tend to be thrown into tension and therefore become straighter on drying. Figure 5.6 shows exaggerated sketches of the effect of drying a number of sections cut from a log.

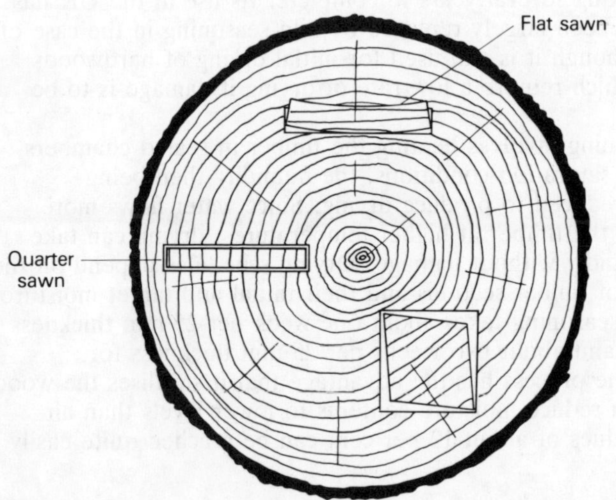

Fig. 5.6 The effect of drying various sections cut from a log. The cheapest way of conversion of timber is to make parallel cuts through the log, known as through-and-through cutting. Most of the resultant timber will then be flat sawn rather than quarter sawn

Seasoning

Seasoning may be defined as the controlled reduction of the moisture content of timber to a level appropriate to end use. Correctly seasoned timber should not be subject to further significant movement once in service. Seasoned timber is also immune to fungal attack, is stronger, has lower density and is therefore easier to handle or transport, is easier to work, glue, paint or preserve than wet timber. The importance of a controlled reduction of moisture will be clear when it is appreciated that moisture loss always takes place at or near the surface of the timber, hence shrinkage occurs preferentially at these positions. Surface layers are therefore thrown into tension as they contract, resulting in 'fissures' in the form of checking (longitudinal surface rupture) or splitting (longitudinal rupture passing through the piece). Serious splits in large timbers are sometimes called 'shakes'. Evaporation tends to occur more quickly from the ends of timber during seasoning, so that checking and splitting are often more pronounced at ends.

Traditionally a large amount of timber was 'air seasoned' by stacking in open formations in a roofed enclosure. Drying takes place, due to the effects of wind and sun, in a time which depends on the type and section size of timbers, the size of air gaps between them and climatic conditions. The process minimises damage but is slow, often taking several years to complete. Its use in the UK has now therefore been largely replaced by kiln seasoning in the case of softwoods, although it is still used for initial drying of hardwoods such as oak which require a low rate of drying if damage is to be avoided.

Kiln seasoning involves heating the timber in sealed chambers, initially under saturation conditions, the humidity then being progressively reduced to produce drying. Since water flows more freely through the timber at higher temperatures, drying can take place more rapidly without damage. Drying schedules depend on the type and size of timber sections and their initial and target moisture content. Kiln seasoning takes about one week per 25 mm thickness for softwoods and about two weeks per 25 mm thickness for hardwoods. The process has the advantage that it sterilises the wood and that it can reduce moisture contents to lower levels than air seasoning – values of about 12 per cent can be reached quite easily.

Factors affecting the distortion of timber prior to use

These include the following (see Fig 5.7 for explanation of terms).

1. *Species of timber*. Some timbers having similar moisture movements in the radial and tangential directions – for example Douglas Fir and Utile – are inherently less prone to distortion than timbers having high relative movements – for example European redwood and beech.
2. *Method of conversion*. Quarter sawn timber distorts less on moisture change than flat sawn timber, though the latter has a

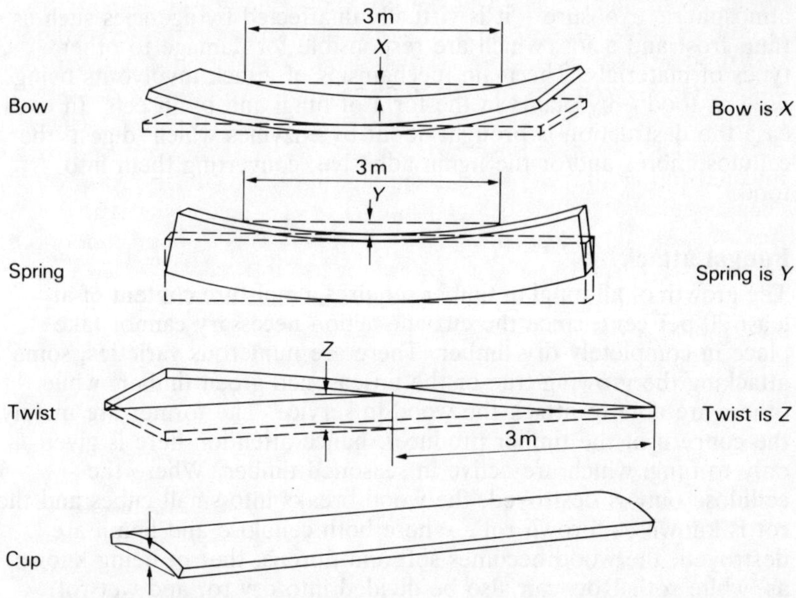

Fig. 5.7 Types of distortion in timber and their measurement

more interesting grain pattern. Pieces of timber which contain the pith are also more prone to distortion, especially springing. Where the piece is not cut parallel to the longitudinal axis, bowing, springing and twisting are likely.

3. *Slope of grain*. Twisting is often caused when the grain is not straight or when the density of the wood varies – for example, due to unequal growth on different sides of the tree. Timber having uniform and straight grain is less likely to undergo distortion.
4. *Stacking procedure*. Each piece of timber in a stack must be adequately supported by 'stickers' prior to and during seasoning in order to avoid distortion due to self-weight. Twisting of timber can be largely avoided if it is held firmly in stacks during seasoning.
5. *Moisture changes prior to installation*. Rapid moisture changes after seasoning – for example wetting or severe drying on occupation of new properties – can lead to serious distortion. Such changes should be avoided.

Durability of timber

Timber has remarkably good resistance to deterioration by

atmospheric exposure – it is virtually unaffected by agencies such as rain, frost and acids, which are responsible for damage to other types of materials. The main mechanisms of attack involve its being used as food – by plants in the form of fungi and by insects. In each case the destruction is brought about by enzymes which 'digest' the cellulose fibres and/or the lignin adhesive, converting them into food.

Fungal attack

The growth of all fungi in timber requires a moisture content of at least 20 per cent, since the enzyme action necessary cannot take place in completely dry timber. There are numerous varieties, some attacking the growing tree or the unseasoned green timber, while others are able to attack the wood in service. The former are mainly the concern of the timber producer, hence attention here is given only to fungi which are active in seasoned timber. Where the cellulose only is destroyed, the wood breaks into small cubes and the rot is known as 'brown rot'. Where both cellulose and lignin are destroyed, the wood becomes soft and fibrous, the rot being known as 'white rot'. Rots can also be divided into dry rot and wet rot. There are many species falling into the latter category but they are separated from dry rot because remedial treatment of dry rot must be much more carefully carried out.

Dry rot

(*Serpula lacrymans*, formerly called *Merulius lacrymans*). Dry rot, a brown rot, is so named because it finally leaves the wood in a dry, friable condition. Growth begins when rust-red spores come into contact with damp timber, the fungus developing as branching white strands (hyphae), which form cotton-wool-like patches (mycelium) and finally soft, fleshy, spore-producing, fruiting bodies (sporophore). Once established, the hyphae can grow into adjacent timber, brickwork and plaster in search of moisture or food. They may become modified into vein-like structures (rhizomorphs) 2 or 3 mm in diameter, which are able to transport moisture from damper areas to continue the attack in drier timber. Dry rot thrives at normal indoor temperatures but is killed at temperatures of over 40°C – hence it does not grow in positions subject to solar radiation. It becomes dormant at temperatures approaching freezing. Drying out of timber renders the fungus dormant and it may die after one year in this state, though the process may take longer if the ambient temperature is reduced.

The fungus is more common in wetter parts of Great Britain, such as the North and West, though in any region it is most likely to occur in old, derelict or damaged buildings which are more prone to dampness problems. London has a high incidence of dry rot outbreaks, probably for this reason.

Dry rot can be a serious problem once established, since it is often very difficult to eradicate the hyphae completely, especially in brickwork or plaster or where access is limited.

Essential remedial measures are:

1. Cut out and burn all visibly affected timber, together with an extra 600 mm of apparently sound neighbouring timber which may contain hyphae.
2. Remove any affected plaster, again working beyond the visibly affected area.
3. Preserve sound exposed timber and treat surrounding brick or concrete with a fungicide.
4. Replace affected timber with preserved, seasoned timber.
5. Use zinc oxychloride in paint or plaster coatings applied to affected wall surfaces. This has a fungicidal action.
6. Rectify the cause of the dampness.

Wet rot

As the name suggests, wet rots require higher moisture contents in order to thrive, optimum values being in the region of 50 per cent. There are many types of wet rot, the most common in the UK being *Coniophora puteana* (formerly *Coniophora cerebella*) and *Phellinus contiguus* (alternative name Porio contigua).

Coniophora puteana ('cellar fungus') is commonly found in very damp situations in buildings – especially basements or cellars. The fungus is of the brown variety and leads to cube formation, especially in large timber sections, though a skin of sound timber may be present. Surface undulations in timber may be the first sign of damage. Affected wood turns dark brown or black but fruiting bodies are rare.

Phellinus contiguus is responsible for a considerable increase in window joinery decay which has occurred over the last 20 years or so. It is a white rot, hence wood breaks into soft strands. The cause of the increase in this type of rot is probably the use of sapwood in joinery, which, together with poor design and inadequate glues leads to water penetration at joints. Since most joinery of this type is painted, the first signs of attack are often undulations in or splitting of the paint film.

Damage from these fungi is more serious in the Southern half of Great Britain, due to the added effect of certain wood-boring weevils which are found in association with wet rots in these regions, increasing the rate of deterioration.

The essential difference in remedial treatment of dry and wet rots is that the latter do not normally infect neighbouring dry timber, brickwork or plaster, hence it is necessary only to cut away and replace affected timber. It is nevertheless still important to remove the cause of dampness and preservation of new timber is always recommended in case any temporary dampness should recur.

Insect attack

Insects, such as the beetles that commonly infest timber in construction, have a characteristic life cycle: egg, caterpillar (larva), chrysalis and finally adult beetle. Beetles then emerge from the timber and fly to new timber to lay eggs and repeat the cycle, which may take several years. Most damage is done by the larvae, which burrow through the wood leaving fine powder ('frass') behind. Flight holes are the normal visual means of locating infested areas but quite advanced deterioration may be accompanied by serious strength loss with only a small number of holes. Dust is often ejected from these holes and an indication of the degree of current activity can be judged from the colour of exit holes and dust produced – a lighter colour indicates recent attack.

Table 5.1 shows some common types of insect. The powder post beetle is mainly a problem in timber yards, while the others can thrive in indoor, seasoned timber. Note that sapwood is much more susceptible to insect attack than heartwood. The seriousness of attack also varies according to species; for example the common furniture beetle is extremely widespread but normally takes many years to produce a noticeable number of flight holes or advanced deterioration.

The house longhorn beetle is relatively rare but in parts of Southern England, and particularly in W. Surrey, attacks have been

Table 5.1 Some types of insect attack on seasoned timber

Beetle	Life cycle	Visual signs	Timber attacked
Common furniture (*Anobium punctatum*)	3–5 years Emergence, May–Aug.	Beetles 5 mm long, granular dust, ½ mm diam. flight holes	Sapwood of untreated hardwoods or softwoods
House longhorn (*Hylotupes bajulus*)	3–11 years	A few large holes up to 10 mm, surface swelling, beetles 10–20 mm in length	Sapwood of softwoods (Surrey)
Death watch (*Xestobium rufovillosum*)	4–10 years. Emergence, March–June	Large bun-shaped pellets, ticking during mating period, May–June	Mainly hardwoods, especially if old or decayed
Powder post beetle (*Lyctus* species)	1–2 years Emergence, June–Aug	10 mm exit holes, fine dust	Sapwood of wide-pored hardwoods, partly or recently seasoned

severe. Additionally, since the life cycle is up to 11 years in length and beetles leave a sound surface skin, serious damage can occur before many flight holes become visible. Roof timbers are mainly affected and Building Regulations now require effective protection of roofing timbers to be used in certain Local Authority areas in these regions.

The death watch beetle is chiefly a problem in partially decayed oak members of older churches and other historic buildings. Treatment in such cases can be difficult, due to access problems and the very large sections often employed.

Preservative treatments for timber (BS 1282)

Preservatives should be toxic to fungi and insects, chemically stable, able to penetrate timber and non-aggressive to surrounding materials, particularly metals. Preservatives can be classified according to type:

Tar oil preservatives (*BS 144; BS 3051*)
Creosotes are the best known examples – they are derivatives of wood or coal, though coal distillates are superior. These are only suitable for external use, since they give rise to a noticeable colour and smell and render timber unsuitable for painting. They are, however, cheap and can be applied to timber with a fairly high moisture content. They tend to creep into porous adjacent materials such as cement renderings and plaster.

Water-borne preservatives (*BS 3452, 3453, 4072*)
These consist of salts based on metals such as sodium, magnesium, zinc and copper and also arsenic and boron. Copper-chrome-arsenate is a common example. They are very tolerant of moisture in the timber, are odourless, non-flammable, non-creeping and do not stain timber, which may be painted on drying out. In some varieties, insoluble products may be deposited in the wood, resulting in excellent retention properties.

Although water-based preservatives are fairly cheap, they have the disadvantage that they swell the timber and will cause corrosion of metals in contact until drying-out has occurred. For this reason they are best used as a preliminary protection followed by kiln drying, rather than as an *in situ* treatment.

Organic solvent preservatives (*BS 5707*)
Examples are chloronaphthalenes, metallic naphthanates and pentachlorophenol. Penetration is excellent provided timber is fairly dry, hence they are often preferred where only brush or spray application are feasible. They are non-creeping, non-staining, non-corrosive to metals, non-swelling and quick-drying. Painting is usually possible, once dried. They are widely used for remedial

treatment, though many organic solvents are highly flammable and present a fire risk until dried, especially when used in confined areas such as roof spaces. They are more expensive than the other types.

Application methods

The technique of application is just as important as the choice of a suitable preservative, since any preservative, poorly applied, will fail to penetrate well into timber sections. The difficulty increases with the size of timber sections and some timbers such as Douglas fir have naturally low permeability to preservatives. Where machining or drilling operations are to be carried out, they should be completed prior to application of preservatives in order that maximum penetration is obtained at all exposed surfaces. The following techniques can be used:

Brushing or spraying

These give only limited penetration of timber, although they may be the only feasible methods for *in situ* remedial work. However, if several coats are applied and the treatment is repeated periodically, a useful degree of protection is achieved.

Dipping

This involves immersion in the preservative for a period, which, if long enough, can give considerable penetration of preservative. In the 'open tank' method of dipping, the preservative is heated and then cooled while the timber is submerged; this gives even better results. It is nevertheless not suited to hardwoods or low permeability softwoods.

Double vacuum process

A vacuum is applied to timber in a sealed chamber and the preservative then introduced. The vacuum is released, forcing the preservative into the wood. After a soaking period, the vacuum is reapplied to eject excess preservative. This process is now widely used in conjunction with organic preservatives for external joinery such as window frames.

Pressure impregnation

This is often used for injection of water-based and tar oil-based preservatives. In the empty cell process, the air surrounding the timber is compressed, the preservative introduced and then a still higher pressure applied, forcing preservative into the wood. On releasing the pressure, excess preservative is ejected. If the timber is not pressurised prior to injection of the preservative (in some cases, a vacuum is first applied), the retention of preservative is increased (full cell method). This method is more expensive in terms of the quantity used and, since saturated, will take longer to dry afterwards. Good protection is nevertheless achieved.

Diffusion processes

In the boron diffusion method, freshly converted green timber with a moisture content exceeding 50 per cent is dipped into a concentrated borate solution. The timber is covered to prevent evaporation and left for some months for the solution to diffuse through the timber. The timber is then seasoned in the normal way. This method provides effective penetration of 'difficult' timbers, though applications are limited by the fact that, in damp conditions, the preservative leaches out by the same diffusion process which is used for its injection.

Current preservation requirements

A number of timbers have high inherent durability, even when damp, so that preservation against fungal attack may not normally be necessary. Such timbers include heartwood of Afrormosia, African Mahogany, European Oak, Sapele, Teak, Utile (hardwoods) and Western Red Cedar and Sequoia (softwoods). Note that sapwood is never regarded as durable. Other types of timber will require preservative treatment if subject to damp or there is a significant risk of damage by insects. Table 5.2 shows the requirements of various timber components of dwellings, as given in Building Regulations (1976) and (in the private sector) the National House Building Council. Since the effectiveness of a method of treatment depends on the method of application as well as on the type of preservative used, various requirements are given under each function category for the treatment to be used. For example, when copper-chrome-arsenate is used, this should be applied under pressure to comply with BS 4072. Note that most structural members of dwellings – as in the floors and pitched roof spaces, are not normally required to be preservative treated, hence the importance of good design and construction if dampness leading to fungal attack is to be avoided.

Timber for structural uses

The short-term tensile strength of perfect timber, taken in relation to its self weight, compares very favourably with that of steel, values of over 100 N/mm^2 being common in a material which has a density equal to about 7 per cent that of steel. The compressive strength of timber is much lower, due to the tendency of fibres to buckle on compression, but quite high bending strengths are nevertheless obtainable, timber being particularly useful for bending applications,

Table 5.2 Situations in which solid timber is required to be preservative treated

Function	Component	Building Regulations	National Housebuilding Council (private sector)
Weather boarding	External weather-resisting timber boarding (unless manufactured from heartwood of certain hardwoods or Western Red Cedar or Sequoia softwoods. (Only certain softwood species are acceptable for weather-boarding, see Building Regulations)	*	–
Carpentry	Softwood timber in construction of, or fixed within a roof, including ceiling joists: Certain areas of S. England subject to house longhorn beetle attack	*	–
	Lintels in brick or blockwork (external walls) Battens as fixings for claddings Any embedded timber Bottom plates in timber frame dwellings Joists, battens, firrings, noggings, wall plates, strutting & blocking in flat roofs (unless timber is at least of moderately durable species) in high risk areas = e.g. kitchens, bathrooms. Joists built into external solid walls	–	*

Function	Component	Building Regulations	National Housebuilding Council (private sector)
Joinery	Door frames, windows, surrounds to metal windows External doors (not flush doors)	–	*
Floors	Wooden fillets embedded in concrete for use as fixings for timber floors	*	–

where self-weight accounts for a substantial proportion of total weight – as in roofing and domestic flooring. The main problems in utilising timber efficiently are as follows:

1. Strengths, even of perfect ('clear') specimens are very variable, coefficients of variation $\left(= \frac{\text{standard deviation}}{\text{mean strength}}\right)$ of over 20 per cent often being obtained.
2. *Long-term* strengths are much (typically 40%) lower than *short-term* strengths, owing to the tendency of timber to creep.
3. The strengths of individual pieces of bulk timber are greatly affected by the presence of defects, such as knots and fissures, and by factors such as the rate of growth and slope of grain.
4. Strength depends on species and, since identification is not always easy, working stresses may have to be based on poorer quality species available.

Considerable progress has been made in the last 15 years towards overcoming some of these difficulties by the introduction of techniques for grading each piece of timber according to its likely performance. Stress grading may, at the present time, be carried out visually or by machine, each method being specified in BS 4978.

Visual stress grading

Each piece of timber is examined visually for a number of defects which would limit strength, the timber hence being categorised into one of three grades – Special Structural (SS), General Structural (GS) and Reject. The SS grade is estimated to have strength between 50 and 60 per cent of that for clear (perfect) timber of the same species and the GS grade approximately 30 to 35 per cent. Timber should be graded by a qualified grader and stamped with the grade and mark of a recognised authority – the Timber Research and Development Association (TRADA) is the main such body in the UK.

(For experimental details, see experiment 5.3 at the end of the Chapter.) The main factors to be considered are given below. (Key terms relating to visual stress grading are given in Fig. 5.8 and requirements for SS and GS grades are given in Table 5.3.)

Knots

The term 'knot area ratio' (KAR) is used to estimate the weakening effect of knots, being defined as the proportion of any cross-sectional area which is occupied by knots. Since knots near to an edge have a more serious effect, a margin condition is defined as being present when more than *half* the top or bottom quarter of any section is occupied by knots (Fig. 5.9). KAR values in excess of one-third (margin condition) or one-half (no margin condition) lead to rejection of that piece.

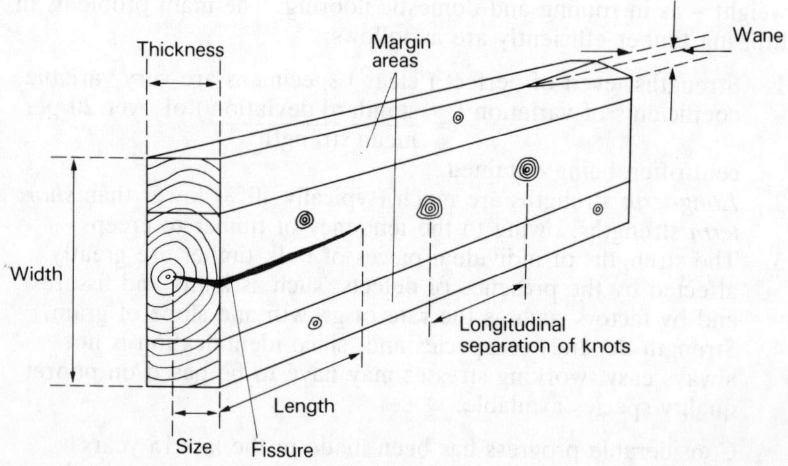

Fig. 5.8 Key terms relating to visual stress grading

Table 5.3 BS 4978 requirements for visually stress-graded timber

Property		**SS**	**GS**
KNOTS	Margin condition	KAR $\frac{1}{5}$ or less	KAR $\frac{1}{5}$–$\frac{1}{3}$
	No margin condition	KAR $\frac{1}{3}$ or less	KAR $\frac{1}{2}$–$\frac{1}{3}$
		Where 2 knots or groups of knots have KAR values over 0.9 × permissible value, they must be separated by a distance equal to not less than $\frac{1}{2}$ width of piece	
FISSURES	Size not more than $\frac{1}{2}$ thickness	Unlimited	Unlimited

Property		SS	GS
	More than ½ thickness less than thickness	Length not to exceed 600 mm or ¼ length of piece, whichever is lesser	Length not to exceed 900 mm or ¼ length of piece, whichever is lesser
	Equal to thickness of piece	Permitted only at ends. Length must not exceed width of piece	Length must not exceed 600 mm. If at end length must not exceed 1½ × width of piece
SLOPE OF GRAIN		Must not exceed 1 in 10	Must not exceed 1 in 6
WANE		Must not exceed ¼ of dimension on which it occurs	Amount of wane not to exceed ⅓ of dimension of surface in which it occurs except that not nearer either end than 300 mm wane may be up to ½ dimension within single length not exceeding 300 mm
RATE OF GROWTH		Not less than 4 annual growth rings per 25 mm	Not less than 4 annual growth rings per 25 mm
DISTORTION	Bow	Not to exceed ½ thickness in 3 m	As for SS
	Spring	Not to exceed 15 mm in any 3 m length	As for SS
	Twist	Not to exceed 1 mm per 25 mm of width in any 3 m length	As for SS
	Cup	Not to exceed 1/25 of width	As for SS

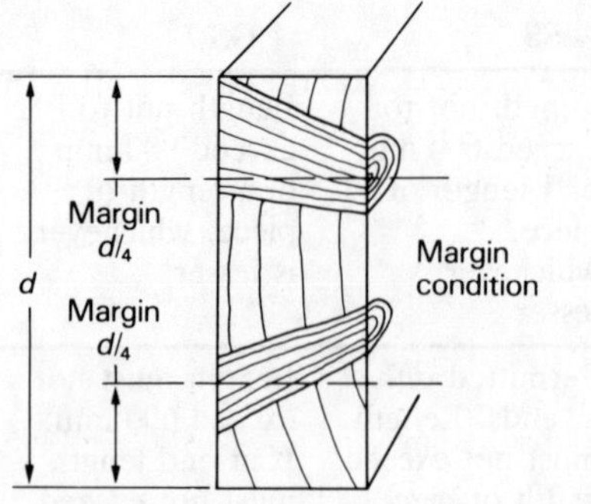

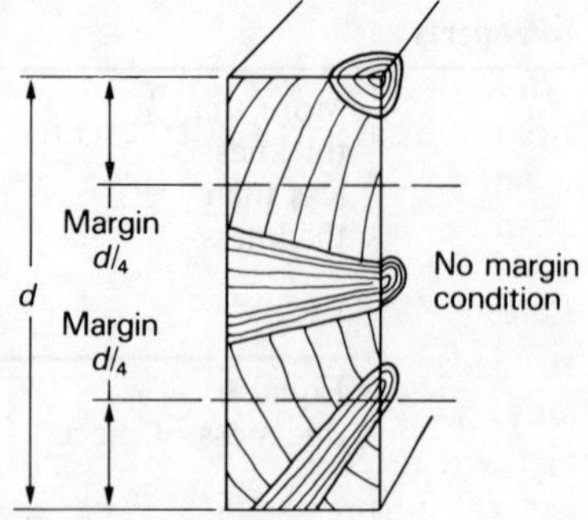

(a) Since more than one half of a margin area is occupied by knots, the knot area ratio must not exceed:

$^1/_3$ for GS grade
$^1/_5$ for SS grade

The KAR for this section is about $^1/_2$ – the piece is therefore 'reject'

(b) Since less than one half of a margin area is occupied by knots, the knot area ratio must not exceed:

$^1/_2$ for GS grade
$^1/_3$ for SS grade

The KAR for this section is between $^1/_3$ and $^1/_2$ – it corresponds to the GS grade

Fig. 5.9 Knot area ratios (a) margin condition (b) no margin condition

Fissures

These result from seasoning problems and are most common in larger sections, especially near the end of the piece. The size of a fissure is equal to the depth of cracks and the length of deeper fissures must be controlled in areas of higher bending moment, since they reduce shear resistance, and hence bending strength, parallel to the grain.

Slope of grain

This results where the tree does not grow straight or where the log is not cut parallel to growth direction. A plane of weakness is produced where the grain intersects the surface, leading to the possibility of tensile or shear failure (Fig. 5.10).

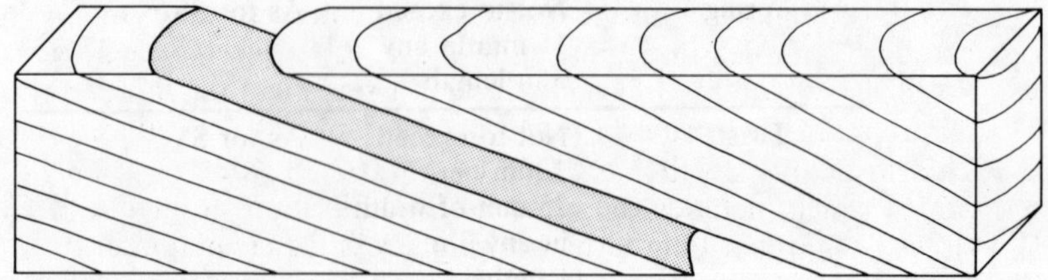

Fig. 5.10 Planes of weakness resulting when log is not cut parallel to grain direction

Wane

Wane occurs when a corner of the piece is cut too close to the outer circumference of the tree (Fig. 5.8). Its presence reduces bending strength in centre regions or bearing strength near the ends of a beam.

Rate of growth

It has been found that faster grown softwoods have lower strength and stiffness than slower grown examples of the same species. Growth rates depend on climatic and other conditions and often vary greatly during the life of the tree but the rate of growth requirement guards against excessively fast grown timber being used. (This rule does not apply to hardwoods.)

Distortion

The four types of distortion together with the method of measurement have already been described (Fig. 5.7). Several of these are often found in the same piece. Some types are more probable and more serious than others for a given application; for example cupping is found in floorboards and skirting boards, while bowing, springing and twisting often occur, structural timber. Bowing and twisting are a particular nuisance in wall plates, as are springing and twisting in hip rafters. It should be noted that, if timber is graded while wet and especially if recently removed from a banded pack, significant further distortion can occur afterwards during drying.

Other defects

These may include wormholes, sapstain and abnormal defects such as fungal decay or 'brittleheart'. See BS 4978 for guidance on such defects.

Derivation of permissible stresses (CP 112)

The safe working stresses for any particular piece of a given species have been derived by the following process:

1. Tests were carried out on small clear specimens – green (wet) or dry according to requirements to give a failure strength in bending, compression, tension or shear, as required (BS 373).
2. From the variability of results in (1), a statistical minimum failure strength (formerly based on 1% failures) is produced.
3. This strength is further reduced by a factor of safety – usually 2.25 – which includes the effect of load duration, to give a 'basic stress' – that is a long-term working stress for clear timber.
4. Each piece is visually graded and hence a working stress for that piece is arrived at by multiplying by a figure between 30 and 35 per cent (GS grade) or between 50 and 60 per cent (SS grade).

Table 5.4 Bending test results and working stresses given in CP 112 for three common softwoods

	Density, 18% mc (kg/m^3)	Short-term bending, clear 12% m/c timber (N/mm^2)	Standard deviation in bending stress	Basic bending stress	SS grade stress CP 112	GS grade stress CP 112
European whitewood (spruce)	510	72	10.2	14.5	7.3	5.1
Douglas fir (UK)	590	91	16.9	17.9	9.0	6.3
Pitch pine (Caribbean)	720	107	14.5	18.6	9.3	6.5

CP 112 gives working stresses for various timber species calculated in this way. Table 5.4 shows test results, together with working stresses in bending for three common softwoods. For timber to be used in joists, bending strength (modulus of rupture), shear strength parallel to grain and compression perpendicular to grain are the most important properties but for other applications different properties may need to be considered. Additionally, elastic moduli are important, since these determine joist deflections. Note that in CP 112, factors of safety are not applied to elastic moduli – mean and minimum (1%) values are given direct, according to stress grade.

Machine stress grading

This is based on the correlation which has been found between bending strength (modulus of rupture) and modulus of elasticity, as determined by deflection tests on samples subject to bending (Fig. 5.11). A major attraction of the method is that it obviates the need for obtaining strengths of small clear specimens and then reducing values by a proportion dependent on grade – the 1 per cent strength value is obtained directly from the correlation of Fig. 5.11, the only additional factor required being the factor of safety. Fig. 5.11 was derived for European redwood (*Pinus sylvestris*) and and European whitewood (*Picea abies*), which together form a very large proportion of the UK market at present.

Modern stress grading depends heavily on computer-operated machines which rapidly measure deflections under load of successive portions of each timber piece as it passes through. Timber is normally loaded on face rather than on edge for practical reasons and the machine automatically compensates for any out-of-straightness. A coloured dye representing the stress grade is sprayed

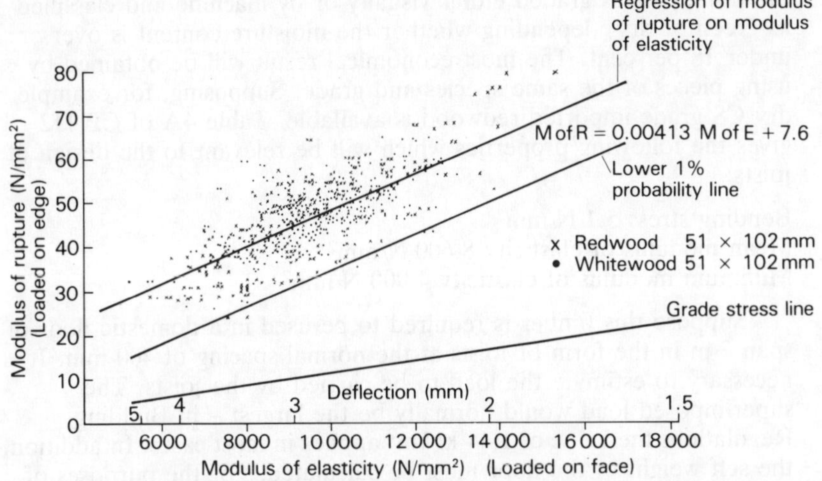

Fig. 5.11 Correlation between elastic modulus and modulus of rupture for timber (source: *The strength properties of timber*, Princes Risborough Laboratory of BRE, MTP Construction 1974)

on successive portions of the timber as it passes through. A final strip is sprayed at the end of each piece representing the worst (and therefore the final) grade for that piece. Visual inspection is also carried out for defects such as fissures, wane, resin pockets etc. At the present time there are four machine grades – M75 and M50 (originally defined in CP 112) and MSS (Machine Special Structural) and MGS (Machine General Structural) specified in BS 4978. The grades MSS and SS; MGS and GS respectively are comparable, strengths in decreasing order being M75, MSS/SS, M50, MGS/GS. A further advantage of machine grading is that better grades are obtained than by visual grading of the same batch and there is less reject material.

Stress grading machines must comply with an approving authority if grading in accordance with BS 4978 and machines are subject to unannounced periodic inspection in order to ensure that standards are maintained.

Design of structural timber sections

This is covered at present by CP 112, which deals with a variety of structural components from solid timber as well as structures from laminated timber, plywood and hardboard. By way of illustration, the principles of design of solid timber joists will be considered.

The species of timber to be used must first of all be identified, the timber stress graded either visually or by machine and classified as green or dry, depending whether the moisture content is over or under 18 per cent. The most economical result will be obtained by using pieces of the same species and grade. Supposing, for example, dry CS grade imported redwood is available. Table 4A of CP 112 gives the following properties which will be relevant to the design of joists:

Bending stress 5.1 N/mm^2
Mean modulus of elasticity 8 600 N/mm^2
Minimum modulus of elasticity 4 900 N/mm^2

Suppose this timber is required to be used in a domestic floor of span 3 m in the form of joists at the normal spacing of 400 mm. It is necessary to estimate the load to be carried by the joists. The superimposed load would normally be the largest – in Building Regulations the value of 1.44 kN/m^2 applies in most cases. In addition, the self weight of the floor must be calculated. For the purposes of calculation the following might be assumed:

Size of joists: 50 × 200 mm (the depth may not be correct but the error resulting will be small because the self-weight of joists is generally a small proportion of total weight)
Thickness of floor boards: 20 mm
Density of timber: 600kg/m^3

Weight of joists

$$= \underset{\text{(thickness)}}{0.05} \times \underset{\text{(depth)}}{0.20} \times \underset{\text{(span)}}{3} \times \underset{\text{(density)}}{600} \times 9.81$$

=177 N

Weight of floorboards per joist

$$= \underset{\text{(thickness)}}{0.02} \times \underset{\text{(spacing)}}{0.4} \times \underset{\text{(span)}}{3} \times \underset{\text{(density)}}{600} \times 9.81$$

= 141 N

(The mass of a ceiling, if used, would need to be included).
Total self weight = 318 N
or 0.318 kN

Total superimposed weight per joist $= 1.44 \times \underset{\text{(spacing)}}{0.4} \times \underset{\text{(span)}}{3}$

$= 1.728$ kN

Hence total load supported = 1.728 + 0.318 = 2.046 kN
For normal spans the bending stress limits the load which can be carried by joists.
The bending moment(M) is given by

$$M = \frac{WL}{8} \qquad \begin{aligned} W &= \text{load (U.D.)} \\ L &= \text{span} \end{aligned}$$

Working in Newtons and millimetres

$$M = \frac{2046 \times 3000}{8}$$
$$= 7.67 \times 10^5 \text{ Nmm}$$

Also

$M = fZ \quad Z$ = section modulus $\quad b$ = breadth

$= \frac{bd^2}{6} \quad d$ = depth

f, the bending stress, is 5.1 N/mm^2, though CP 112 indicates that, when four or more members act together such that the load is shared – as in a boarded floor, the bending stress can be increased by 10 per cent. Hence in this case the permissible bending stress if $5.1 \times 1.1 = 5.61\ N/mm^2$.

$$\text{Therefore } Z = \frac{M}{f}$$
$$= \frac{7.67 \times 10^5}{5.61}$$
$$= 1.37 \times 10^5 \text{ mm}^3$$

For $b = 50$ mm

$$d = \frac{\sqrt{6Z}}{b}$$
$$= \frac{\sqrt{6 \times 1.37 \times 10^5}}{50}$$
$$= \sqrt{1644}$$
$$= 128 \text{ mm}$$

The standard size to cover this requirement would be 150 mm.

For larger spans, the deflection may be the limiting criterion and so this should be checked also:

Deflection (UD load) $= \frac{5}{384} \cdot \frac{WL^3}{EI}$

$$= \frac{5 \times 12}{384} \cdot \frac{WL^3}{Ebd^3}$$

Where E = modulus of elasticity

I = second moment of section

$= \frac{bd^3}{12}$ (rectangular section)

Hence deflection $= \frac{60}{384} \times \frac{2046}{8600} \times \frac{3000^3}{50 \times 150^3}$

$= 5.95$ mm

(Note that E_{mean} is used here because load sharing is assumed. In other cases, or where the dead load forms a substantial proportion of the total load, E_{min} should be used.)

Code of Practice 112 limits deflection of joists to 0.003 × span –

in this case 0.003 × 3000 = 9 mm. Hence in this case the joist is satisfactory.

Note: 1. Exceptionally, where very short spans are used under high loads, the complimentary shear stress may need to be calculated and compared with the permissible value given in CP 112.

2. The bearing area at the ends of joists should be sufficient to ensure that the bearing stress in the timber (compression perpendicular to grain) does not exceed the value allowed.

Code of Practice 112, which currently covers the design of structural timber, is being revised, though in the new edition which appears as BS 5268 there are no fundamental differences in the approach to the design of timber joists. Permissible stresses or elastic moduli may, however, alter and for convenience nine strength classes have been introduced. Most softwoods currently used for structural timber will lie in the strength class range SC 1 to SC 5, depending on species and stress grade. The remaining classes will comprise the denser hardwoods.

Experiments

Experiment 5.1 Identification of common woods

Identification of a given piece of wood, especially if a softwood, can be extremely difficult, since there are many hundreds of species obtainable and properties within each species often vary. The following may nevertheless assist as a guide to identifying some of the commonly available softwoods and hardwoods.

It is usually essential to have a smooth surfaced sample of the wood to be identified – this could be in the form of a small rectangular piece. One radial and one tangential face should be planed smooth and one transverse section cut smooth with a *very sharp* knife or chisel. With careful cutting a clean, dark surface, free of tearing, should be obtainable. Sanding will also produce a smooth surface but this takes longer and the dust tends to obscure finer detail such as resin ducts. Moistening the end of the timber may help in finding these. Low power magnification of, for example, 10 times will assist greatly in seeing and identifying detail in transverse sections. It may also be an advantage for some assessments such as knot distribution to have a larger piece of timber as well as the smaller sample.

A distinction should first be made between hardwoods and softwoods. On the transverse plane, softwoods can be recognised by the absence of pores – for example, Fig. 5.12 (Douglas fir).

Hardwoods can be further subdivided according to the nature of

Table 5.5 Softwood Identification (Species given in approximate order of darkening colour)

Type	Growth rings	Density (kg/m^3)	Colour	Other features
European whitewood (European spruce) *picea abies* (Fig. 5.13)	Well defined. Springwood merges gradually into late wood	510	Very light yellow/white	A few resin ducts irregularly spaced in late wood
Sitka spruce *Picea stichensis*	Springwood merges gradually into thin bands of dark red/ brown summerwood	400	Very light brown	Irregular resin ducts – latewood rapid growth – rings well spaced – low density
European redwood (Scots pine) *Pinus sylvestris* (Fig. 5.3)	Well defined. Thin/medium bands of dark red summerwood	520	Sapwood light brown. Heartwood deeper red/brown	Newly-cut surface smells resinous. Regular resin ducts. Knots in groups separated by clear timber
Parana pine *Araucaria augustifolia*	Poorly defined. Early wood merges gradually into latewood	530	Sapwood light, heartwood light to dark brown with red streaks	No resin ducts.Dense, fine, straight grain
Western hemlock *Tsuga haterophylla*	abrupt transition from springwood to pink/brown summerwood	500	Yellow/ brown	Resin ducts absent
Douglas fir *Pseudotsuga taxifolia* (Fig. 5.12)	Well defined springwood. Quite thick well-defined bands of dense hard red/brown summerwood difficult to cut. Growth rings often wavy	545	Darker than most softwoods except cedar. Sapwood yellow, heartwood red/brown	Resin pockets visible on transverse section under microscope. May be resinous smell
Western red cedar *Thuja plicata*	Clear rings. Narrow bands of latewood	370	Sapwood yellow, heartwood fairly dark brown	Distinctive aromatic smell. No resin ducts. Note the low density

pores – whether ring-porous or diffuse-porous (Fig. 5.4 and 5.15). The density of dry specimens should also be measured by weighing and dividing by volume. Tables 5.5, 5.6 and 5.7 give characteristic descriptions of the key properties of common softwoods, ring-porous hardwoods and diffuse-porous hardwoods respectively. Figures

Fig. 5.12 Transverse section of Douglas fir (*Pseudotsuga taxifolia*). Softwood. Note dense summerwood bands (× 8 magnification)

Table 5.6 Identifying features of some common ring porous hardwoods

Type	Growth rings/rays	Density (kg/m^3)	Colour	Other features
Ash *Fraxinus excelsior*	Growth rings distinct. Fairly coarse pores in springwood. Hard, dense summerwood. Rays invisible	690	Very light – whitish	Quite hard, dense wood
Oak *Quercus robus* (Fig. 5.4)	Rays very clear. Large pores in springwood	690	Light yellow/ brown	'Silver grain' on quarter-sawn surfaces (effect of rays). Hard, dense
Sweet Chestnut *Castanea sativa*	Well-defined thin rings of large pores. Rays indistinct	600	Light/ medium brown	Similar to oak if flat sawn. Silver grain absent when quarter-sawn. Less dense than oak

Table 5.7 Identifying features of some common diffuse porous hardwoods

Type	Growth rings/rays	Density	Colour	Other features
Beech *Fagus sylvatica* (Fig. 5.14)	Thin, well-defined rays on transverse section. Grain fairly faint. Pores not visible except under microscope	710	Light yellow/ pink	Rays produce fine, well-distributed lines on flat sawn section
Maple *Acer saccharum*	Summerwood distinct though only slightly darker than springwood. Rays distinct. Fine, well-scattered pores	690	Light biscuit brown	Fine smooth surface; attractive lustre. Hard, dense
African mahogany *Khaya ivorensis* (Fig. 5.15)	Well-spaced medium-size pores. Thin rays – clearly visible under microscope	660	Dark red/brown	Pores produce long fine indentations on radial and tangential surfaces

5.12–5.15 show transverse sections of a number of common woods and these may assist in identifying the species concerned. Reference to scanning electron microscope photographs of Figs 5.3 and 5.4 may also be helpful.

Experiment 5.2 Measurement of the moisture movement of timber

This can be quite easily carried out, provided suitable size specimens are available. Ideally three pieces of timber of each species should be available of size approximately 6 × 75 × 100 mm, each cut with its long dimension parallel to one of the three respective principal directions in the wood (Fig. 5.16). Knot-free samples are preferable and the end grain of the flat-sawn piece should be as straight as possible if cupping is to be avoided. Pieces containing the pith should, in any case, be avoided.

Note that quarter-sawn specimens are fragile and must therefore be handled with care. An airtight cabinet with sufficient space for all the specimens and glass containers of sulphuric acid are also required, together with vernier calipers accurate to 0.1 mm.

Fig. 5.13 Transverse section of whitewood (*Picea abies*). Softwood. Note the small, light coloured resin ducts irregularly spaced in latewood (× 8 magnification)

Fig. 5.14 Transverse section of beech (*Fagus sylvatica*). Diffuse porous hardwood. Note prominent rays (× 8 magnification)

Fig. 5.15 Transverse section of African mahogany (*Khaya ivorensis*). Note the well-spaced pores and thin rays. The growth rings are indistinct in this sample (× 8 magnification)

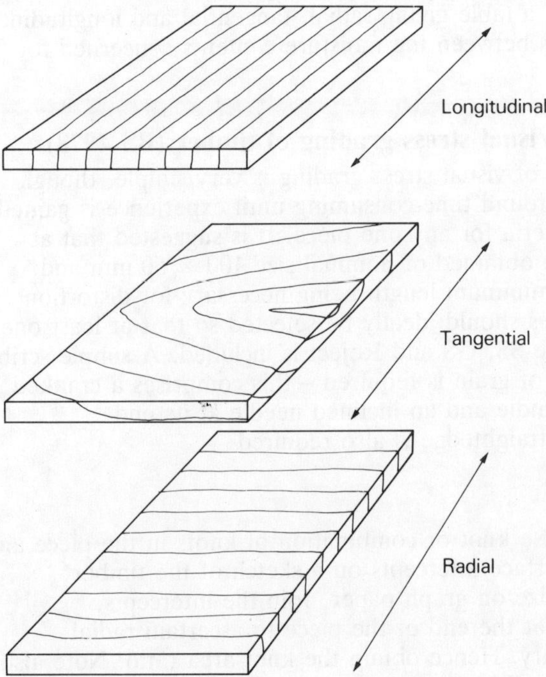

Fig. 5.16 Methods of cutting timber for moisture movement measurement

Procedure

The samples should first be conditioned to a given low relative humidity – say, 30 per cent, which would need sulphuric acid of relative density 1.43 (take care!). Equilibrium may take some days to reach and samples should be weighed periodically until mass becomes constant. Mark pieces at a convenient position on the longest dimension and take caliper readings at this position. Readings should be taken several times to ensure repeatability and the mass of samples noted.

The samples are then returned and the humidity increased to, say, 90 per cent, which would need sulphuric acid of relative 1.14. Again, weigh samples periodically until the weight is constant. Soaking to 'speed up' the operation is not recommended as it leads to moisture gradients and may damage the sample.

When constant weight is achieved the caliper readings and masses are again taken. Find the difference between the readings corresponding to the two humidities and represent the movement as a percentage. (Note that the difference in readings in the longitudinal direction will be very small.)

Finally, oven-dry the timber at 105°C and find the dry mass. Hence find the moisture contents of the timber at the two humidities. Compile a table giving radial, tangential and longitudinal moisture movements between the moisture contents concerned for each species.

Experiment 5.3 Visual stress grading of timber (BS 4978)

The basic technique of visual stress grading is very simple, though the process may be found time-consuming until experience is gained as to the critical criteria for any one piece. It is suggested that at least three pieces be obtained of nominal size 100 × 50 mm and length 3.0 m – this minimum length being necessary for distortion measurements. Pieces should ideally be selected so that at least one sample of each grade SS, GS and Reject is included. A simple scribe for measuring slope of grain is required – this comprises a cranked rod with a swivel handle and an inclined needle at its end (Fig. 5.17). A 3 m straightedge is also required.

Procedure

Knots. Find the worse knot or combination of knots in the piece and mark positions of surface intercepts on a sketch of the timber section, drawn full size on graph paper. Join the intercepts, inspecting the grain at the end of the piece to ascertain radial directions, if necessary. Hence obtain the knot area ratio. Note also whether a margin condition is present (Fig. 5.9).

Fissures. Inspect for fissures and record:

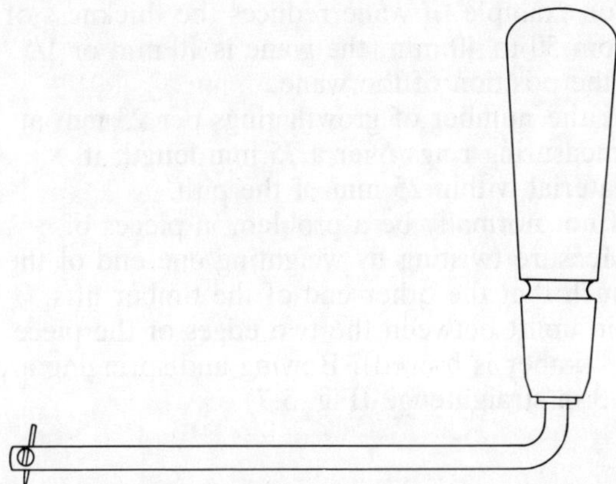

Fig. 5.17 Scribe with swivel handle for measuring slope of grain

(a) position;
(b) size (depth) as a fraction of the thickness of the piece;
(c) length

Slope of grain. This should be measured on one face and edge. Press the needle of the scribe into the wood and draw along in the apparent direction of the grain. The needle will form a groove and give the precise direction. Avoid excess pressure which would prevent steady movement, or inadequate pressure which will cause the needle to 'jump' across the fibres. Note that growth ring direction and grain direction do not normally coincide. Measure the slope of grain as Fig. 5.18. The direction of fissures, when present, also indicates grain direction.

Wane. The wane on any face is equal to the amount of that dimension which is missing. Express this as a fraction of the

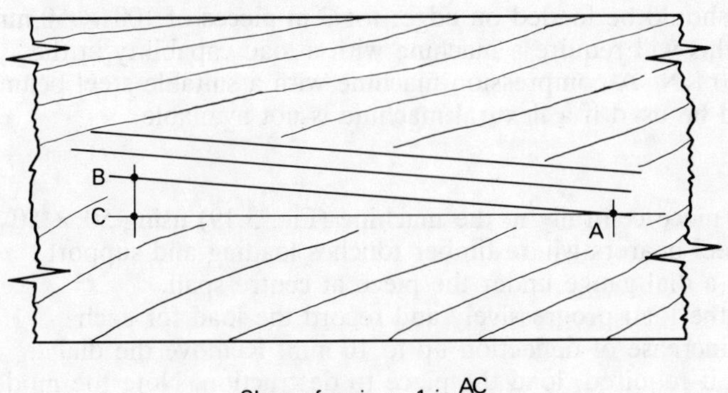

Slope of grain $= 1 \text{ in } \frac{AC}{BC}$

Fig. 5.18 Method of measurement of slope of grain

dimension concerned. For example, if wane reduces the thickness of a 100 × 50 mm piece from 50 to 40 mm, the wane is 10 mm or 1/5 of the dimension. Note the position of the wane.

Rate of growth. Measure the number of growth rings per 25 mm at right-angles to growth, measuring rings over a 75 mm length if possible and omitting material within 25 mm of the pith.

Distortion. Cupping will not normally be a problem in pieces of section 100 × 50 mm. Measure twisting by weighting one end of the piece flat on the floor, such that the other end of the timber lifts. Measure the difference in uplift between the two edges of the piece (both ends will lift if the timber is bowed). Bowing and springing are easily measured using a 3 m straightedge (Fig. 5.7).

Assessment of grade

Compare results in respect of knots, fissures, slope of grain, wane, rate of growth and distortion with the requirements of Table 5.3. To comply with a given grade, pieces must satisfy all requirements. Any piece failing a GS requirement is designated REJECT.

Experiment 5.4. Machine stress grading

This experiment is not an attempt to simulate commercial machine grading tests in which performance of each localised section of the piece is assessed. It should be possible, however, to correlate results of this simple test with visual grading results, especially where the latter grades are determined on the basis of rate of growth or knot characteristics. For this reason it is recommended that the experiment be carried out on pieces of timber which have already been visually graded.

It is, of course, unnecessary to test timber to destruction – deflection tests are adequate, though destructive tests will yield bending stress results which can be compared with the stresses given in Table 5.4.

Pieces should be loaded on edge; for 3 m pieces of 100 × 50 mm softwood, this will require a machine with a load capability in the region of 10 KN. A compression machine with a suitable steel beam insert could be used if a flexural machine is not available.

Procedure

Locate the piece centrally in the machine (Fig. 5.19) using 50 × 50 × 6 mm steel bearers where timber touches loading and support rollers. Fix a dial gauge under the piece at centre span.

Apply the load progressively and record the load for each millimetre increase of deflection up to 10 mm. Remove the dial gauge and, if required, load the piece to destruction. Note the mode of failure.

Repeat for the other pieces.

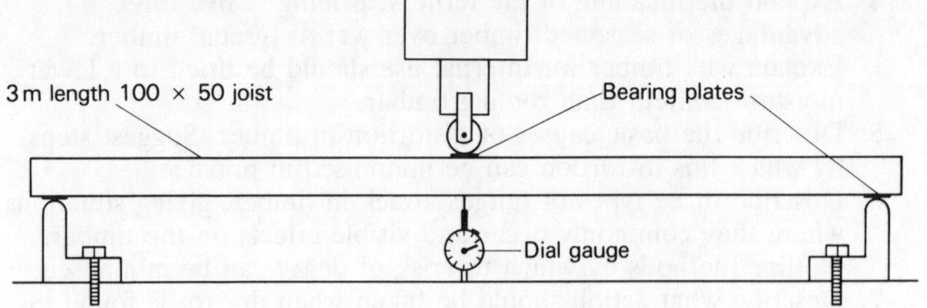

Fig. 5.19 Loading arrangement for machine stress grading

Results

Plot graphs of load (Y axis) against deflection (X axis) and draw the best straight line through the points. Obtain the gradient of the graph in N/mm. Note that higher gradients signify stiffer material.

The elastic modulus of the timber may be calculated:

$$E = \frac{WL^3}{48\delta I} \qquad (\delta = \text{deflection}) \quad \text{(other symbols as used earlier)}$$

$$= \frac{W}{\delta} \cdot \frac{L^3}{48I}$$

$$= (\text{gradient of graph}) \times \frac{L^3}{48I}$$

The stress at failure of the timber is

$$f = \frac{M}{Z} = \frac{WL}{8Z}$$

Calculate the stress at failure. Look for correlation between the elastic modulus and strength values for each piece and the visual stress grade result.

Questions

1. Describe the nature and function of the following:
   (a) vessels (hardwoods);
   (b) fibres (hardwoods);
   (c) tracheids (softwoods);
   (d) rays.
2. (a) Describe the visual differences between hardwood and softwood by inspection of Fig. 5.3 and 5.4.
   (b) Distinguish between ring porous and diffuse porous hardwoods and give one common example of each.
3. Comment on the strength, durability and availability of softwoods compared with hardwoods. Hence give main applications of each group in construction.

4. Explain the meaning of the term 'seasoning'. Give three advantages of seasoned timber over wet or 'green' timber. Explain why timber for internal use should be dried to a lower moisture content than roofing timber.
5. Describe the basic causes of distortion in timber. Suggest steps by which this distortion can be minimised in practice.
6. Describe three types of fungus attack in timber, giving situations where they commonly occur and visible effects on the timber. Outline methods by which the risk of decay can be minimised.
7. Describe what action should be taken when dry rot is found in the joists supporting a suspended ground floor.
8. Define the terms 'knot area ratio' (KAR) and 'margin condition'. Give the BS 4978 requirements for KAR values for 'General Structure' and 'Special Structural' grades. Estimate the KAR values of the sections shown in Fig. 5.20 and hence classify them in this respect.
9. Explain the principle of machine stress grading. Give two advantages of machine stress grading over visual stress grading.
10. (a) A uniformly distributed load of total value 25 KN is to be supported by 10 timber joists spanning 3 m. A joist size of 175 × 50 mm has been suggested. If the permissible bending stress in the timber is 5.1 N/mm^2, calculate whether this size of joist would be satisfactory, from a stress standpoint.
    (b) If the elastic modulus of the timber is 8600 N/mm^2, calculate the maximum deflection and check whether it is within the permissible limit of 0.003 × span.

References

Building Regulations (1976) HMSO.
National House Building Council Manual

British Standards

CP 112: *The Structural Use of Timber.*
BS 144: 1973, *Coal Tar Creosote for the Preservation of Timber.*
BS 373: 1957, *Testing Small, Clear Specimens of Timber.*
BS 1282: 1975, *Guide to the Choice, Use and Application of Wood Preservatives.*
BS 3452: 1962, *Copper/Chrome Water-Borne Wood Preservatives and Their Application.*
BS 3453: 1962 (1979), *Fluoride/Arsenate/Chromate/Dinitrophenol Water-borne Wood Preservatives and Their Application.*
BS 4072: 1974, *Wood Preservation by Means of Water-borne Copper/Chrome/Arsenic Compositions.*
BS 4978: 1973, *Timber Grades for Structural Use.*
BS 5707: Parts 1–3: *Solutions of Wood Preservations in Organic Solvents.*

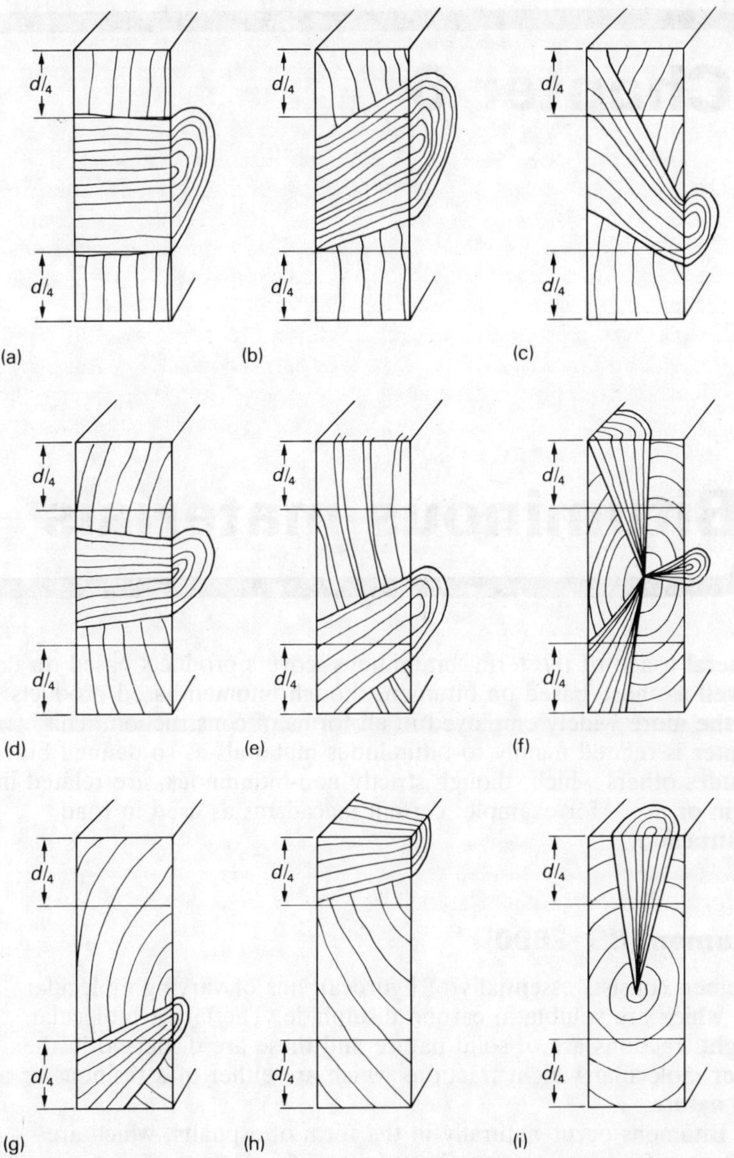

Fig. 5.20 Knot area ratio (KAR) classification

Chapter 6

Bituminous materials

General usage of the term 'bituminous' covers products based on tar as well as those based on bitumen, though bitumen-based products are the more widely employed in all forms of construction. This chapter is related mainly to bituminous materials as so defined but includes others which, though strictly non-bituminous, are related in origin or use – for example, certain macadams as used in road construction.

Bitumen (BS 3690)

Bitumen consists essentially of hydrocarbons of varying molecular size which are soluble in carbon disulphide. The larger molecular weight fractions are of solid nature and these are dispersed in the lower molecular weight fractions which are either of a resinous or an oily nature.

Bitumens occur naturally in the form of asphalts, which are mixtures of bitumen, minerals and water found in the form of rock or lake asphalt. The majority of bitumen is, however, produced as a residue from the fractional distillation of crude petroleum. (The *condensed distillate* of this process – that is, the part which evaporates, is known as '*tar*'.)

The properties of bitumens vary greatly according to composition which, in turn, depends on the manufacturing method and crude material. However, all bitumens are thermoplastic – they soften on heating, though they have no well-defined softening or melting point. On cooling they tend to become progressively more brittle. Other properties important to their use are adhesive qualities and resistance to water, dilute acids and alkalis. They dissolve in many organic solvents, though this may not always be an advantage.

The following are the main types of bituminous materials.

Blown bitumen

'Blowing' is normally used for the production of 'straight-run' bitumens – obtained by the controlled heating of crude petroleum. Since heating the crude bitumen above about 400 °C would tend to produce decomposition, distillation is achieved by heating to a lower temperature assisted by blowing air or steam into the fractionating column. The more volatile products are removed by evaporation and the bitumen settles as a viscous fluid to the base of the columns. By varying the temperature and duration of distillation, a great variety of grades can be produced, although in practice there are two basic grades – hard and soft – which may be blended according to requirements.

The essential feature of straight run bitumens is that they are solid at ordinary temperatures and must therefore be heated prior to application, whether in roofing, flooring or roads. They are nevertheless widely employed since they have the advantage that hardening takes place immediately on cooling, so that there is only a minimal delay between construction and use. For grading purposes blown bitumens are described by their penetration and/or their softening point. The penetration is the distance that a standard shaped needle will penetrate a sample of bitumen when loaded in a standard manner (100 g load for 5 s at 25 °C). The penetration is measured in units of 0.1 mm, e.g. '200 pen' bitumen means 20 mm penetration (see experiment 6.1). Penetrations for most purposes lie in the range 30 to 300. The softening point temperature is found by a ring and ball test (see experiment 6.4). When bitumens have a penetration of less than, say, 100, the softening point test tends to give a more sensitive indication of hardness, the softening point increasing from about 45 °C for '100 pen' bitumens to over 60 °C for very low pen bitumens. There is, however, no unique relationship between these two parameters and bitumen specifications often refer to both.

Cutback bitumens

These comprise straight-run bitumen to which a volatile fluxing oil such as kerosene or creosote is added in order to reduce viscosity. The handling and placing of products based on cutback bitumens can take place at much lower temperatures than straight-run bitumens. Subsequent hardening is by solvent evaporation, hence it is generally considerably slower than that of straight run bitumens. Their main application is in cold-rolled asphalts. Cutbacks are graded using the standard tar viscometer in which the time in seconds for 50 ml of cutback to flow through a standard orifice at a standard temperature is measured (experiment 6.3). Values range typically from 50 to 200 s.

Bitumen emulsions

A bitumen emulsion contains minute bitumen particles dispersed in water by means of an emulsifying agent. These agents impart electric charges to the particle surface, thereby causing them to repel and preventing the formation of a continuous solid mass. Two types of emulsifier may be used: anionic emulsifiers, which impart a negative charge to the bitumen and cationic emulsifiers which impart a positive charge.

The mechanism of solidification ('breaking') of emulsions is by water loss, which inactivates the emulsifier. In the case of cationic emulsions, breaking may be assisted by the neutralisation of the positive charge by negative charges often present on solid mineral materials such as silica. Hence cationic emulsions tend to break more quickly than ionic emulsions and may break without drying of the water. Anionic emulsions are nevertheless cheaper and are more commonly used. Breaking is normally accompanied by a change in colour from brown to black.

Bitumen emulsions are widely used to produce damp-proof membranes, as curing membranes in concrete roadbases and as tack-coats in road surfacing. They have the advantage of adhering to damp surfaces, though 'breaking' in such situations would normally be delayed. Thin films only must be used – ponding of an emulsion will result in very long drying times. Where thicker coatings, such as in damp-proofing, are required, these should comprise several coats, each being allowed to dry before application of the next.

Road tar (BS 76)

Road tar is obtained by the destructive distillation of coal (or, less commonly, wood or shale) at about 1000 °C. The tar is driven off as a thick brown vapour, which is condensed and collected. The other products of distillation are gas, and oil factions such as benzole.

The condensate is referred to as crude tar and this must be treated to produce road tars. Treatment comprises distillation at temperatures up to 350 °C in which light oil, naphthalene and creosote are progressively driven off. The remaining material (residue) is described as base tar or pitch and this is fluxed back with selected tar oils to give a road tar with the desired viscosity and distillation characteristics.

According to BS 76, there are two types of road tar – type S and type C. Type S tars contain more volatile oils and therefore tend to set more rapidly on the road, being used mainly in surface dressings. Type C tars are less volatile and are intended for use with coated macadam. Tars are classified principally according to their viscosity as measured by the standard tar viscometer (experiment 6.2). Water content is also important, BS 76 requiring a maximum of 0.5 per cent in order to prevent frothing on heating.

Tars differ from bitumens in the following main respects:

1. They are generally more susceptible to temperature change, tending to soften quite quickly at higher temperatures and being subject to embrittlement at very low temperatures. Hence the viscosity of tar which is chosen for a particular function will depend on seasonal temperature variations as well as traffic load requirements.
2. Tars and pitches undergo 'weathering' in service – a combination of oxidation and evaporation of volatile fractions. This is an advantage in roads since smooth tar films, brought to the road surface by heavy traffic, weather away slowly and leave the aggregate exposed.
3. The solubility of tars in organic solvents (such as petrol) is much lower than that of bitumen, hence tars are more suitable for surfacings which are subject to contamination by diesel or lubricating oils – such as hard standings for buses or commercial vehicles.

The main application of tar is as a surface dressing for roads, since it has the advantage over bitumens (with the exception of cationic emulsions) of superior adhesion in damp conditions. Dense tar surfacings, which are rather similar to hot rolled asphalts, are also used in situations where the advantages of a tar binder are required.

Low temperature tar

This term is misleading, since it may erroneously be taken to imply a tar for cold application. In fact the term refers to the method of production; a carbonising temperature of 600–750 °C being employed instead of 1000 °C or more, as for conventional tars. The lower temperature is used when coal is converted to smokeless fuels as distinct from the higher temperature 'destructive' distillation which is used for the production of 'town' gas. It will be evident that large quantities of low-temperature tar are now available as a by-product of the smokeless fuel industry and this can be blended to give very similar properties to those of conventional tars. BS 76 now makes provision for the use of such tars.

Asphalts and macadams

Asphalts are bituminous mixtures containing a relatively fine particle grading (Fig. 6.1), the fine material together with the binder forming a stiff 'mortar' which provides strength and stiffness in the final product.

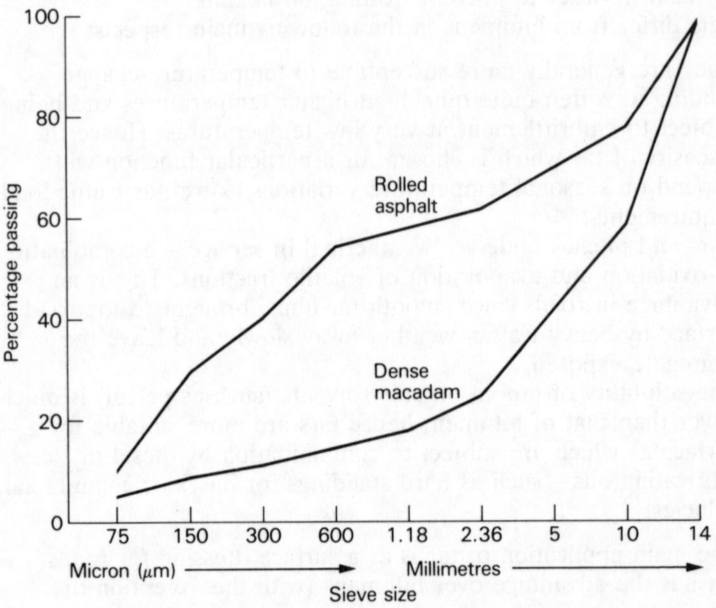

Fig. 6.1 Overall aggregate gradings for typical rolled asphalt and dense bitumen macadam. The rolled asphalt contains some coarse material and a high proportion of fine material. The macadam is composed mainly of coarse material

Macadams are materials which rely mainly on particle interlock rather than a stiff mortar to provide strength and stiffness. They normally contain a wide range of particle sizes (Fig. 6.1). Macadams are often coated with a bituminous binder in which case they would be described as 'coated' macadams. Some macadams for roadbase construction may not have a bituminous binder – they are referred to as 'wet-mix' and 'dry-bound' macadams. The principal forms of asphalts and macadams are as follows:

Mastic asphalt

This is a high-quality surfacing material with a relatively large binder content – between 6 and 20 per cent of a low penetration bitumen.

The aggregate may be natural rock asphalt (BS 1162, 1418, 1410) or limestone (BS 988, 1076, 1097, 1451), each ground to a powder which all passes a 2.36 mm sieve. Relatively high application temperatures – in the region of 200 °C are necessary and the material is spread by hand – a process involving a good deal of skill. The material is applied in layers to a final thickness in the range 25–50 mm. The product contains less than 1 per cent voids and is impermeable. An important use is in road carriageways subject to the highest traffic intensities, applications including bridge decks, tunnels and deceleration areas. In these situations chippings are rolled in to improve skid resistance.

A further important application is in flat roofing. The asphalt is laid in two layers on isolating felt to allow movement and is held in place by its own weight. The substrate for the asphalt should be rigid – for example concrete, rather than timber, since asphalts tend to crack under excessive flexing, especially after ageing. Solar reflective treatments help reduce embrittlement due to ageing. Mastic asphalt roofs provide much better resistance to pedestrian traffic than built-up felt roofs especially if suitably gritted. They will also withstand vehicle traffic provided support is adequate. Mastic asphalt is also used for flooring and tanking.

Rolled asphalts – BS 594

These comprise a mixture of aggregate, filler and 'asphaltic cement', which may be a bitumen, a pitch bitumen mixture or a mixture of lake asphalt and bitumen. (The latter two binders produce better weathering properties.) Rolled asphalts may have low stone content (about 30%) or high stone content (about 60%). The former are used for road surfacings only, chippings being rolled in after laying. High stone content rolled asphalts are normally used for base courses and roadbases. Rolled asphalts are laid hot by machine in thicknesses of 38–76 mm. They are widely used on heavily trafficked roads and city streets. The optimum binder content in a rolled asphalt is obtained by the Marshall test (see experiment 6.12).

Cold asphalts – BS 4987

These are really macadams and are given the alternative name 'bitumen macadams' in BS 4987. The material is based on cut-back bitumens and is designed to be used cold or warm. Fine and coarse varieties based on 6 mm and 10 mm aggregates respectively are available. Fine varieties are laid in thicknesses of about 20 mm and coarse varieties to 30 mm. Cold asphalts are used for regulating and patching purposes and for footpaths, having the advantage that they can be stored for some time. They make little contribution to the strength of the pavement and will be indented by sustained point loads.

Bitumen macadams – BS 4987

These are based on bitumens of about 100 penetration, together with graded aggregates of size up to 40 mm depending on thickness. They have a higher void content than asphalts (up to 25% depending on type), though this reduces progressively due to compaction by traffic.

The texture of a macadam depends on the maximum aggregate size and on the content of fines – the amount of material passing a 2.36 mm sieve. Open-textured macadams have a maximum size of 10 to 14 mm and fines content not exceeding 15 per cent.

Medium textured macadams have a maximum size of 6–10 mm with 40–60 per cent fines. Fine-textured macadams have a maximum size of 6 mm with 75 to 100 per cent fines. Dense macadams have a fines content of about 37 per cent and typically 28 mm or 40 mm maximum size.

Open and medium-textured macadams are free-draining; they are used for both the basecourse and wearing course of road surfacings. When used in the latter, they reduce traffic spray in wet weather, though an underlying impervious layer is essential to prevent rain penetration to the roadbase. They are used for resurfacing, when the existing road provides this waterproof layer. Dense bitumen macadams provide higher strength and are impermeable. They are used as roadbases, basecourses and wearing courses and are suitable for all but the heaviest traffic categories.

Wet-mix and dry-bound macadams – BS 63

Wet-mix macadam is based on crushed rock or slag graded from 40 mm downwards and mixed with 2 to 6 per cent of water in order to minimise segregation and assist compaction. Compaction is carried out using a vibrating roller and the final void content should be less than 10 per cent. Wet-mix macadam is used as a roadbase material for flexible roads.

Dry-bound macadam is also used for roadbases and comprises 40 or 50 mm nominal single size material. It is laid dry to a depth of 75 to 100 mm and compacted by a 2.5 tonne steel-tyred roller. Dry fine aggregate of size 5 mm downwards is then spread about 25 mm thick on the compacted stone and vibrated into the voids using a plate or roller. The process is repeated until no further fine aggregate will penetrate and the surface is then swept clean and finally rolled. Over-vibration must be avoided, otherwise segregation will occur.

Wet-mix macadam suffers from the disadvantage that accurate metering of water is necessary, while the dry-bound macadam process is more involved and requires preliminary drying of materials. The load-carrying capacity of roads constructed from each of these materials in the UK is now limited by current Road Works Specifications and there is evidence that the rate of deformation in dry-bound roadbases in particular is comparatively rapid.

Defects in bituminous pavements or surfacings

Cracking

This is likely to lead to serious problems in all types of surfacing. Cracked surfacings permit water penetration. which, in the case of roads, may lead to weakening of foundations and hence reduced load-bearing capacity. The penetration of water will also accelerate deterioration due to the effect of frost and de-icing salts. In roofs, moisture penetration leads to all the associated problems of dampness both in the roof structure and in the building itself.

Cracking is caused essentially by movements which exceed those the material can absorb. In flexible roads laid on cement-bound bases, a pattern of well-spaced cracks frequently forms in the bituminous surfacing, corresponding to cracks previously formed in the roadbase. These 'reflected' cracks can be minimised if, during construction, measures are taken which will result in a relatively large number of fine cracks in the base, so that movements at any one crack are reduced. Thicker or more flexible surfacings also reduce the extent of the problem. Once such cracking patterns are produced, they are difficult to cure permanently but are relatively easy to seal and resurfacing will effect a short-term remedy. Similar types of crack may occur in asphalt roofs where the isolation membrane between the surfacing and deck is absent or ineffective. Joints in the decking, together with dressings, flashings and weatherings require careful design and execution to avoid excessive movement leading to cracks. Where a few well-defined cracks exist, it may be possible to cut back, make provision for movement and apply fresh asphalt. Where significant water penetration has occurred however, complete replacement will be necessary.

Finer cracks or crazing may result when a bituminous surfacing is not able to absorb thermal movements it is subject to. This may, in the first instance, be due to the use of a bitumen or tar having too low a penetration value, though a further cause is often overheating prior to use, which results in the loss of fluxing oils. Solar radiation causes further progressive loss of these oils and roofs which are prone to rapid heating and cooling benefit from protective coatings of reflective material such as light-coloured chippings. Crazing is a surface effect and does not, initially, lead to water penetration though it accelerates overall failure of the material, since cracks concentrate the tensile stresses occurring when cold weather causes thermal contraction. Most crazing occurs in cold weather, since this results in tensile stress at a time when the tensile strain capacity of the material is at its minimum. Surface crazing may be at least temporarily alleviated by means of surface treatments, which also require protection from solar radiation. Deeper crazing, resulting in moisture penetration, will necessitate replacement of the material.

Blistering

This occurs mainly in asphalt or built-up felt roofs and is caused by the presence of moisture under the surface. The blistering occurs in hot weather when heat vaporises the water, which swells the softened asphalt. Frequently the blisters remain on subsequent cooling – for example if rain stiffens the asphalt and prevents it resettling. Blisters are initially waterproof but may eventually leak in cold weather if damaged mechanically.

The asphalt is also invariably thinner at these positions, increasing vulnerability. Minor blisters may be left, or patched in dry weather. Severe blistering is indicative of a design or construction fault which calls for replacement. The problem occurs most commonly with 'wet' substrates such as concrete which are not effectively isolated by a membrane from the asphalt. By the use of such a membrane, together with dry conditions during construction, blistering should be avoided.

Deformation

Surface deformation in roads is the result of prolonged or severe mechanical stress. It is quite common in deceleration areas of roads such as near roundabouts, traffic lights or bus stops, especially on downward gradients. The cause is the use of either too much binder, too soft a binder or incorrect aggregate grading and it leads to corrugations of the surfacing. These then exacerbate the problem as upward-sloping sections of each undulation become subject to higher stresses under a given vehicle braking load. To effect a cure it is necessary to replace the surfacing with one designed to have the extra stiffness required.

A more serious form of deformation may occur in which the roadbase is also affected. This is caused by structural failure of the pavement as a whole and results in large depressions in the road surface. In such situations the surfacing and roadbase must be removed and replaced to an uprated specification.

Embedment

Embedment is a term commonly used in the context of road surfacings and it describes the sinking of chippings into the binder and, in some cases, the underlying material. Particularly important is surface dressing where the binder and chipping size employed should be such that, after compaction by traffic, the lower half of each surface chipping is embedded (Fig. 6.2(a)). Where embedment is less than this (Fig. 6.2(b)), there will be a tendency for chippings to break loose ('scabbing'). Conversely, excessive use of binder, combined with a soft substrate, may lead to total embedment and hence to 'fatting-up' with loss of surface texture and skid resistance (Fig. 6.2(c)). Where this occurs, a further surface dressing can be

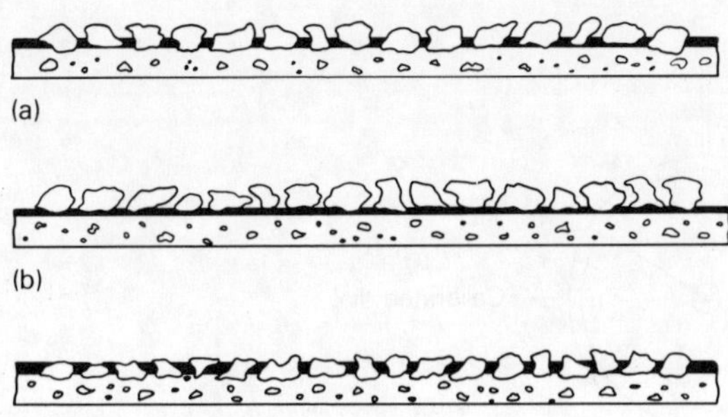

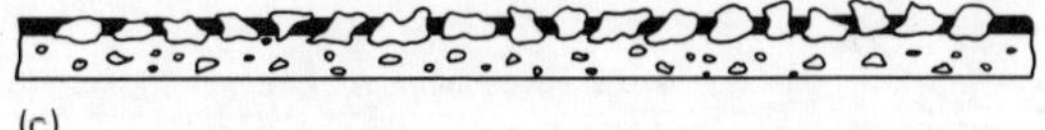

Fig. 6.2 Varying degrees of embedment of chippings applied as surface dressing (a) satisfactory – approximately half each stone covered (b) too low leading to 'scabbing' (c) too high leading to 'fatting up'

applied with relatively low binder content, together with increased chipping size (up to 20 mm) in order to result in the correct degree of embedment after compaction by traffic.

Experiments – Tests on bitumen/tar binders

Introductory comment

These tests are based on British Standard specifications, although some have been abbreviated or simplified to take account of the limited time usually available. Further simplifications can be undertaken where the principle only of the test is being illustrated, though the experimenter should refer to the text of BS specifications where an accurate and valid test result is required.

Experiment 6.1 Determination of the penetration of bitumen (BS 4691)

This test is used to determine the consistence of penetration grade 'straight-run' and stiffer 'cut-back' bitumens at the standard temperature of 25 °C.

Apparatus

Penetration apparatus as shown in Fig. 6.3. The dial gauge should be capable of reading to 0.1 mm and the mass of the needle and spindle assembly should total 100 g. Needles should be of hardened stainless steel, of 1 mm diameter with a 9° taper at one end to a truncated tip 0.15 mm in diameter. Sample containers should be of diameter 55 mm and internal depth 35 mm for penetrations less than 200 or diameter 70 mm and internal depth 45 mm for penetrations between 200 and 350. They may be of metal or glass. A water bath capable

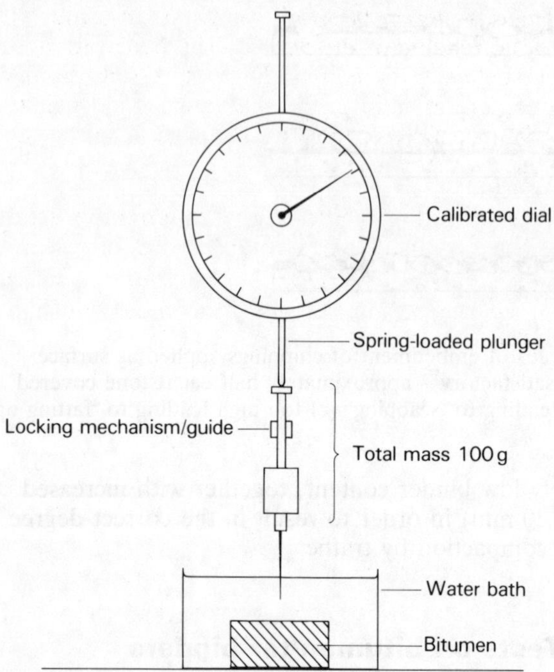

Fig. 6.3 Penetration apparatus

of maintaining a temperature of 25 °C ± 0.1 °C, stop-watch and thermometer are also required.

Preparation of specimens

Heat the sample until just sufficiently fluid to pour, stirring to avoid local overheating. Stirring also helps remove air bubbles which may be present in blown bitumens. Avoid prolonged heating (over 30 min). Pour into the sample container judged to be appropriate to the original consistence of the material, tapping to remove air. The container should be almost full. Allow to cool for 1 to 2 h, according to container size and then insert into the water bath containing at least 10 litres of water and leave for a similar time to allow the temperature to reach 25 °C.

Procedure

The test should be carried out on the specimen while submerged in the water bath or while submerged in a suitable smaller vessel containing water at 25 °C. In each case check that the sample is firmly mounted and unable to rock. Lower the clean penetrometer needle until it just touches the bitumen. This may be facilitated by using the shadow of the needle or its reflected image. Take the reading of the dial gauge. Release the needle and start the stop-watch. After 5 s note the reading of the needle. The penetration is equal to the difference between the two readings expressed in units of 0.1 mm. Make three determinations. the simplest method being to use a fresh clean needle at a different part of the surface for each determination. Find the average reading.

Experiment 6.2 Determination of the equiviscous temperature (e.v.t.) of tar using the standard tar viscometer (BS 76)

This test is designed for softer bituminous materials such as cut-back bitumen. The e.v.t. is the temperature at which the viscosity of the materials of a standard value.

Apparatus

Standard tar viscometer (Fig. 6.4). The essential features are as follows:

Tar cup, in the form of an open-topped brass cylinder with an

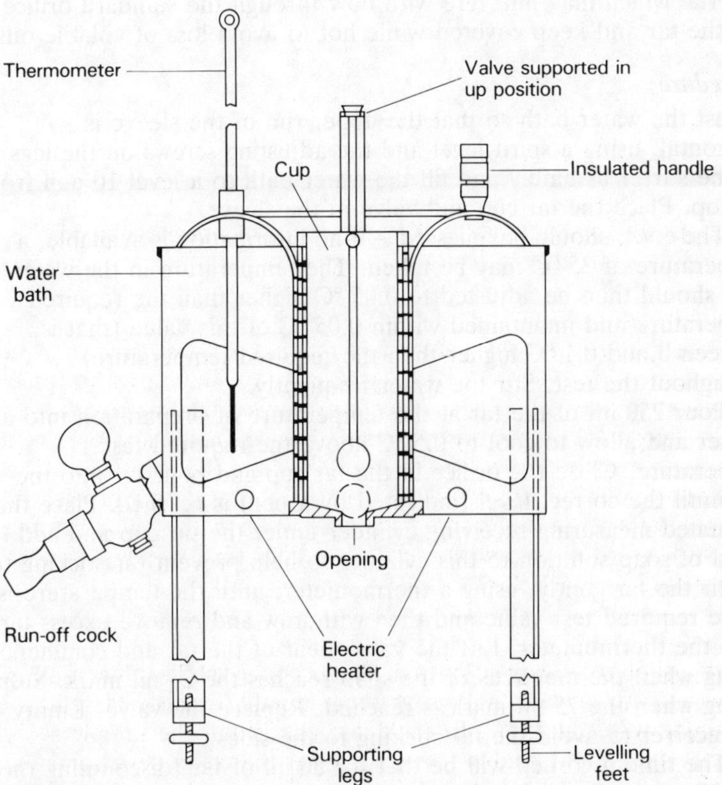

Fig. 6.4 Section through standard tar viscometer

accurate opening of diameter 10 mm at the base. This opening can be closed by a sphere attached to an operating rod.
Water bath, which contains an accurate central sleeve into which the tar cup fits. It has three legs which are adjustable for levelling, a run-off cock, electric heater and stirring vanes. The latter are attached via a further concentric cylinder to a curved upper shield provided with a handle for rotating. This shield also provides support for the tar cup valve.

A 100 ml graduated measuring cylinder, thermometer and stop-watch are also required.

Sample preparation

Immerse a container of the sample in water at a temperature of not more than 30 °C above the expected equiviscous temperature. If no information is available as to the expected e.v.t., a preparation temperature of 65 °C may be used as a starting point, heating further, if necessary, to obtain adequate fluidity. BS 76 requires the warm sample to be strained through a 600 μm sieve to remove any material which may interfere with flow through the standard orifice. Stir the tar and keep covered while hot to avoid loss of volatile oils.

Procedure

Adjust the water bath so that the upper rim of the sleeve is horizontal, using a spirit level and the adjusting screws on the legs. Fit the stirrer assembly and fill the water bath to a level 10 mm from the top. Place the tar cup and valve in the sleeve.

The e.v.t. should be 'guessed' – if no information is available, a temperature of 35 °C may be taken. The temperature in the water bath should then be adjusted to 0.05 °C higher than the required temperature and maintained within 0.05 °C of this value (that is, between 0 and 0.1 °C higher than the required temperature) throughout the test. Stir the water frequently.

Pour 250 ml of the tar at the temperature of preparation into a beaker and allow to cool to 0.5 °C above the required test temperature. Close the orifice in the tar cup and pour tar into the cup until the correct level (indicated by a peg) is reached. Place the graduated measuring receiving cylinder under the tar cup and add 20 ml of soap solution to this cylinder to help prevent tar sticking to it. Stir the tar gently, using a thermometer, until the temperature is at the required test value and then withdraw and remove excess tar from the thermometer. Lift the valve clear of the tar and commence timing when the meniscus of the soap reaches the 25 ml mark. Stop timing when the 75 ml mark is reached. Replace the valve. Empty the receiver to avoid the tar sticking to the sides.

The time recorded will be that for 50 ml of tar (discounting the first 25 ml) to flow from the cup. At the equiviscous temperature, the time taken would be 50 s. For times in the range 33 to 75 s.

Table 6.1 will enable the correct e.v.t. to be obtained. Suppose, for example, a time of 65 s was obtained at a test temperature of 35 °C. The correction from the table is + 1.6 °C and so the e.v.t. is 36.6 °C. If the time obtained is outside the values indicated in heavy type in the table, the experiment should be repeated using Table 6.1 as a guide to select a new test temperature.

Typical values of equiviscous temperature for tars

Surface dressing	Heavy traffic	42–46 °C
	Average roads	38–42 °C
	Light traffic	34 °C
Coated materials	Dense roadbase (heavy traffic)	54 °C
	Basecourse, estate roads	38 °C

Experiment 6.3 Determination of the viscosity of cutback bitumen (standard tar viscometer BS 2000: Part 72)

The apparatus for this test is basically the same as that for Experiment 6.2, although for low viscosity cutbacks a 4 mm cup is used. There are some differences in procedure. The cup size and testing temperature should be as follows:

Viscosity (seconds) (10 mm cup at 25 °C)	Cup size to be used (mm)	Testing temperature (°C)
Greater than 500	10	40
15–500	10	25
Less than 15	4	25

A trial test may be necessary to determine the correct cup size and temperature, though most cutbacks have viscosities in the range 50–200 s.

Procedure

According to BS 2000, the temperature of the cutback should be adjusted to within 0.5 °C of the test temperature by use of a separate water bath. This requires the orifice of the viscometer to be closed by a cork inserted from beneath and the thermometer and valve to be located by a second cork with a central hole (for the thermometer) and slot fitted into the top. The cutback should be free from water and should first be heated to 60 °C for 3 h, taking care to avoid loss of volatile constituents. Then cool to the approximate test temperature. After fitting the corks, fill the viscometer cup with the cutback until it is level with the peg. Immerse in the separate water bath for 1.5 h at the correct temperature.

Table 6.1 Correction in °C to be applied to temperatures of test to give evts

Viscosity (s)	0	1	2	3	4	5	6	7	8	9
10	− 10.4	− 9.8	− 9.2	− 8.7	− 8.2	− 7.7	− 7.3	− 6.9	− 6.5	− 6.1
20	− 5.7	− 5.4	− 5.1	− 4.8	− 4.5	− 4.3	− 4.0	− 3.8	− 3.5	− 3.3
30	− 3.1	− 2.9	− 2.7	− **2.5**	− **2.3**	− **2.2**	− **2.0**	− **1.9**	− **1.7**	− **1.5**
40	− **1.4**	− **1.2**	− **1.1**	− **0.9**	− **0.8**	− **0.6**	− **0.5**	− **0.4**	− **0.3**	− **0.1**
50	**0**	+ **0.1**	+ **0.2**	+ **0.3**	+ **0.5**	+ **0.6**	+ **0.7**	+ **0.8**	+ **0.9**	+ **1.0**
60	+ **1.1**	+ **1.2**	+ **1.3**	+ **1.4**	+ **1.5**	+ **1.6**	+ **1.7**	+ **1.7**	+ **1.8**	+ **1.9**
70	+ **2.0**	+ **2.1**	+ **2.2**	+ **2.3**	+ **2.3**	+ **2.4**	+ 2.5	+ 2.5	+ 2.6	+ 2.7
80	+ 2.8	+ 2.8	+ 2.9	+ 3.0	+ 3.0	+ 3.1	+ 3.1	+ 3.2	+ 3.3	+ 3.3
90	+ 3.4	+ 3.5	+ 3.5	+ 3.6	+ 3.6	+ 3.7	+ 3.7	+ 3.8	+ 3.9	+ 3.9
100	+ 4.0	+ 4.0	+ 4.1	+ 4.1	+ 4.2	+ 4.2	+ 4.3	+ 4.3	+ 4.4	+ 4.4
110	+ 4.5	+ 4.6	+ 4.6	+ 4.7	+ 4.7	+ 4.8	+ 4.8	+ 4.9	+ 4.9	+ 5.0
120	+ 5.0	+ 5.1	+ 5.1	+ 5.2	+ 5.2	+ 5.2	+ 5.3	+ 5.3	+ 5.4	+ 5.4
130	+ 5.5	+ 5.5	+ 5.5	+ 5.6	+ 5.6	+ 5.7	+ 5.7	+ 5.7	+ 5.8	+ 5.8
140	+ 5.9	+ 5.9	+ 6.0	+ 6.0	+ 6.0	+ 6.1	+ 6.1	+ 6.1	+ 6.2	+ 6.2

Note That part of the table giving corrections for tars having viscosities between 33 s and 75 s inclusive (indicated by bold type) may alone be used in calculating the evt to be reported. The remainder of the table will be useful in ranging tests

Set up the viscometer water bath and adjust to the correct temperature, stirring frequently.

Transfer the viscometer cup to the viscometer water bath and remove the thermometer and corks. Check that the level of cutback is correct.

Time 50 ml of cutback through the orifice, as described in experiment 6.2, except that light mineral oil is used in the graduated receiver instead of soap solution. Hence obtain the viscosity of the cutback expressed in seconds.

Experiment 6.4 Determination of the softening point of bitumen using the ring and ball method (BS 4692)

This test is designed to be used with 'straight run' (penetration grade) bitumens.

Apparatus

The apparatus enables tests to be carried out on two samples of the material. It comprises a support frame 25.4 mm above a lower plate, together with two tapered rings, two ball centring guides and two steel balls.

A heat-resistant glass container, 300 μm sieve, thermometer, electric heater, mechanical (electric or magnetic) stirrer, thermometer and knife are also required. Distilled water is normally suitable as the heating medium; glycerol/dextrin debonding mixture (or a suitable grease).

The assembly is shown in Fig. 6.5.

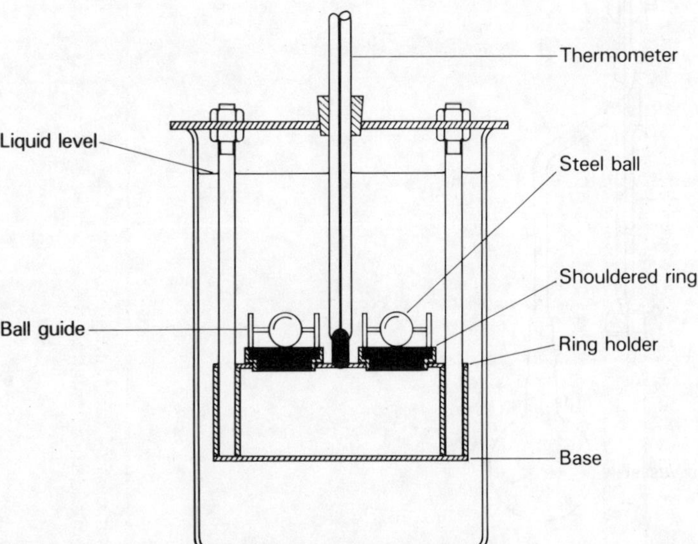

Fig. 6.5 Softening point apparatus

Sample preparation

If the sample contains water, BS 4692 requires that it be heated briefly to a temperature of 130 °C.

Heat the sample until fluid; with the exception of low penetration bitumens, a temperature of 130 °C should suffice. Stir until free of air bubbles and filter, if necessary, through a 300 μm sieve (though this should normally not be necessary). Heat the tapered rings to about the same temperature and place on a metal plate coated with a debonding mixture of glycerol and dextrin. Fill the rings with a *slight* excess of the liquid bitumen but *avoid* overflowing. Cool in air for 30 min and cut away the excess with a warm knife.

Procedure

Assemble the apparatus as in Fig. 6.5, with ball guides in position and fill the glass container to 50 mm above the upper surface of the rings with freshly-boiled distilled water at a temperature of 5 °C. After 15 min place the steel balls, which should be at a similar

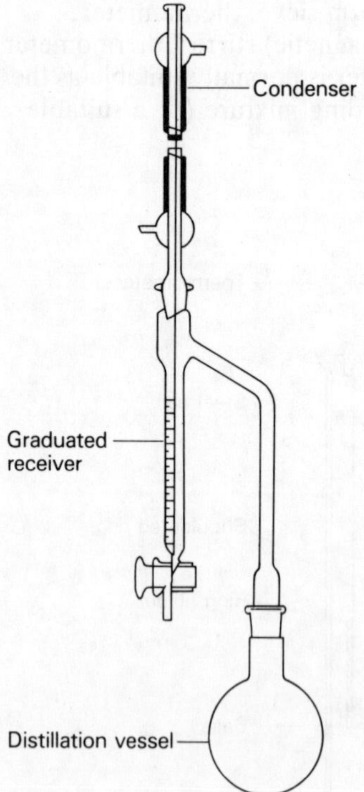

Fig. 6.6 Dean and Stark reflux apparatus

temperature, in the ball guides. Heat the bath, stirring continuously so that the temperature rises at 5 °C ± 0.5 °C per minute. Record the temperature at which each sample surrounding the ball touches the bottom plate. The temperatures obtained from the two samples should be within 1 °C of each other. Obtain the average temperature – this is the softening temperature.

Typical softening temperatures

Penetration value	35	50	100	300
Approx. softening temperature (°C)	58	53	46	34

(It should be emphasised that the relationship is approximate and that many specifications for bitumens require both penetration *and* softening point determinations.)

Experiment 6.5 Determination of the water content of a tar (BS 76, BS 4385)

Excess water in tar can cause frothing at high temperatures and may affect adhesion.

Apparatus

A Dean and Stark reflux apparatus with 2 ml receiver is required (Fig. 6.6). A glass or metal flask of 500 ml capacity is used as the distillation vessel; 100 ml graduated measuring cylinder; coal tar solvent naphtha; weighing balance accurate to 0.5 g.

Procedure

Weigh 100 ± 0.5 g. of the stirred tar sample into the flask and add 100 ml of solvent.

Attach the flask to the Dean and Stark apparatus and heat so that condensate falls from the end of the condenser at two to five drops per second. Continue until water is no longer visible in the apparatus, except in the bottom of the calibrated tube. The water level should also become constant.

Allow the apparatus to cool and note the volume of water.

The mass of the water in grams can be taken to be the same as its volume in millilitres.

Express the mass as a percentage of the original mass of tar.

Note. BS 76 limits the amount of water present to 0.5 per cent.

Experiment 6.6 Determination of the insoluble residue in a bituminous binder (BS 4690)

It is important to have a knowledge of the proportion of insoluble material in the binder when analysing coated materials – especially asphalts.

Apparatus

Filtration apparatus including: Filter flask – suitable for vacuum filtering; Gooch funnel; Gooch crucible – of vitreosil silica, translucent with perforated base (a rubber adaptor is needed for holding the Gooch crucible in the filter funnel); muffle furnace, desiccator, oven; asbestos – acid washed for the Gooch crucible; balance accurate to 0.05 g; trichloroethylene solvent. This is toxic, hence adequate ventilation is necessary. All sources of heat should be kept away from trichloroethylene, since it emits phosgene gas on heating.

Specimen preparation

If the sample contains water, it should be heated to 120–130 °C with constant stirring until the binder ceases to foam.

Procedure

Weigh the Gooch crucible. Disperse some of the asbestos in distilled water and then pour some of the suspension into the crucible and allow to settle. Apply light suction to draw off the water, leaving a firm mat. Wash with water, dry in an oven at 100 °C and then ignite in a muffle furnace at 650 °C. Cool the crucible in a desiccator and weigh. Repeat the ignition and cooling until constant weight (W_1) is obtained. The mass of the mat is the difference between the original crucible mass and the final mass. This should be 5 ± 0.1 g.

Weigh 2 to 5 g of the dry binder to the nearest 0.01 g (W_2) and place in a 200 ml flask. Add 100 ml of solvent. Stir and leave for one hour. Assemble the filter apparatus and moisten the asbestos mat with solvent. Pour the contents of the flask into the crucible and filter gently. The filtrate should be clear. Wash the residue in the flask into the crucible with the solvent in a wash bottle. Wash the material in the crucible with further solvent until the filtrate is colourless. Dry the crucible in an oven at 105 to 115 °C for one hour; cool in a desiccator and weigh (W_3).

The percentage of insoluble residue is then

$$\frac{W_3 - W_1}{W_2} \times 100$$

Note. The insoluble residue in bituminous binders for roads should not exceed 0.5 per cent.

Experiment 6.7 Determination of the flash point of bitumen (BS 4689)

It is essential that the flash point of bitumens be sufficiently high to avoid the risk of combustion of bituminous mixtures at working temperatures.

Apparatus

The Cleveland cup apparatus is used (Fig. 6.7); this comprises an open test cup mounted on a heating plate and held in a frame to which a thermometer and test flame applicator are also accurately fixed. The apparatus may be heated by Bunsen burner. To avoid objectionable fumes, the apparatus may be mounted in a fume cupboard but draughts must be avoided. The thermometer should be of standard type range − 6 to 400 °C, graduated in 2 °C intervals.

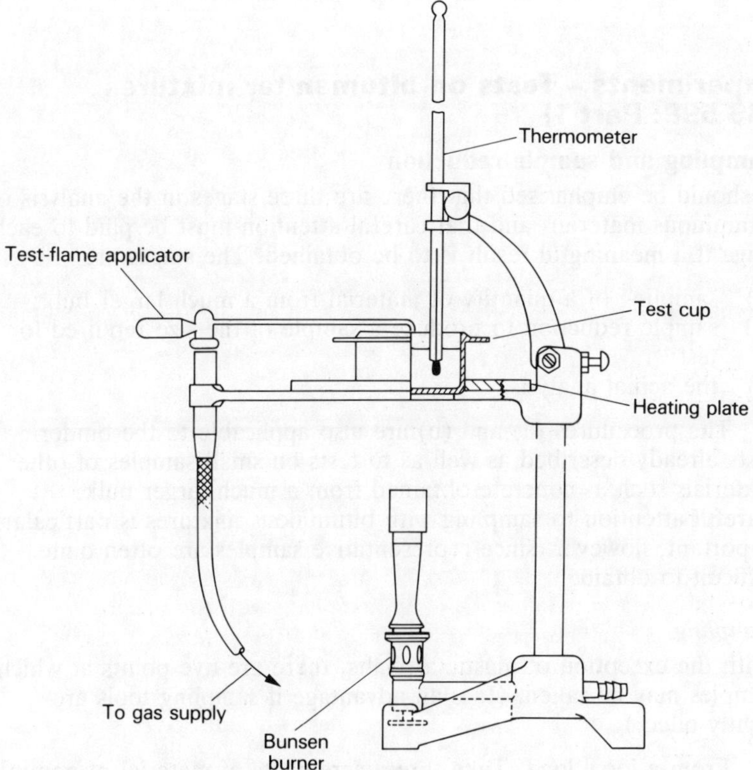

Fig. 6.7 Cleveland open cup apparatus

Procedure

Position the thermometer bulb 6 mm from the bottom of the clean cup and towards the opposite side from the test flame burner arm. Heat the sample as necessary to make it sufficiently fluid and then fill the cup so that the meniscus is level with the top. Light the test flame and adjust to a diameter of 4 mm. Heat the sample at approx.

15 °C per minute and as it approaches the flash point (as indicated by smoke emission) decrease the heating rate to about 5 °C per minute. At about 30 °C below the flash point pass the test flame across the surface of the bitumen, about 1 mm above it, taking about 1 s to pass the surface. Repeat for each 2 °C temperature rise until a flash appears on the surface of the bitumen. The temperature at this point is the flash temperature.

The heating procedure may require a 'trial run' in order to obtain correct heating rates and the point at which the test flame is applied.

Experiments – Tests on bitumen/tar mixtures (BS 598: Part 1)

Sampling and sample reduction

It should be emphasised that there are three stages in the analysis of bituminous materials and that careful attention must be paid to each stage if a meaningful result is to be obtained. The stages are:

(a) sampling of a quantity of material from a much larger bulk;
(b) sample reduction to produce a sample of the size required for test;
(c) the actual analysis.

The procedures (a) and (b) are also applicable to the binder tests already described as well as to tests on small samples of other materials such as concrete obtained from a much larger bulk. Careful attention to sampling with bituminous mixtures is particularly important, however, since representative samples are often quite difficult to obtain.

Sampling

With the exception of mastic asphalts, there are five points at which samples may be taken. (It is an advantage if sampling tools are lightly oiled.)

1. From a lorry load. Take three increments of material of nominal size 20 mm or smaller or four increments of larger sizes from about 100 mm below the surface of the material. The increments should be of about 7 kg each and as widely spaced as practicable, though not from the sides of the vehicle. Avoid lumps of coarse surface material falling into the holes during sampling.
2. From a mixer. The sample pan should preferably be fixed mechanically to the mixer so that it can be passed accurately through the centre of the stream on discharge. Take two or three increments according to aggregate size, avoiding the

beginning and end of the discharge.

3. From a paver hopper. Take three or four increments after approximately one half of the lorry load is discharged into it. (Samples from the paver hopper tend to be variable, the paver itself usually improving uniformity by further mixing.)
4. From the augers (screws) of the paver. Take two increments alternately from each side of the paver while augers are fully charged and in motion.
5. From the laid-but-not-rolled material. (Not recommended for wearing course material or where the nominal aggregate size is within 20 mm of the thickness being laid.) Place two 375 mm square steel trays not more than 10 mm deep each side of the centre line of the paver path. The corner of each tray is connected by steel wire to the area clear of the paver. After the passage of the paver, lift the wire to locate the trays and carefully remove. Combine the two samples. (This method has the disadvantage of causing additional inconvenience during the paving operation.)

Mastic asphalts may be sampled from at least six blocks of the material, or during discharge from the mixer, the principles of collection from a mixer being as given above for other materials.

The minimum sample masses required for the various materials are given in Table 6.2. Too large a sample is undesirable, since extra subdivision is then required.

Table 6.2 Minimum size of bulk sample for different nominal size materials

Material	Minimum Mass (kg.)
Nominal size larger than 20 mm	24
Nominal size 20 mm and smaller	16
Mastic asphalt	6

Sample reduction

Riffling and quartering of the received bulk samples may be used for reducing the size to that required for testing, though a riffle box is to be preferred, since errors resulting from quartering are larger. The riffle box may be lightly oiled or heated if sticky materials are being subdivided.

The masses required for analysis are given in Table 6.3.

Experiment 6.8 Hot extractor method of analysis of bituminous mixtures (BS 598: Part 2)

The purpose of this method is to determine the binder content of a

Table 6.3 Masses of bituminous mixtures required for analysis

Nominal aggregate size (mm)	Mass of sample (kg)
50	3 to 5
40	2.5 to 4
28	2 to 3
20	1 to 1.5
14	0.8 to 1.2
10	0.5 to 1.0
6	0.2 to 0.5
3	

bituminous mixture and to obtain the grading of the mineral fraction. It is especially suitable for the analysis of older materials which are likely to have a significant water content. (The method is not suitable for the analysis of mastics since the filler would block the filter paper. It may take up to two days to carry out correctly, although, provided suitable apparatus is available, it does not require great skill.)

Apparatus

The sample container is in the form of a cylindrical vessel made from brass gauze of mesh 1 to 2 mm or equivalent, mounted in the upper part of a flanged pot fitted with an upper cover and gasket. This is connected to a reflux condenser and 12.5 ml Dean and Stark graduated receiver. An electric hot plate should be used for heating; No. 1 Whatman filter paper; oven, desiccator; weighing balance to 0.05 g accuracy; trichloroethylene; pipette.

Procedure

Fit a No. 1 Whatman filter paper into the gauze container to form a complete lining; dry at 100 ° to 120 °C, cool in a desiccator and weigh (M_1). Place the gauze container in the pot. Place a sample of the correct mass (Table 6.3) in the container and weigh to 0.05 g accuracy (M_2). Pour adequate trichloroethylene over the sample but do not submerge. Bolt the cover with its gasket in place, connect the receiver and condenser and heat so that two to five drops of condensate fall per second from the end of the condenser onto the sample and through the filter paper. Water will collect in the receiving tube – if this becomes full, a measured quantity must be removed by means of a pipette, after temporarily stopping the distillation. (Alternatively, if a stop cock is provided on the receiver, the water may be drawn off.) Continue heating until extraction is complete and no further water is collected. Measure the total water collected in g (W). Remove the aggregate in the container and dry to constant mass at 100 °C to 120 °C. Allow to cool and weigh the cylinder and contents (M_3). The binder content, expressed as a percentage, is then

$$\frac{M_2 - (M_3 + W)}{M_2 - (M_1 + W)} \times 100$$

In the following simplified method for determining the aggregate grading any fine matter which may have passed through the No. 1 Whatman filter paper is ignored.

Transfer the aggregate from the filter paper to a metal bottle of suitable size, brushing the filter paper gently to remove as much aggregate as possible. Add solvent to the aggregate and wash through a 75 μm sieve under a 1.18 mm protective sieve. Filter the material passing through both sieves using a weighed No. 5 Whatman filter paper. Dry this filter paper and weigh again to give the approximate amount of filler. Combine and dry the remaining aggregate and grade by the same principles that concreting aggregates are graded.

The sieves that are to be used will depend on the type and size of the material being tested. (See BS 594 for rolled asphalts specifications and BS 4987 for coated macadams specifications.)

Compare the aggregate grading with those of Fig. 6.1.

Experiment 6.9 Sieving extractor method of analysis of bituminous materials (BS 598: Part 2)

This method is more rapid than the hot extractor method – it may be completed in 1 to 3 hours. It has, however, two disadvantages:

1. Shaking the material through sieves may break down softer aggregates such as limestones, leading to a misleading grading.
2. Wet sieving tends to lead to a finer particle grading than dry sieving which forms the basis of standard specifications.

This test is unsuitable for mastic asphalts.

If water is present, the percentage by mass will be required, using a technique such as that of experiment 6.8.

Apparatus

Sieving extractor apparatus comprising a nest of specially constructed sieves, with gaskets, attached to a base by clamps. The apparatus is capable of being rocked by electric motor and has a drain cock for the solvent. A domed top can be fitted above the nest of sieves and clamps are provided so that the whole apparatus is leak-proof. Centrifuge; metal bottle of 2.5 litre capacity with rubber stopper; recovery apparatus comprising water bath and flat-bottom flask which can be connected to a vacuum pump fitted with pressure gauge. Volumetric flasks; dichloromethane; dried silica gel; weighing balance.

Procedure

Weigh the sample to 0.05 per cent accuracy (M). See Table 6.3 and 6.4 for the correct sample size, sieve sizes to be used and volume of solvent. Note that the deeper sieves (25 mm depth) are required for some materials. Assemble the clean sieves on the base of the sieving extractor with size decreasing downwards and domed head uppermost. Tighten firmly. Add the required measured volume (V) of dichloromethane to the sieves. After checking for freedom from leaks, add the sample to the top sieve, together with a weighed quantity of silica gel (say 25 g) to absorb any water which may be present. Shake for 10 min for coarser materials and 20 min for finer materials.

Remove the liquid proof extractor head and run off the solution into a metal bottle. Shaking may continue during this process, provided escape of solution is prevented.

Separate insoluble matter from the binder by centrifuging. Transfer a volume v to a flat-bottomed flask weighed to 0.01 g accuracy.

Place the flask in the recovery apparatus and boil at reduced pressure (not less than 600 mb), shaking so that the binder is deposited as a thin layer on the walls of the flask.

For highly viscous residues, reduce the pressure to 200 mb for 3.5 min. For low viscosity residues, increase pressure to atmospheric and then reduce to 600 mb for 3.5 min.

Cool the flask and weigh to 0.01 g accuracy. For an accurate result, 0.75 to 1.25 g of binder should be left. The soluble binder, expressed as a percentage by mass (S) is given by

$$S = \frac{10\,000\, Z\, V}{v\, M\,(100 - P)} \left[1 + \frac{Z}{dv}\right]$$

where M is the mass of undried sample (g)
Z is the mass of binder recovered
V is the total volume of solvent
v is the volume of the solution used for binder recovery
d is the relative density (1.0 for bitumen; 1.15 for tar mixtures)
P is the percentage by mass of water in the sample

The remaining aggregate should be washed, using about 750 ml of dichloromethane, the sieves than being dried in a drying cupboard. Material passing the 75 μm sieve (filler) may be measured by filtration while remaining aggregate is graded in the normal way, using sieves appropriate to the material (see BS 594 for rolled asphalts specifications and BS 4987 for coated macadams specifications).

Experiment 6.10 Surface dressing; rate of spread of coating chippings (BS 594)

This test is meaningless unless carried out from a full-size spreading

Table 6.4 Recommendations for the size of sample, sieves and volume of solvent to be used for test by the sieving extractor method

Type and size of material	Sample mass (g)		Recommended sieves (12.5 mm and 25 mm deep) (mm)			(µm)					Minimum volume of solvent (ml)
40 mm nominal size											
Macadams	2500–3750		3.35	–	1.18	600	300	–	–	75	3500
Rolled asphalt	2500–3750		–	2.36	–	600	300	212	150	75	3500
28 mm nominal size											
Macadams	1500–2250		3.25	–	1.18	600	300	–	–	75	2500
Rolled asphalt	1500–2250		–	2.36	–	600	300	212	150	75	3500
20 mm and 14 mm nominal size	**20 mm**	**14 mm**									
Macadams	1000–1500	800–1200	3.35	–	1.18	–	300	–	–	75	2000
Dense tar surfacing	1000–1500	800–1200	3.35	–	1.18	–	300	–	–	75	3000
Rolled asphalt	1000–1500	800–1200	–	2.36	–	600	–	212	150	75	2500
Coated chippings	2000–3000	2000–3000	3.35	–	1.18	–	300	–	–	75	2000
10 mm nominal size and smaller											
Macadams	700–1100		3.35	–	1.18	–	300	–	–	75	2000
Cold asphalt, coarse	600–900		–	2.36	–	600	–	–	150	75	2000
Cold asphalt, fine	600–900		–	2.36	–	600	–	212	150	75	2500
Mastic asphalt percentage retained 2.36 mm > 5	500–750		–	2.36	–	600	–	212	150	75	2500
Mastic asphalt percentage retained 2.36 mm < 5	300–500		–	2.36	–	600	–	212	150	75	2500
Rolled asphalt percentage retained 2.36 mm > 10	700–1100		–	2.36	–	600	–	212	–	75	2500
Rolled asphalt percentage retained 2.36 mm < 10	700–1100		–	2.36	–	600	–	212	–	75	2500
Coated chippings	2000–3000		3.35	–	1.18	–	300	–	–	75	2500

machine in the course of surface dressing. This is often quite easily arranged with a local authority.

Apparatus

Five to ten 300 mm square trays with four attached lifting hooks; suspension chains and spring balance (which may be calibrated direct in kg/m^2).

Procedure

Number and weigh the trays, using the chains and spring balance and position five to 10 trays in the path of the spreader vehicle.

From an experimental point of view, the most convenient method is to run the chipping spreader 'dry' for a short length – that is, without the surface being first sprayed with binder. If this is not possible, trays can be inserted between sprayer and chipping spreader, though they must be debonded from the binder by sheets of paper under each tray.

After passage of the chippings spreader, retrieve the trays and weigh. Determine the average rate of spread of the chippings:

$$\text{Rate of spread} = \frac{\text{Average mass of chippings per tray}}{0.3 \times 0.3} \text{ kg/m}^2$$

The rate should then be converted into m^2 coverage per tonne. Typical rates of spread are:

20 mm chippings	50–65 m^2/tonne
14 " "	65–85 " "
10 " "	85–110 " "
6.3 " "	115–150 " "

Experiment 6.11 Determination of rate of spread of binder in surface dressing (RN 39: Appendix 2)

This test can only realistically be carried out using a full-scale sprayer in the course of surface dressing operations. This should, however, be fairly easy to arrange with a local authority.

Apparatus

Five or more light metal trays 200 mm square by 5 mm deep; weighing balance accurate to 0.1 g; two-pronged fork and stick for tray removal.

Procedure

Number and weigh the trays. Place at least five trays on flat horizontal surfaces in the path of the binder distributor, well clear of vehicle wheels or other obstructions.

After the sprayer has passed, remove the trays with the fork, holding each tray onto the fork with the stick. Wrap in weighed sheets of paper and weigh to 0.1 g accuracy. The tray weights will give a good indication of the average rate of spread and of the variation from place to place. The mean rate of three or more trays should not vary from the specified value by more than 10 per cent.

The rate of spread (litre/m²)

$$= \frac{0.025 \times \text{mass of binder (g)}}{\text{Relative density}}$$

Assumed relative density is 1.0 for cut-back bitumen and 1.15 for tar. Rates of spread depend on the type of surface and traffic load values, varying between 1.4 litre/m² for lightly trafficked, hard surfaces and 1.1 litre/m² for heavy traffic.

Table 6.5 Marshall test: Correction factors for stability values with variations in height or volume

Height of specimen (mm)	Volume of specimen (ml)	Stability correction factor
62	502–503	1.04
	504–506	1.03
	507–509	1.02
	510–512	1.01
63.5	513–517	1.00
	518–520	0.99
	521–523	0.98
	524–526	0.97
65	527–528	0.96

Experiment 6.12 Measurement of the strength performance of asphalts using the Marshall test (BS 594)

The Marshall test is an arbitrary test for measuring the effect of binder content on the strength of asphalts for a given aggregate type. In a full analysis 12 or more specimens must be made with varying binder contents. Time will normally be against this and the simplest approach is probably to illustrate the principle of the test by the use of one previously manufactured sample.

Apparatus

Oven capable of maintaining a temperature in the range 80–200 °C; mechanical mixer – 5 litre capacity, fitted with paddles; the bowl of the heater can be heated by an external purpose-designed electric element; compaction mould required for making specimens; compaction pedestal and hammer; extractor for removing specimens from mould; water bath – thermostatically controlled; balance to weigh at least 2 kg to 0.1 g accuracy and adapted for weighing specimens in water; Marshall load frame.

Procedure

The sample should be of correct size to produce one compacted specimen 101.6 mm in diameter by 63.5 mm high.

Heat the sample in the oven at a temperature of approximately 165 °C, depending on binder type and mix thoroughly in the heated mixer. Place the material in the lightly-oiled heated circular mould complete with collar, using tough absorbant paper at the top and bottom to prevent sticking. Apply 50 blows of the compaction hammer and then reverse the mould and collar and apply 50 blows to the other face.

Cool the specimen, in its mould, in water and remove using the extractor. Measure the height and if it is not within the range 63.5 ± 1.5 mm, reject and repeat. Dry and then weigh in air (W_1) and again in water (W_2) by means of an adapted weighing balance or by suspending from a spring balance. The volume of the specimen is ($W_1 - W_2$) g.

Place the specimen in a water bath at 60 °C for one hour and then test sideways in compression, using the specially designed testing heads and loading at 50.8 mm/min. Read the maximum load L.

Obtain the stability correction factor from Table 6.5

Calculate the stability (S)

$S = L \times$ stability correction factor.

Calculate the compacted density of mix (CDM).

$$\text{CDM} \quad = \frac{W_1}{W_1 - W_2} \text{ g/ml}$$

If the binder content is known, calculate the compacted density of aggregate (CDA):

$$\text{CDA} \quad = \text{CDM} \ \frac{(100 - \text{A})}{100} \text{ g/ml}$$

When designing mixtures, the results of CDM, CDA and S are plotted for various binder contents, those contents giving maximum values of each of the three parameters being determined. The average of these three binder contents is then taken as optimum. Typical values of CDM, CDA and S at optimum binder content are 2.13 g/litre, 1.90 g/litre and 4.0 kN respectively.

Optimum binder contents are usually in the region of 10 per cent by weight.

Questions

1. Distinguish between bitumen and tar
   (a) in terms of manufacture;
   (b) in terms of properties/uses.
2. Comment on
   (a) the weathering properties;
   (b) the temperature susceptibility;
   (c) the action of organic solvents
   on bitumen compared with tar.
3. Distinguish between blown bitumen and cutback bitumen. Give basic properties and applications of each.
4. Explain what is meant by a bitumen emulsion and describe briefly how they 'break' or set. Hence indicate why ponding should be avoided. Give two applications of bitumen emulsions in construction.
5. Distinguish between asphalts and bitumen macadams as used in road construction. Give the special properties and applications of mastic asphalts.
6. Suggest possible causes of cracking in asphalt roofs and indicate how, by good design and construction, the risk of cracking can be minimised.
7. Explain what is meant by blistering in asphalt or built-up felt roofs. Suggest
   (a) how the risk of blistering can be reduced;
   (b) what remedial steps may be taken.
8. Explain the meaning of the term 'embedment' in relation to surface dressings on roads. Indicate what circumstances would lead to 'fatting up' and 'scabbing' in surface dressings.
9. Describe tests which could be used for measuring
   (a) the hardness;
   (b) the behaviour at elevated temperatures
   of a bitumen. Explain the relationship between these properties.

References

British Standards

Binder

BS 76: 1974, *Tars for Road Purposes*.
BS 3690: Part 1: 1982, *Bitumens For Road Purposes*.

Mixtures

BS 63: Part 1: 1971, *Single-sized Roadstone and Chippings*.
BS 594: 1973, *Rolled Asphalt*.

BS 988, 1076, 1097, 1451: 1973, *Mastic Asphalt for Building (Limestone Aggregate)*.

BS 1162, 1418, 1410: 1973, *Mastic Asphalt for Building (Natural Rock Asphalt Aggregate)*.

BS 4987: 1973, *Coated Bitumen Macadams*.

Tests

BS 598: Parts 1 and 2: 1974, *Sampling and Examination of Bituminous Mixtures for Roads and Other Paved Areas*.

BS 2000 Part 47: 1983, *Method for Determination of Solubility of Bituminous Binders*.

BS 2000: Part 72: 1982, *Visosity of Bitumen and Cut-back Road Oil*.

BS 4385: 1980, *Method of Determination of Water in Petroleum Products and Bituminous Materials. Distillation Method*.

BS 4689: 1980, *Method of Determination of Flash and Fire Points of Petroleum Products. Cleveland Open Cup Method*.

BS 4691: 1974, *Method for Determination of Penetration of Bituminous Materials*.

BS 4692: 1971, *Method of Determining the Softening Point of Bitumen (Ring and Ball)*.

Chapter 7

Plastics

This chapter is concerned with the general structure of matter, showing how certain chemical properties are obtained and in particular those properties that characterise plastics.

Atomic structure of matter

All matter is made up of units called atoms. Just over 100 different atoms have been identified from the simplest, hydrogen, to the very heavy man-made radiocactive ones that are so unstable that they only exist for a minute fraction of a second. All these atoms, with their diverse properties, are made from varying combinations of only three different particles; protons, neutrons and electrons.

1. *Protons* can be considered as particles of unit mass and unit positive electrical charge.
2. *Neutrons* can be considered as particles of unit mass with no electrical charge.
3. *Electrons* can be considered as particles with zero mass (actually about 1/1836 of that of the proton or neutron) with unit negative electrical charge.

Each atom consists of a nucleus of the heavy particles (neutrons and protons) around which rotate the electrons some distance away. There are normally equal numbers of protons and electrons within any atom, the rotating electrons being held in orbit by the attraction of the protons. It can be considered that neutrons merely add mass.

The simplest atom is that of hydrogen with one proton and a single electron, as shown in Fig. 7.1. It will be seen that the electron rotation forms a ring around the nucleus. There is only room for up to two electrons in this shell. Hydrogen atoms have therefore one spare space in this shell. Certain isotopes of hydrogen are possible, notably deutrium and tritium, which are identical except that they have in addition one and two neutrons respectively. They are chemically identical to hydrogen, physically twice or three times as heavy.

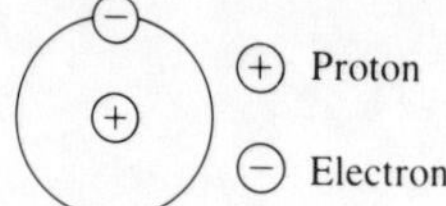

Fig. 7.1 Hydrogen atom

The second atom, helium, has two protons and two neutrons in the nucleus with a pair of electrons filling the shell, as shown in Fig. 7.2. Helium is an inert element which does not combine or react with anything because its electron shell is full. The next element lithium, must have three electrons, two of which will fill the first and smallest shell and one lone one in the next shell (Fig 7.3). There are spaces for up to eight electrons in this second shell. Beryllium has four protons, five neutrons and four electrons with six vacant spaces in this second shell. This is continued until the second electron shell is full at neon. After this, a third shell must be started which can hold up to eight electrons. Beyond this it becomes more complex

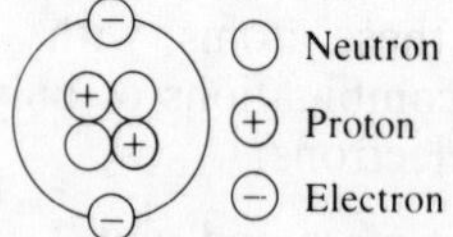

Fig. 7.2 Helium atom

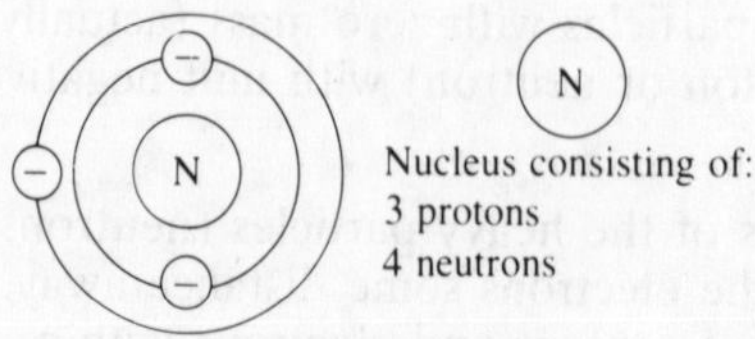

Fig. 7.3 Lithium atom

with larger shells. It will be clear to the reader that a regular pattern is developing and all the elements can be classified into what is known as the Periodic Table (Table 7.1). Table 7.2 gives a list of the known elements with their chemical symbols.

Molecular bonding and valency

Atoms having full electron shells are by far the most stable (unreactive) – for example helium and neon. Atoms having partially complete shells are relatively unstable (reactive) and therefore tend to combine with other atoms in order to obtain full electron shells. This may be achieved by electron transfer, so that electron shells become either empty or full (ionic bonding); or by sharing of electrons (covalent bonding). The valency of an element is equal to either the number of electrons in its outer shell or the number of

Table 7.1 Periodic table of the elements

	Groups									
	I	II	III	IV	V	VI	VII		VIII	
1	1 H								2 He	
2	3 Li	4 Be	5 B	6 C	7 N	8 O	9 F		10 Ne	
3	11 Na	12 Mg	13 Al	14 Si	15 P	16 S	17 Cl		18 A	
4	19 K	20 Ca	21 Sc	22 Ti	23 V	24 Cr	25 Mn	26 Fe	27 Co	28 Ni
	29 Cu	30 Zn	31 Ga	32 Ge	33 As	34 Se	35 Br		36 Kr	
5	37 Rb	38 Sr	39 Y	40 Zr	41 Nb	42 Mo	43 Tc	44 Ru	45 Rh	46 Pd
	47 Ag	48 Cd	49 In	50 Sn	51 Sb	52 Te	53 I		54 Xe	
6	55 Cs	56 Ba	57–71 *	72 Hf	73 Ta	74 W	75 Re	76 Os	77 Ir	78 Pt
	79 Au	80 Hg	81 Tl	82 Pb	83 Bi	84 Po	85 At		86 Rn	
7	87 Fr	88 Ra	89–96 †							

* Rare earths † Actinide series

Table 7.2 Chemical symbols and atomic weights of the elements

Element	Symbol	Atomic weights	Element	Symbol	Atomic weights
Actinium	Ac	227	Iridium	Ir	193.1
Aluminum	Al	26.98	Iron	Fe	55.85
Americium	Am	(243)	Krypton	Kr	83.80
Antimony	Sb	121.76	Lanthanum	La	138.92
Argon	A	39.944	Lead	Pb	207.21
Arsenic	As	74.91	Lithium	Li	6.94
Astatine	At	(210)	Lutetium	Lu	174.99
Barium	Ba	137.36	Magnesium	Mg	24.32
Berkelium	Bk	(245)	Manganese	Mn	54.93
Beryllium	Be	9.013	Mercury	Hg	200.61
Bismuth	Bi	209.00	Molybdenum	Mo	95.95
Boron	B	10.82	Neodymium	Nd	144.27
Bromine	Br	79.92	Neon	Ne	20.183
Cadium	Cd	112.41	Nickel	Ni	58.69
Calcium	Ca	40.08	Niobium	Nb	92.91
Carbon	C	12.01	Nitrogen	N	14.01
Cerium	Ce	140.13	Osmium	Os	190.2
Cesium	Cs	132.91	Oxygen	O	16
Chlorine	Cl	35.46	Paladium	Pd	106.7
Chromium	Cr	52.01	Phosphorus	P	30.98
Cobalt	Co	58.94	Platinum	Pt	195.23
Copper	Cu	63.54	Polonium	Po	210
Curium	Cm	(243)	Potassium	K	39.1
Dysprosium	Dy	162.46	Praseodymium	Pr	140.92
Erbium	Er	167.2	Protactinium	Pa	231
Europium	Eu	152.0	Radium	Ra	226.05
Fluorine	F	19.00	Radon	Rn	222
Gadolinium	Gd	156.9	Rhenium	Re	186.31
Gallium	Ga	69.72	Rhodium	Rh	102.91
Germanium	Ge	72.60	Rubidium	Rb	85.48
Gold	Au	197.2	Ruthenium	Ru	101.7
Hafnium	Hf	178.6	Samarium	Sm	150.43
Helium	He	4.003	Scandium	Sc	44.96
Holmium	Ho	164.94	Selenium	Se	78.96
Hydrogen	H	1.008	Silicon	Si	28.09
Indium	In	114.76	Silver	Ag	107.88
Iodine	I	126.91	Sodium	Na	22.997
Strontium	Sr	87.63	Titanium	Ti	47.9
Sulphur	S	32.07	Tungsten	W	183.92
Tantalum	Ta	180.88	Uranium	U	238.07
Tellurium	Te	127.61	Vanadium	V	50.95
Terbium	Tb	159.2	Xenon	Xe	131.3
Thalium	Tl	204.39	Ytterbium	Yb	173.04
Thorium	Th	232.12	Yttrium	Y	88.92
Thulium	Tm	169.4	Zinc	Zn	65.38
Tin	Sn	118.7	Zirconium	Zr	91.22

vacancies, whichever is smaller. Lithium has a valency of one because it has one electron in its second shell; Beryllium has a valency of two and so on. Oxygen has six electrons in its second shell (valency two), hence it combines readily with two hydrogen atoms, borrowing each of their single electrons to make eight in total and giving water – H_2O. Molecular bonding is most useful from a building point of view because without such bonding it would not be possible to produce any of the wide range of solid materials which are essential to the industry.

Carbon

It can be seen from the Periodic Table that carbon comes in the centre of the second row, with six protons and six electrons. The second shell contains four electrons and four vacant spaces, which give carbon a valency of four and an ability to combine in many different ways (Fig. 7.4). Tetravalent bonds are nearly always covalent, that is, they tend to share electrons within a chain or ring.

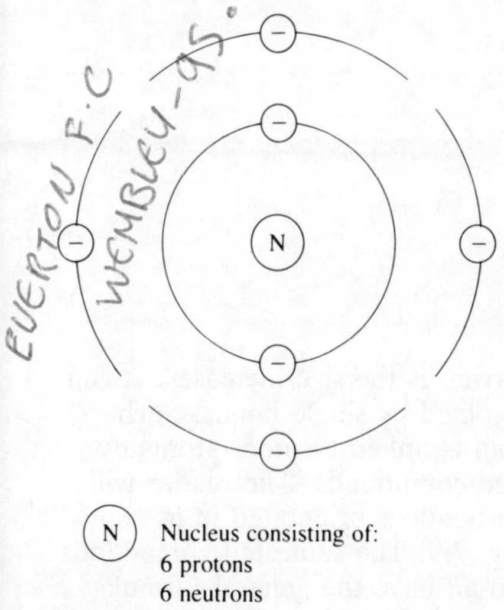

Fig. 7.4 Carbon atom

The simplest carbon compound is methane, where one carbon atom is combined with four hydrogen atoms, as shown in Fig. 7.5. Another possibility is for two or more atoms of carbon to combine with hydrogen to form ethane (Fig. 7.6), propane (Fig. 7.7), or butane (Fig. 7.8).

This can obviously be extended indefinitely to form very long

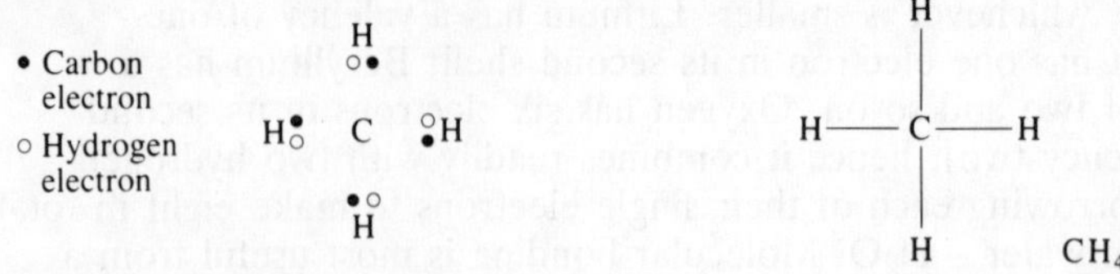

Fig. 7.5 Methane

```
   H   H
   |   |
H—C—C—H
   |   |
   H   H     C2H6
```

Fig. 7.6 Ethane

```
   H   H   H
   |   |   |
H—C—C—C—H
   |   |   |
   H   H   H     C3H8
```

Fig. 7.7 Propane

```
    H    H    H    H
    |    |    |    |
H — C — C — C — C — H
    |    |    |    |
    H    H    H    H      C4H10
```

Fig. 7.8 Butane

chain molecules, which become heavier as the size increases. It can be seen that the carbon atoms are joined by single bonds. Such compounds, where each carbon atom is linked to other atoms by single bonds, are known as saturated compounds. The reader will realise that each of the four carbon bonds is orientated in a particular direction, as shown in Fig. 7.9. The saturated compounds described are known as alkanes and all have the general formula C_nH_{2n+2}.

Unsaturated compounds

If an organic compound has one or more of its carbon atoms linked chemically by a double or triple bond, then it is said to be unsaturated. Ethylene is one of the simplest of the saturated organic compounds, as shown in Fig. 7.10. Because the four valency 'arms' of the carbon atom are spaced in three dimensions evenly around a sphere to form a double bond, this involves considerable stress. The

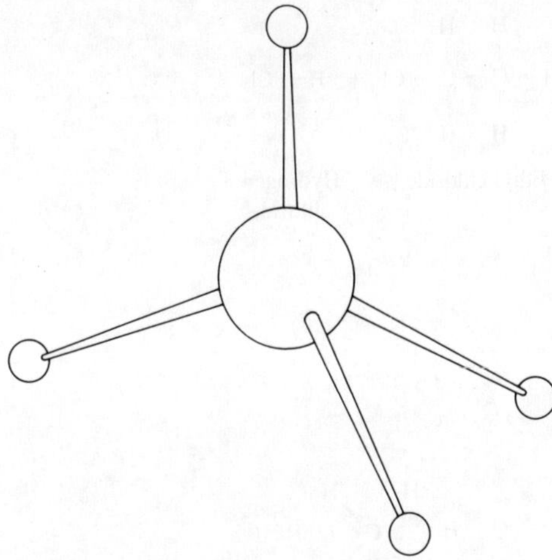

Fig. 7.9 Four carbon bonds

```
H         H
  \     /
   C=C
  /     \
H         H
```

Fig. 7.10 Ethylene, C_2H_4

result is that these multiple bonds in unsaturated compounds are easily broken leaving vacant 'arms' ready to combine with other groups or elements. This fact is utilised in the production of some very long-chain polymers. If one of the bonds is ruptured, then conditions are created under which an addition reaction may take place, as shown in Fig. 7.11.

```
                                     H    H
H        H                           |    |
  \     /                            
   C—C       +  Cl—Cl ——→Cl—C—C—Cl
  /     \                            |    |
Cl       H                           H    H

 Ethylene        Chlorine        Dichloroethylene
```

Fig. 7.11 Addition reaction

An alternative method of forming a compound is by substitution, as shown in Fig. 7.12. In this case a chlorine atom is substituted in place of a hydrogen atom.

An example of a triple bond is shown in Fig. 7.13 – acetylene.

Yet another way of combining the carbon atoms is in the form of a ring. Three common ones are shown in Fig. 7.14.

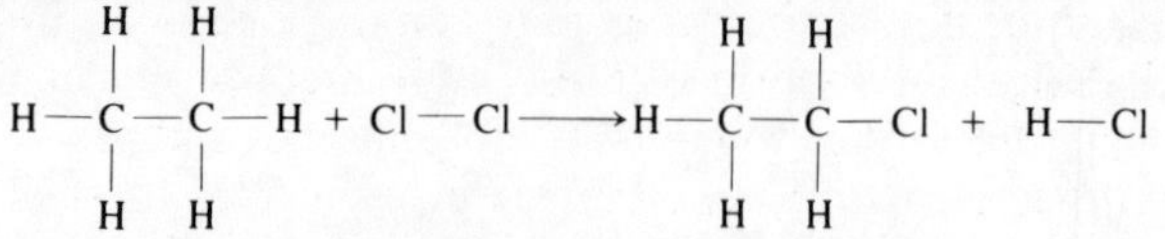

```
    H   H                                   H   H
    |   |                                   |   |
H — C — C — H + Cl — Cl ———→ H — C — C — Cl  +  H — Cl
    |   |                                   |   |
    H   H                                   H   H
```

Ethane Chlorine Ethyl chloride Hydrogen chloride

Fig. 7.12 Substitution reaction

H—C≡C—H C_2H_2

Fig. 7.13 Acetylene

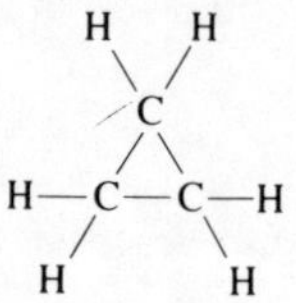

```
  H   H
   \ /
    C
   / \
H—C———C—H
 /     \
H       H
```

Cyclopropane

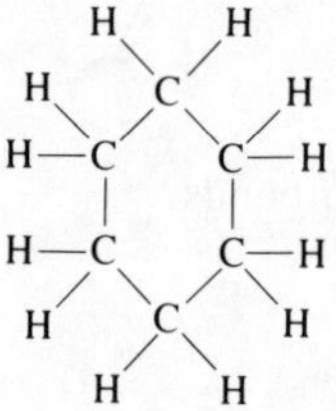

```
        H     H
         \   /
   H       C       H
    \    /   \    /
  H—C           C—H
    |           |
  H—C           C—H
    /    \   /    \
   H       C       H
         /   \
        H     H
```

Cyclohexane

```
          H
          |
   H      C      H
    \   //  \   /
      C        C
      |        ||
      C        C
    /   \\   /   \
   H      C      H
          |
          H
```

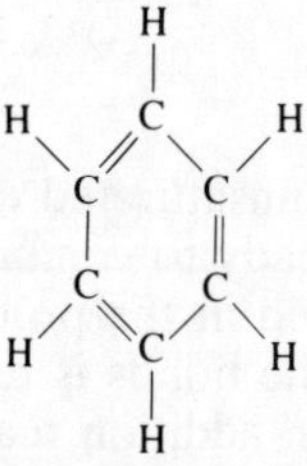

Benzene

Fig. 7.14 Ring molecules

Polymerisation

Polymerisation is the linking together of simple molecules to form larger ones. The original molecular unit is usually a monomer and the resulting molecule is known as a polymer. The process is accompanied by a gradual change from the liquid state into the solid state.

Addition polymerisation occurs when molecules of a monomer such as ethylene react additively to produce long chain molecules with possibly as many as 20 000 links in the chains.

Condensation polymerisation is a type of polymerisation which usually involves two different types of monomers. The molecules of at least one of these monomers contain two or more reactive groups of atoms while the molecules of the other may contain one or more reactive groups. Chemical interaction of these monomers produces a plastics material which has either long chain molecules or a three dimensional cross-linked structure. In either case, molecules of such simple substances as water (H_2O) or hydrogen chloride (HCL) are eliminated. It is in this respect that condensation polymerisation differs from addition polymerisation. Some examples of radicals can be seen in Figs 7.15 and 7.16. Figure 7.17 shows the polymerisation of phenol and formaldehyde producing 'bakelite' – one of the earliest plastics to be produced.

Types of plastics

There are two groups of plastics: thermoplastics and thermosetting plastics

Thermoplastics

These can be softened by heating after they have been cured and

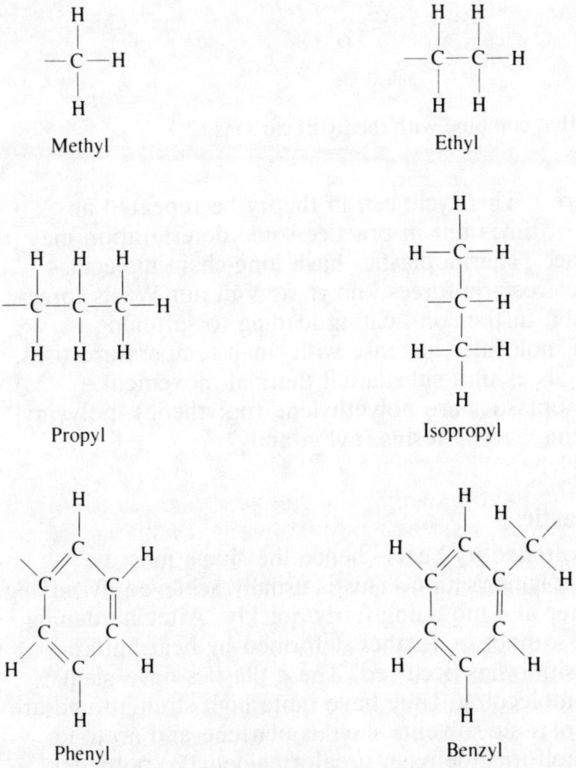

Methyl

Ethyl

Propyl

Isopropyl

Phenyl

Benzyl

Fig. 7.15 Hydrocarbon radicals

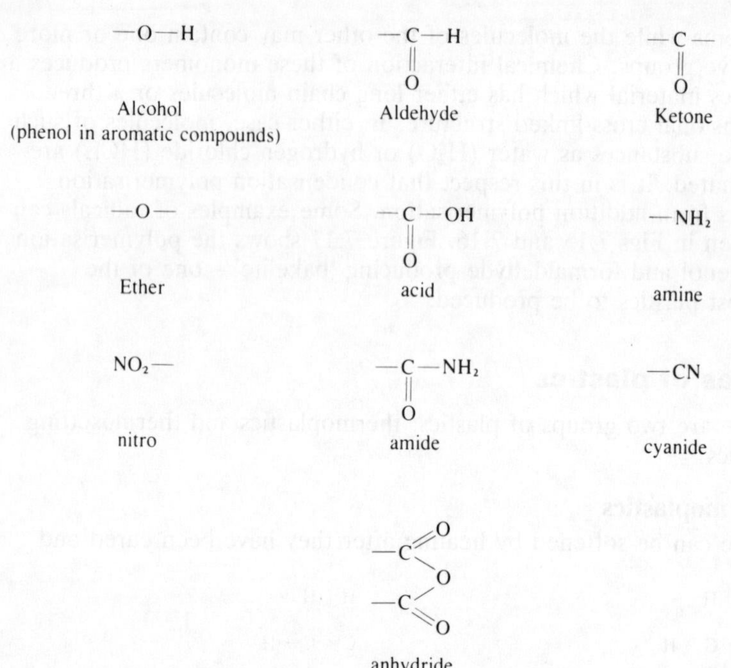

Fig. 7.16 Radicals that combine with the hydrocarbons

remoulded, if desired. This cycle can in theory be repeated an indefinite number of times but in practice some deterioration may eventually take place. Thermoplastics have long-chain molecules linked by weak electrostatic forces known as Van der Waals forces. These forces weaken further on heating leading to softening. Distances between molecules increase with small temperature rises, hence these materials exhibit substantial thermal movement. Examples of thermoplastics are polyethylene (polythene), polyvinyl chloride, polystyrene, acrylic resins, nylon and polytetrafluoroethylene.

Thermosetting plastics

These cannot be softened by heat – hence the shape must be prepared prior to polymerisation. This is usually achieved by mixing a resin and hardener and moulding fairly quickly. After hardening, the moulded shape cannot be further deformed by heat until a chemical decomposition has occurred. These plastics have giant three-dimensional molecules. They have quite high strength and are insoluble in many organic solvents such as benzene and acetone. Examples are phenolformaldehyde, ureaformaldehyde, polyester resins and epoxy resins.

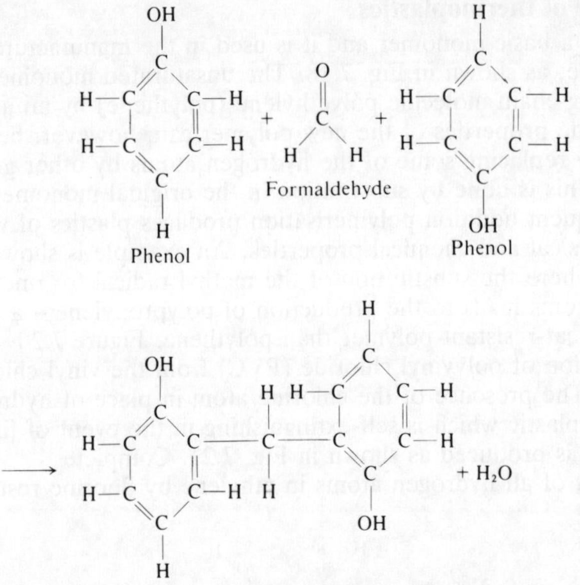

Phenol + Formaldehyde + Phenol

→ Preliminary condensation products $+ H_2O$

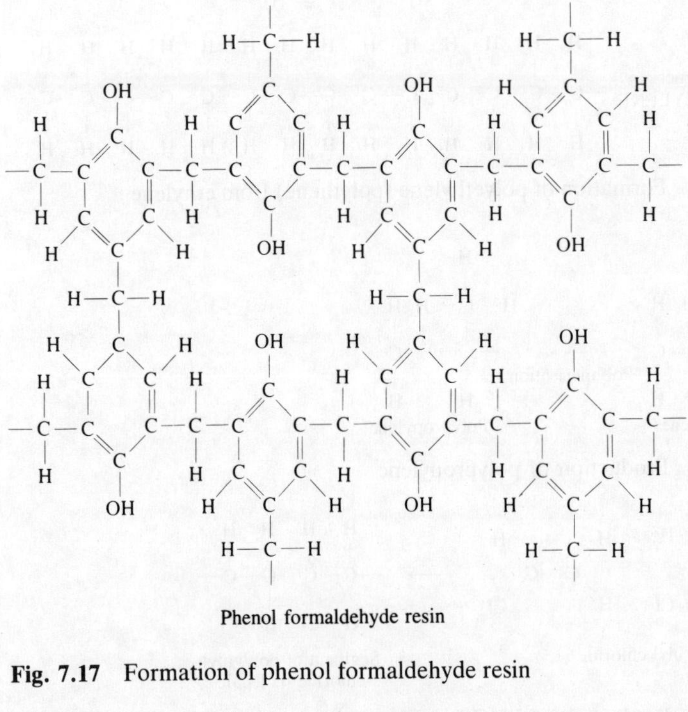

Phenol formaldehyde resin

Fig. 7.17 Formation of phenol formaldehyde resin

Production of thermoplastics

Ethylene is a basic monomer and it is used in the manufacture of polyethylene, as shown in Fig. 7.18. The unsaturated monomer forms a long-chain molecule polyethylene (polythene) by an addition reaction. The properties of the new polymer can, however, be modified by replacing some of the hydrogen atoms by other groups of atoms. This is done by substitution in the original monomer and then subsequent addition polymerisation produces plastics of widely varying physical and chemical properties. An example is shown in Fig. 7.19, where the substitution of the methyl radical for one of the hydrogen atoms leads to the production of polypropylene – a stiffer and more heat-resistant polymer than polythene. Figure 7.20 shows the production of polyvinyl chloride (PVC) from the vinyl chloride monomer. The presence of the chlorine atom in place of hydrogen produces a plastic which is self-extinguishing in the event of fire. Polystyrene is produced as shown in Fig. 7.21. Complete replacement of all hydrogen atoms in ethylene by fluorine results in

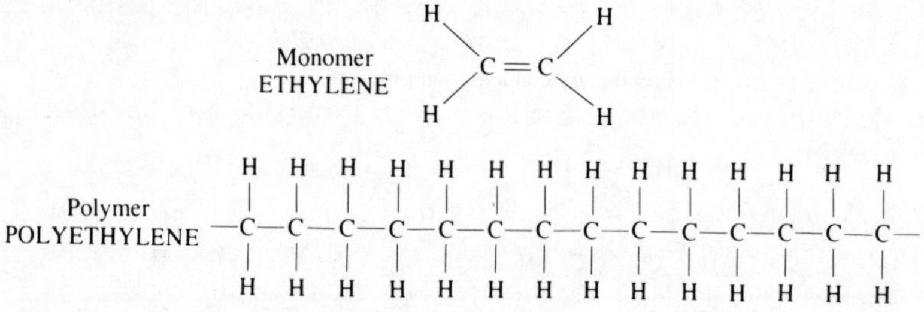

Monomer ETHYLENE

Polymer POLYETHYLENE

Fig. 7.18 Formation of polyethylene (polythene) from ethylene

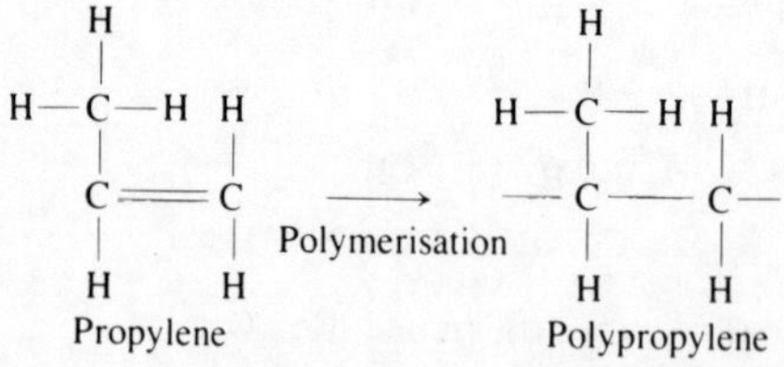

Propylene → Polymerisation → Polypropylene

Fig. 7.19 Production of polypropylene

Vinyl chloride

Segment of polyvinyl chloride molecule

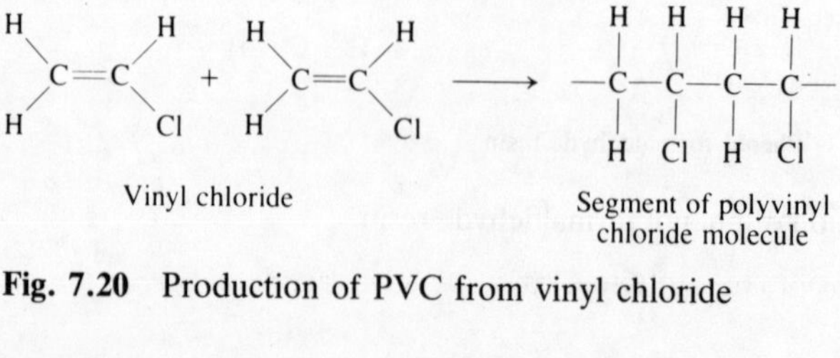

Fig. 7.20 Production of PVC from vinyl chloride

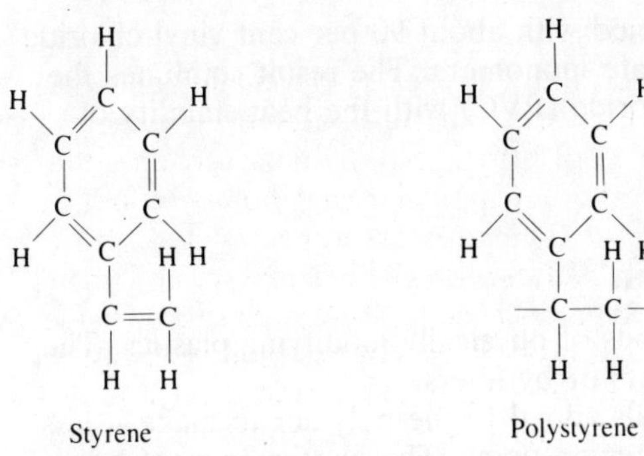

Fig. 7.21 Production of polystyrene

the tetrafluoroethylene monomer. Addition polymerisation produces polytetrafluoroethylene (PTFE), as shown in Fig. 7.22. This plastic possesses a number of very useful properties including:

1. high chemical resistance;
2. a softening point of 327 °C (compared with polythene in the range 76–120 °C);
3. non-flammability;
4. very low coefficient of friction making it suitable for non-lubricated bearings.

Copolymerization

A copolymer is formed when two or more different monomers are jointly polymerised. The result is often a product with better properties than the separate polymers. An example is vinyl chloride and vinyl acetate copolymer (Fig. 7.23).

```
F  F            F  F
|  |            |  |
C=C   ——→   —C—C—
|  |            |  |
F  F            F  F
```

Tetrafluoroethylene   Polytetrafluoroethylene

Fig. 7.22 Production of PTFE by additional polymerisation

```
 H  H  H  H  H  H  H  H  H  H  H  H
 |  |  |  |  |  |  |  |  |  |  |  |
—C—C—C—C—C—C—C—C—C—C—C—C—
 |  |  |  |  |  |  |  |  |  |  |  |
 H  Cl H  Cl H  Cl H  Cl H  O  H  Cl
                            |
                            C=O
                            |
                            CH3
```

Fig. 7.23 Segment of chain of vinyl chloride/vinyl acetate copolymer

This copolymer is formed with about 90 per cent vinyl chloride and 10 per cent vinyl acetate monomers. The result combines the toughness of polyvinyl chloride (PVC) with the heat stability of polyvinyl acetate (PVAC).

Physical modification

There are two main methods of physically modifying plastics. They are by the use of plasticisers or by fillers.

Plasticisers are materials added to the polymer to make it less brittle and to lower its softening point. The plasticiser must be a good solvent for the polymer but must have a low vapour pressure to ensure that the enhanced properties are permanent. Perspex (Fig. 7.24) may be made more flexible by the addition of the high molecular weight compound dibutyl phthalate to the original methyl methacrylate monomer. Polyvinyl chloride is also frequently plasticised for use in floor coverings and electrical insulation.

Fillers are inert solids which are added to resins or polymers to modify their properties. Examples include wood flour, cotton, alpha cellulose or glass fibres which reduce brittleness and increase impact strength. Asbestos fibres or mica flakes improve heat and chemical resistance. Fillers are usually cheaper than the pure resin and therefore their use lowers the cost of the end product.

Extenders are fillers often used to lower the cost of plastics with no change in the other properties of the material.

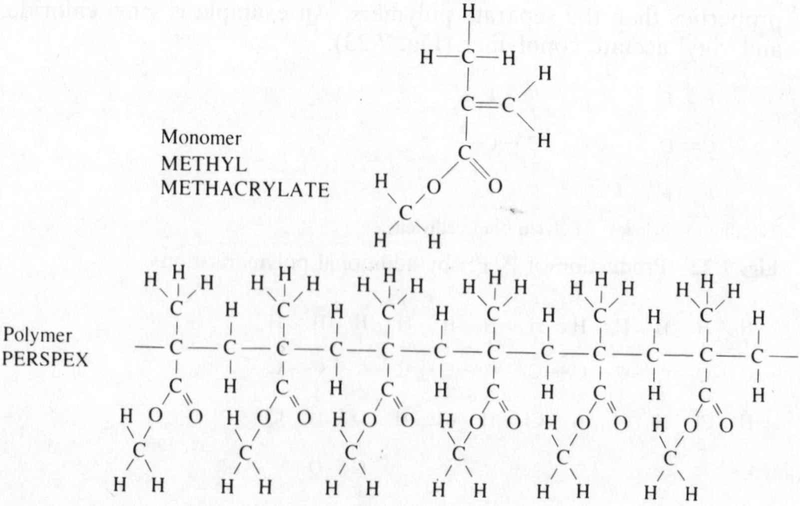

Monomer
METHYL
METHACRYLATE

Polymer
PERSPEX

Fig. 7.24 Formation of perspex by the polymerisation of methyl methacrylate

Properties required of plastics in building

Plastics are used for many different situations in building, applications ranging from underground pipes to places where they are exposed to external light and weather or internal decorative situations. The properties required will vary with the application, so it is important to select the correct plastic for each use.

Dimensional stability

Plastics have lower strength and rigidity than steel and many other building materials. This must inevitably limit their structural application. They are also subject to creep, which means that under a given load the deformation increases with time. Creep accelerates as load increases and thus the elastic modulus falls with time and load. As a result of these limitations, tests have been carried out on standard components to ensure that acceptable durability is achieved. Life expectancies of at least 50 years would be expected for plastic pipes. Bursting tests may be carried out to find the bursting times at various pressures (stresses). By extrapolation an acceptable life can be ensured for the product.

In general, unreinforced plastics are not used for structural application because of the large sections needed and hence high costs involved, though unplasticised PVC has been used for a number of lightweight structures such as swimming pool roofs.

Weather resistance and colour fastness

The importance of colour fastness will vary with application. Indoors there should be little problem provided the correct pigmentation has been used. However, outdoors the ageing of plastics is far more complicated and will be affected by temperature, humidity (moisture absorption or evaporation) and ultra-violet radiation. Accelerated tests in the laboratory are difficult and most have proved unreliable in terms of correlation with natural weathering. Stabilisers as well as correct pigmentation are often essential to ensure there are no deleterious weathering effects. In many cases the damage may be superficial with no reduction in mechanical properties. Surface effects will clearly be more serious in the case of thin sheet materials. Polythene, polypropylene and PVC are all subject to UV degradation, though each can be stabilised.

Fire safety

Many plastics represent a fire hazard, due either to their flammability or to ability to produce smoke and fumes. There are, however, wide variations between plastics. Some can have the hazard reduced by the addition of 'fire retardant' agents. The effects of ageing may reduce the fire retardant properties of some materials. In choosing plastics, their fire safety for the particular application must be considered, together with mechanical properties and appearance. For example, the use of smoke-producing polystyrene in halls and stairways would be very unwise.

Resistance to water and water vapour

Nearly all plastics have very low water absorption properties as well as low water vapour permeability. Indeed there are few other materials which have a comparable performance. Thus they are used for membranes in construction, protection of materials on site and, in some cases, protection of the whole building under construction or repair.

Thermal insulation

Plastics have a low thermal conductivity (high thermal resistance). This can be further improved by expanding or foaming certain materials such as polyurethane or polystyrene (see Cellular plastics).

Thermal expansion

For most plastics the coefficient of thermal expansion is much higher than for alternative materials; for example that for low density polythene is about 18 times that for steel. Care must be taken in the choice of material to ensure that allowance has been made for thermal expansion by the addition of expansion joints.

Sound insulation

Good sound insulation is normally most easily achieved by means of mass. As plastics materials have a low specific gravity, the economic achievement of adequate mass is impossible. Thus the alternative of multiple construction becomes essential and careful technical detailing important.

Brittleness

Brittleness may be a problem with some plastics, especially at low temperatures when flexibility and therefore their ability to absorb energy are reduced. Softer plastics such as polythene, nylon, PTFE and plasticised PVC are generally tougher than harder plastics such as polystyrene and acrylic plastics. The effect of reduced temperature on brittleness also depends on type – for example polythene is tough even at low temperatures, whereas PVC becomes quite brittle at sub-zero temperatures. Painting can also reduce the toughness of PVC. Thermosetting plastics are in general brittle, though they can be improved, for example, by the incorporation of fibres as in glass reinforced polyester (grp).

Elastomeric properties

The term elastomeric is reserved for materials, such as rubbers, which have the capability to undergo very large distortion under stress while still remaining elastic – that is they return to their original shape when the stress is removed. Elastic strains of over 400 per cent are easily obtainable in some elastomers. These materials are based on long-chain polymers at a temperature above their softening point. The chains tend to adopt a zigzag profile in this state, resulting from preferred bond directions in the carbon backbone. On stretching, these chains become straighter (Fig. 7.25). There is a great variety of synthetic elastomers now produced with widely varying properties, according to type. Examples include synthetic isoprene rubbers – which have good elastic properties; styrene butadiene (SB) rubber – better weathering resistance than natural rubber; butyl rubber – good sunlight resistance; polychloroprene – good chemical stability; nitrile rubbers – good resistance to oils etc.; polysulphide rubbers – good all-round chemical and atmospheric stability.

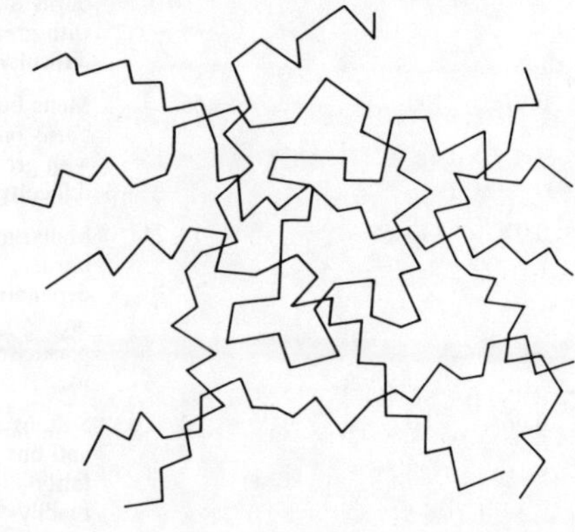

(a)

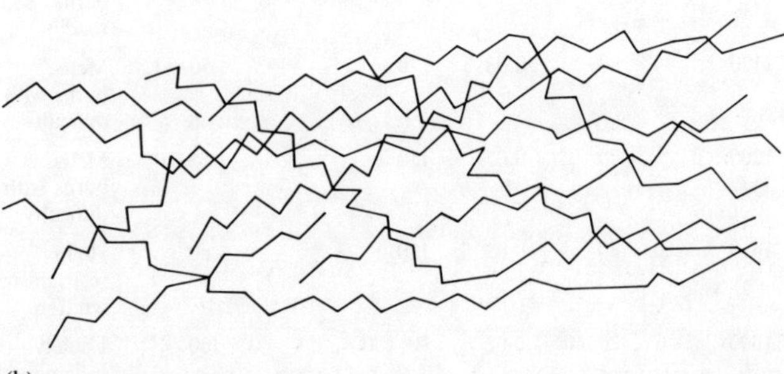

(b)

Fig. 7.25 (a) Random zig zag profile of carbon chain in unstressed elastomer (b) Chain straightening caused by stretching

Properties of common plastics

Table 7.3 summarises chief properties of some common plastics.

Table 7.3 Typical properties of plastics used in building (*Based on BRE Digest 69-courtesy BRE*)

Material (thermoplastic except where stated)	Density (kg/m³)	Linear expansion per °C	Coeff. mm/m × 10^{-6}	Max temperature recommended for continuous operation (°C)	Short-term tensile strength (MN/m²)	Behaviour in fire
Polythene*						Melts and burns like paraffin wax
low density	910	200	0.2	80	7–16	
high density	945	140	0.14	104	20–38	
Polypropylene	900	110	0.11	120	34	Melts and burns like paraffin wax
Polymethyl methacrylate (acrylic)	1185	70	0.07	80	70	Melts and burns readily
Rigid PVC (UPVC)	1395	50	0.05	65	55	Melts but burns only with great difficulty
Post-chlorinated PVC (CPVC)	1300–1500	70	0.07	100	55	Melts but burns only with great difficulty
Plasticised PVC	1200–1450	70	0.07	40–65	10–24	Melts, may burn, depending on plasticiser used
Acetal resins	1410	80	0.08	80	62	Softens and burns fairly readily
ABS	1060	70	0.07	90	40	Melts and burns readily
Nylon	1120	80	0.08	70	50–80	Melts, burns with difficulty
Polycarbonate	1200	70	0.07	110	55–70	Melts, burns with difficulty
Phenolic laminates (thermosetting)	1410	30	0.03	110	80	Highly resistant to ignition
GRP laminates (thermosetting)	1600	20–40	0.02	90–150	100	Usually inflammable Relatively flame-retardant grades are available

Key: UPVC = unplasticised polyvinyl chloride GRP = glass-reinforced polyester PVC = polyvinyl chloride ABS = acrylonitrile/butadiene/styrene copolymer

*High density and low density polythene differ in their basic physical properties, the former being harder and more rigid than the latter. No distinction is drawn between them in terms of chemical properties or durability. The values shown are for typical materials but may vary considerably, depending on composition and method of manufacture

Cellular plastics

These now play a most important part in modern building primarily on account of their excellent thermal insulation, good acoustic properties and versatility – they can be preformed or used *in-situ*. They may be subdivided into 'foamed' plastics, which may have an open or closed cell structure, and 'expanded' plastics having a mainly closed cell structure. Polyurethanes, urea formaldehyde and phenol formaldehyde are commonly used in foam form for cavity insulation, their cell being open to a degree dependent on type and application. The plastic most commonly used in expanded form is polystyrene.

Table 7.4 gives some properties of typical cellular plastics used in building.

Possible failure modes of cellular plastics

Water penetration

Some rigid foams such as urea formaldehyde – especially those formed *in-situ* – are subject to shrinkage and fissuring or may simply have a significant water absorption, hence there is a possibility of rain penetration when used as cavity fills. It is advisable, therefore, when using these foams that the external skin of the building is checked for watertightness. Foam cavity filling is not generally recommended in situations of extreme exposure.

Fire damage

Both polystyrene and the adhesives commonly used for fixing the material are normally highly flammable, though more expensive flame retardant grades are available. Suitable precautions must be taken during the storage of the material on construction sites and it should not be used where there is a fire risk – for example in the neighbourhood of boilers or stoves. The fire risk may be increased by painting. Foamed urea and phenol formaldehydes are much more resistant to ignition.

Softening

Expanded polystyrene or its fixing adhesive may become soft or tacky, due to the effects of

(a) heat – for example when used as insulation in corrugated roofing;
(b) plasticisers, which may be present in neighbouring materials such as PVC cable (which then becomes brittle), some dpc materials and paints.

Compression

Cellular plastics have comparatively low compressive strength and may therefore be damaged by pressure or impact. When used

Table 7.4 Typical properties of cellular plastics used in building

Material	Density (kg/m³)	Compressive stress at yield point ($\times 10^4$ N/m²)	Coeff of linear expansion ($\times 10^{-6}$ per °C)	Thermal conductivity (W/m °C)	Max temp for continuous operation (°C)	Seven days' water absorption (Vol. %)	Water vapour resistivity† (MNs/g)
Expanded polystyrene							
bead board	16	7	50–70	0.035	80*	3.0	270
bead board	24	12	70	0.033	80*	2.5	420
extruded	32	27	70	0.035	75*	1.5	1300
extruded with surface skin	40	27	70	0.032	75*	1.0	1300
Expanded pvc	40	27	35	0.035	50	3.0	800
Expanded pvc	72	90	50	0.043	50	3.8	1300
Foamed urea-formaldehyde	8	Negligible	90	0.038	100	Fairly high	22
Foamed phenol-formaldehyde	48	14	20–40	0.036	150	High (open cell)	35
						Fairly low (95% closed cell)	240
Foamed rigid polyurethane	32	17	20–70	0.020	100	2.5	360
(fluorinated hydrocarbon blown)				0.025			

* These temperatures may be slightly lower for flame-retardant grades. Manufacturers' advice should be sought in cases of doubt.
† 15 MNs/g is considered a suitable resistance for a vapour barrier in building applications but because of the risk of interstitial condensation within a cellular material, an additional vapour-sealing skin may be required.

directly under felt as a roofing insulation, boards must be used for access. Denser or precompressed grades of material should be used as insulating floor skins. Protection to wall surfaces can be obtained by means of plaster coatings.

Applications of plastics in building

A large variety of plastics are used for building applications. It is convenient to simplify the list by considering them under three headings. Thermosetting plastics and thermoplastics are the main areas, with some use of elastomers. Table 7.5 is a list of the main applications with the types of materials which are appropriate in each case. It can also be seen that the type of plastic employed is related to both the requirements of the manufacturing technique and the end use.

The main properties required of plastics used in building have been considered earlier. As with most building materials, they must be durable. Externally they may be affected by sunlight, temperature, moisture, oxygen and the presence of pollutants. Internally daylight, artificial light, temperature, moisture, the use of cleaning materials, abrasives and chemicals may affect them. Underground they may be protected from these but be subject to higher stresses and in some situations rats and termites. It is worth appreciating that many plastics used outdoors will deteriorate roughly four times as fast in a tropical climate as they do in Britain. As temperatures are raised by 10 °C, the rate of deterioration is likely to be twice as fast.

Unlike many other building materials, most plastics have not been available for long enough to know their full potential. Accelerated tests in the laboratory situation are often not reliable.

Table 7.6 describes some common cellular plastics and their applications. Table 7.7 shows a comparison of properties with those of mild steel and concrete.

Examples

Damp-proof membranes

Polythene has a high resistance to the penetration of moisture and is readily available in sheet form. It is therefore ideal for use as damp-proof membranes and courses. It needs to be thick enough to avoid puncture prior to use. It will degrade due to the effect of ultraviolet light within a few years if exposed. This, however, is not a problem when used as a damp-proof membrane. Black polythene may be preferable if there is significant exposure to sunlight. In normal use it should easily last the life of the building.

Water pipes

These are normally either made of polythene or unplasticised (rigid) PVC.

Table 7.5 Plastics and rubbers used in the building industry

(1)	(2)							(3)												(4)							
	Resins **Thermosetting materials**							**Thermoplastic materials**												**Rubbers** General-purpose			Special-purpose				
Applications	*Phenolic resin (PF)*	*Urea resin (UF)*	*Melamine resin (MF)*	*Unsaturated polyesters (UP)*	*Epoxies (EP)*	*Polyurethanes (PUR)*	*Silicones (SI)*	*Polyvinylchloride, unplasticised (UPVC)*	*Polyvinylchloride, plasticised (PVC)*	*Polyvinyl Acetate (PVAC)*	*Polystyrene (PS)*	*Polyethylene (PE)*	*Polypropylene (PP)*	*Polyisobutylene (PIB)*	*Acrylanitrile-butadiene-styrene (ABS)*	*Acrylics*	*Polyamides (e.g. nylons) (PA)*	*Cumarone-indene resin*	*Cellulose acetate (CA)*	*Natural & synthetic isoprene rubber*	*Styrene butadiene rubber*	*Polybutadiene rubber*	*Ethylene propylene rubber*	*Butyl rubber*	*Polychloroprene*	*Nitrile rubber*	*Polysulphide rubber*
CONCRETE STRUCTURES																											
Moulds				X	X																		X	X	X		
Shuttering for columns								X																			
Shuttering for sections				X	X						X																
Lining for shuttering	X							X	X		X	X	X										X	X	X		
Reinforcing bar spacers												X															
Cement mortar for repairs					X					X																	
Membranes chem. resistant										X		X		X									X	X	X	X	X

Seals for expansion joints						X			X				X							X	X			X
Foam blocks for pocket holes											X													
WALLS																								
Sandwich type panels: core	X					X		X			X													
Sandwich type panels: facing	X		X	X	X			X																
Hollow type panels	X							X																
Sheets, flat and profiled	X		X	X				X							X									
Sheets, transparent				X					X						X									
Gaskets (structural)									X											X	X	X	X	X
DOORS																								
Folding doors, flap doors									X								X	X						
Rolling grilles, dipcoated									X							X								
Sandwich type doors, facing	X			X					X															
Sandwich type doors, core						X					X													
Swing door, transparent									X															
Sliding gear																X								
WINDOWS																								
Cold bridge																	X	X		X	X			
Glazing sheets and foils				X					X						X									
Glazing beads								X	X				X											
Weather strips									X				X							X	X	X		
Condensation sections									X											X	X	X		
Sections with metal or wooden core								X	X															
Sections all plastics				X				X	X															
Jointing and caulking material							X		X	X				X				X	X	X	X	X			

Table 7.5 (Cont'd)

	(2)							(3)												(4)							
	Resins							**Thermoplastic materials**												**Rubbers**							
	Thermosetting materials																			General-purpose				Special purpose			
Applications	*Phenolic resin (PF)*	*Urea resin (UF)*	*Melamine resin (MF)*	*Unsaturated polyesters (UP)*	*Epoxies (EP)*	*Polyurethanes (PUR)*	*Silicones (SI)*	*Polyvinylchloride, unplasticised (UPVC)*	*Polyvinylchloride, plasticised (PVC)*	*Polyvinyl Acetate (PVAC)*	*Polystyrene (PS)*	*Polyethylene (PE)*	*Polypropylene (PP)*	*Polyisobutylene (PIB)*	*Acrylanitrile-butadiene-styrene (ABS)*	*Acrylics*	*Polyamides (e.g. nylons) (PA)*	*Cumarone-indene resin*	*Cellulose acetate (CA)*	*Natural & synthetic isoprene rubber*	*Styrene butadiene rubber*	*Polybutadiene rubber*	*Ethylene propylene rubber*	*Butyl rubber*	*Polychloroprene*	*Nitrile rubber*	*Polysulphide rubber*
Windows (cont'd)																											
Sun protection								X	X																		
Sealants and gaskets																				X	X	X	X	X	X		
FLOORS																											
Foam sheets for floating floors											X																
ROOFS																											
Vapour barriers												X															
Roof lights and domes				X												X											
Corrugated and flat sheets				X				X								X											

INSULATION																						
Expanded beads as concrete filler										X												
Foam sheets	X	X				X	X			X												
Foam applied in situ.		X				X																
SANITATION, DRAINAGE AND UTILITIES																						
Cisterns, flush pipes and floats							X				X	X		X				X				
Disposal systems							X				X	X										
Pipes, fittings, fixtures and taps							X				X	X		X				X				
Rain gutters				X			X				X											
Baths				X											X							
Wash basins, troughs				X	X										X							
Sinks				X																		
Shower cabinets				X	X		X								X							
Toilet and urinal bowls				X											X							
Traps, floor drains and syphons							X				X	X										
Electrical switches, junction boxes	X		X				X															
Electrical conduit							X															
Airducts				X			X					X										
Ventilators and grilles							X					X				X						
Flexible joints and seals for pipes & taps											X								X	X		
FINISHING																						
Ceiling – tiles sheet						X				X												
Floor – sheets								X											X	X	X	X
Floor – tiles								X									X		X	X	X	X
Floor – jointless				X	X				X													

Table 7.5 (Cont'd)

Applications	(2) Resins – Thermosetting materials							(3) Thermoplastic materials												(4) Rubbers – General-purpose				Special purpose			
	Phenolic resin (PF)	*Urea resin (UF)*	*Melamine resin (MF)*	*Unsaturated polyesters (UP)*	*Epoxies (EP)*	*Polyurethanes (PUR)*	*Silicones (SI)*	*Polyvinylchloride, unplasticised (UPVC)*	*Polyvinylchloride, plasticised (PVC)*	*Polyvinyl Acetate (PVAC)*	*Polystyrene (PS)*	*Polyethylene (PE)*	*Polypropylene (PP)*	*Polyisobutylene (PIB)*	*Acrylanitrile-butadiene-styrene (ABS)*	*Acrylics*	*Polyamides (e.g. nylons) (PA)*	*Cumarone-indene resin*	*Cellulose acetate (CA)*	*Natural & synthetic isoprene rubber*	*Styrene butadiene rubber*	*Polybutadiene rubber*	*Ethylene propylene rubber*	*Butyl rubber*	*Polychloroprene*	*Nitrile rubber*	*Polysulphide rubber*
Finishing (cont'd)																											
Walls – panel facings	X		X	X				X																			
Walls – veneers	X		X																								
Walls – tiles and sheets								X			X																
Walls – wall cloth									X																		
Walls – waterproofing and pore filling material							X			X																	
Roof sheeting									X														X	X			
Stair nosing								X	X											X	X	X	X				

MISCELLANEOUS																								
Covers (temporary weather protection)								X			X									X	X	X		
Adhesives	X	X	X		X	X			X				X				X	X			X	X	X	X
Fencing dipcoated								X																
Shrink covers (handrails)								X																
Ropes											X	X				X								
Hardware and ironmongery	X	X	X				X					X				X								
Flag poles				X	X																			
Hoses								X									X	X	X	X	X	X	X	

Table 7.6 Cellular plastics and their applications

Material	Description	Availability
Expanded polystyrene 'bead-board'	White rigid material formed by the fusion together of expanded beads of polystyrene. Also obtainable in a pre-compressed form that is more flexible and resilient, and in granular form as unfused expanded beads.	Sheets a few millimetres thick and slabs 13 mm and more thick; also shaped forms for special insulating jobs. Densities normally 16–40 kg/m³ (see also BS 3837 and BS 3932).
Extruded expanded polystyrene	White or light-coloured material formed by a simultaneous extrusion and foaming process.	Boards up to 50 mm thick; also boards with a denser surface skin. Densities normally 32–40 kg/m³.
Expanded polystyrene beads and granules	White material formed by granulating bead board or as unfused expanded beads.	Density normally 12–24 kg/m³.
Expanded polyvinyl chloride (pvc)	Yellow to deep brown rigid material, formed by foaming pvc when in a plastic state, and cooling to solidify.	Boards up to about 100 mm thick, with cells sized 1 mm upwards. Densities 24–128 kg/m³ (see also BS 3869).
Foamed urea-formaldehyde (uf) resins	White friable material, usually formed by foaming an aqueous dispersion of resin and curing it in this condition.	Slabs of density 32 kg/m³ and upwards. For building application, generally foamed *in situ* to produce a 'cotton-wool' texture and density as low as 6 kg/m³.
Foamed phenol-formaldehyde (pf) resin (phenolic foam)	Pink or deep red rigid material, somewhat friable, made by foaming and subsequently curing phenolic resin.	Sheets, blocks, moulded sections of density 48 kg/m³, or higher, if required.
Foamed polyurethanes (urethane foam)	Colourless to deep brown material, sometimes artificially coloured. Prepared from two liquid components which are sometimes pre-expanded before complete chemical interaction and curing occurs.	Rigid or flexible foam in sheet and block form and in shaped forms for special jobs. The rigid foam is also available as a sandwich between layers of thick paper and in other laminates. May also be foamed *in situ* in cavity walls or applied by spraying.
Foamed polyurethane granules	Granulated urethane foam.	

Applications	Comments	Behaviour in fire
Lining of walls and skin roofs, insulation of flat roofs and concrete floors. In floating floor construction to absorb impact sound. Wall and ceiling tiles; insulation of cold water pipework. Shaped formwork for concrete. Cavity wall and roof insulation.	Attractive appearance; good thermal insulation; relatively low softening point; attacked by most organic solvents. If in contact with pvc, interaction causes loss of plasticiser and embrittlement.	Burns fairly rapidly; often softens and collapses. Flame-retardant grades are available
Lining of walls and skin roofs; semi-structural sandwich panels.	Relatively strong; low water-vapour transmission; low softening point.	Collapses, but burns with difficulty.
In situ filling of cavity walls to provide thermal insulation.	Poor physical and mechanical properties.	Resistant to ignition.
Lining of walls and flat roofs and as core material for sandwich panels.	Good fire and high temperature characteristics. Relatively poor physical, mechanical properties.	Highly resistant to ignition.
Shaped insulation for pipework, acoustic applications, sealing and jointing.	Relatively high thermal insulation and water vapour transmission	Generally burn rapidly, producing thick dark smoke; flame-retardant grades are available.
In situ insulation of roofs; as insulating boards for use in roofs, walls, underfloor applications. Core material for sandwich panels. Insulating and stabilising cavity walls. Spray-up foam has been used externally with a weather-resistant coating for walls and roofs.	Excellent thermal insulation; fairly good high temperature and water vapour transmitting characteristics.	

Table 7.7 Comparison of some 'Engineering' Properties (Typical plastics, steel, and concrete as building materials)

(1)	(2)	(3)	(4)	(5)	(6)
Material	**Density**	**Tensile strength MN/m²**		**Modulus of elasticity**	**Coefficient of thermal expansion**
	(kg/m³)	**Short term**	**Permissible design stress**	**(GN/m²)**	**(°C⁻¹**
					(× 10⁻⁶)
Polyvinyl chloride (PVC)	1400	50	11 to 12	3.0	50
Glass-reinforced polyester*	1500 to 2000*	70 to 400*	7 to 50*	5 to 25*	18 to 32*
Mild steel	7800		150	200	12
Concrete (1 : 2 : 4 mixes)**	2500		7 (in compression)	14	7 to 12

* Values given depend on type of reinforcement.
** Concrete is normally used under compression.

Polythene is common for small diameter cold water pipes. If they are to be exposed to light, then they will need to be black to resist degradation. In any event, a small percentage of carbon black is essential to resist degradation and algae growth. The British Standard requires the pipes to be of sufficient thickness to have a life expectancy of 50 years. Failures have normally been due to jointing or incorrect fixing.

The higher strength of rigid PVC makes it more suitable for pipes than polythene, particularly for those of larger diameter. Correct jointing and fixing is essential. Solvent welding is a simple means of providing durable joints in PVC pipes.

Sink wastes and drains

PVC or polythene products which are correctly moulded should prove excellent for normal domestic use. Very hot water from certain washing machines can prove a problem and these polymers are vulnerable to certain wastes such as paint stripper and some cleaning fluids. They may prove unsatisfactory for laboratory or industrial use.

ABS (acrylonitrile butadiene styrene copolymer) has a higher softening point than low-density polythene and is more resistant to organic solvents than PVC, so it is widely used in wastes – especially water traps.

Cold water cisterns

Both polythene and glass fibre (glass reinforced polyester – GRP) are readily available. Polythene degradation due to light is not usually a problem because of its location. The use of black polythene will overcome problems of prolonged exposure to daylight. Correct jointing is essential and the cisterns must be properly mounted on a smooth, level platform to avoid uneven stresses.

Glass-fibre cisterns made with suitable resins can be excellent. It is important that the curing is done correctly to avoid tainting the water.

Rainwater goods

Unplasticised PVC (UPVC) is used normally for this purpose, being obtainable in black, grey or white. Exposure to sunlight and thermal expansion limits the type of plastic and the colours which are suitable.

Window frames

UPVC is now the most widely used plastic material. Experience to date indicates that it should have a durability greater than 20 years. White is likely to be the most durable colour. Thermal movement may eventually cause the breakdown of the joints and result in water penetration.

References

British Standards

BS 1972: 1967, *Polythene Pipe (Type 32) for Cold Water Services.*

BS 3284: 1967, *Polythene Pipe (Type 50) for Cold Water Services.*

BS 3505: 1968, *Unplasticized PVC Pipe for Cold Water Services.*

BS 3532: 1962, *Unsaturated Polyester Resin Systems for Low Pressure Fibre Reinforced Plastics.*

BS 4346: Part 1: 1969, *Injection Moulded Unplasticized PVC Fittings for Solvent Welding for use with Pressure Pipes, including Potable Water Supply.*

BS 4346: Part 1: 1970, *Mechanical Joints and Fittings Principally of Unplasticized PVC.*

BS 4213: 1975, *Cold Water Storage Cisterns (polyolefin or olefin copolymer) and Cistern Covers.*

BS 4514: 1969, *Unplasticized PVC Soil and Ventilating Pipe, Fittings and Accessories.*

BS 4660: 1973, *Unplasticized PVC Underground Drain Pipes and Fittings.*

BS 4305: 1972 (1977), *Baths for Domestic Purposes made from Cast Acrylic Sheet.*

BS 4576: Part 1: 1970, *Half Round Gutters and Circular Pipes*

BS 4203: , *Specification for Extruded Rigid PVC Corrugated Sheeting*: Part 1: 1980, *Specification for Performance Requirements.*

BS 3837: 1977, *Specification for Expanded Polystyrene Boards*.
BS CP 144: Part 3: 1970, *Roof Coverings : Built-up Bitumen Felt*.
BS 3869: 1965, *Rigid Expanded Polyvinyl Chloride for Thermal Insulation Purposes and Building Applications*.
BS 3927: 1965, *Phenolic Foam Materials for Thermal Insulation and Building Applications*.
BS 4840: 1973, *Rigid Methane Foam in Slab Form for Transport Containers, Refrigerator Cabinets and Cold Stores*.
BS 4549: *Guide to Quality Control Requirements for Reinforced Plastic Mouldings: Part 1: 1970, Polyester Resin mouldings reinforced with chopped strand mat or randomly deposited glass fibres*.
BS 3532: 1962, *Unsaturated Polyester Resin Systems for Low Pressure Fibre Reinforced Plastics*.
BS 3496: 1973, *Glass Fibre Chopped Strand Mat for the Reinforcement of Polyester Resin Systems*.
BS 2592: 1973, *Thermoplastic Flooring Tiles*.
BS 3260: 1969, *PVC (Vinyl) Asbestos Floor Tiles*.
BS 3261: *Unbacked Flexible PVC Flooring Part 1: 1973, Homogeneous Flooring*.
BS CP 203: 1969, *Sheet & Tile Flooring (Cork, Linoleum, Plastics and Rubber)*.

Building Research Establishment

BRE Digest 69: *Durability & Application of Plastics*.
BRE Digest 93: *Cellular Plastics for Building*.
BRE Digest 161: *Reinforced Plastics Cladding Panels*.
BRE Digest 33: *Sheet & Tile Flooring made from Thermoplastic Binders*.
BRE Digest 224: *Cellular Plastics for Building*.
BRE Digest 236: *Cavity Insulation*.
BRE Digest 262: *Selection of Windows by Performance*.

Chapter 8

Paints

Introduction

There are many different types of paint available. They may be required to perform several different functions:

1. to provide a protective layer on the material covered;
2. to provide a decorative finish;
3. to fulfil special requirements – for example light or heat reflecting qualities.

It will be clear that not all paints are required or able to perform all functions. For some uses the decorative ability is paramount; in other cases protection is the only important factor. The concepts are simple but, because of the different natural and man-made substances used and the application requirements, the technology is complicated. Paint, like concrete, must be satisfactory in both wet and hardened state.

Painting systems

There are usually three stages used in a painting scheme: (1) primer; (2) undercoat; (3) finishing or topcoat(s). In some cases not all of these stages are needed.

Primer

The function of a primer is to prepare the material by sealing the bare surface, to provide protection against corrosion and dampness and to give a good adhesive surface for the following coats.

Undercoat

The function of an undercoat is to provide a smooth surface, good opacity (hiding power) and good adhesion for the finishing coat. Undercoats and priming coats do not usually wear well without a finishing coat as they are not impermeable to water and do not resist dirt. Undercoats usually contain a large amount of pigment for hiding power.

Finishing coat

The topcoat must provide a durable layer of the required colour. The texture of the finishing coat may be gloss, silk or matt.

It will be appreciated that it is not usually possible to combine all the functions in one can without sacrificing some of the quality.

Constituents of paint

Paint is essentially a suspension of an insoluble powdered solid in a liquid. The powdered solid is known as the pigment and the liquid as the medium, vehicle or binder. However, many other materials must be added to achieve the optimum results both for the application and the finished situation.

Medium, vehicle or binder are terms used to refer to the oils or resins or combinations of the two that form the basis of all paints. Linseed oil is an example of a vegetable oil used as a binder. In all cases it must have the ability to change from a fairly low viscosity liquid into a hard plastic film at the same time as binding together the fine particles of pigment. The actual properties of the binder may be modified to a large extent by the pigment.

Three main properties are required of the solid film:

1. It must have the correct gloss. All binders are glossy but have considerable variation.
2. It must adhere to the substrate (the surface being painted).
3. It needs the correct mechanical properties, which are the qualities of the combined film and substrate and include bending, scratching and impact.

Pigments are fine insoluble crystalline particles which give colour-hiding ability and body to the paint. They may be organic, inorganic, natural or synthetic. If the resulting hardened paint film is to be glossy, the pigment must all be below the surface. The amount of gloss is determined by the type and shape of pigment and the ratio of pigment to binder, usually on a volume basis. In general very glossy paints have less pigment and therefore less hiding power, while very matt ones are underbound. Increasing the pigment proportion increases hardness but decreases flexibility. Other properties, such as corrosion resistance and exterior durability, are all affected by the quality and quantity of pigment. Some desirable properties and types of pigment are shown in Table 8.1. It will be appreciated that films of paint are, by normal everyday standards, very thin at around 25 μm. A pigment particle will be about 1/100 of this thickness, intentionally near that of the wavelength of visible light to obtain maximum opacity.

Table 8.1 Types and properties of pigments

Property	Type	Comment
White paints	Inorganic	Titanium dioxide is the whitest pigment. No organic white pigments are available
Black paints	Inorganic	Carbon is the blackest pigment. No organic black materials are available
Brilliance & clarity	Organic	The most attractive and cleanest looking colours are made with organic pigments
Light fastness	Inorganic	The valency bonds in inorganic compounds are usually more stable to ultra-violet light than those in organic compounds
Non-bleeding	Inorganic	Inorganic compounds are almost insoluble in organic solvents
Heat stability	Inorganic	Very few organic compounds are stable above 300 °C

Extenders are used to improve some of the properties of the paint, although they have little or no pigmentary value. They can, for instance, be used to control the amount of gloss. A semi-gloss paint might need so much pigment to achieve the correct gloss characteristic that it would not pour and would leave heavy brush marks. The addition of a suitable filler can considerably reduce cost and at the same time improve viscosity and finish. Only enough pigment to give colour and hiding power is needed. The amount of extender used varies, depending on the paint, but may be as much as 45 per cent. Materials used as extenders do not affect the colour because their refractive index is very close to that of the medium. Extender particles are much larger than pigment particles.

Solvents are volatile liquids added at a suitable stage to lower the viscosity of the wet paint. They must evaporate very rapidly when the paint is applied to a surface, so that high viscosity is obtained and hence freedom from runs. The solvent can affect the final result and it is vital that the correct type is used for any particular resin system.

Driers are added to oil-bound paints. These are usually oxides which will give out oxygen and thereby increase the rate of oxidation of the binder and thus the rate of drying. The rate of drying can also be increased by using blown linseed oil – linseed oil which has had air blown through it.

Plasticisers are added to some paints to make the hardened film more flexible.

Light stabilisers are added to make the paint colour more stable under sunlight.

Fungicides and insecticides are added to prevent attack by insects and to prevent the formation of moulds. These are needed with household vinyl emulsion paints to prevent mould growth feeding on the cellulose or other colloids in the dry film.

Film formation

Paints may be divided into two groups according to the system by which the hardened film is formed. These are non-convertible and convertible paints.

Non-convertible paints rely entirely upon solvent evaporation for their drying process. They have the advantage of simplicity and ability to dry very fast within a few minutes. However, they tend to produce thin films with poor adhesion and chemical resistance. In addition they can be dissolved by the original solvent, which produces difficulties when recoating unless spraying techniques are used. Nitrocellulose lacquers dry by this process.

Convertible systems are those where low molecular weight, fairly low viscosity material is changed to a high molecular weight hardened film. This is a chemical change, not merely a physical one as with non-convertible systems. The hardening process goes through three stages:

1. Uncured stage, where solvents dissolve the resin. All paints must be in this stage before application.
2. Part-cured stage, where solvents would make the resin swell.
3. Cured stage, where solvents have no chemical effect on the film.

The chemical change is most commonly achieved by means of oxygen from the air. Some paints are produced where the reaction takes place between ingredients within the paint. The two-pack system is one example. This is not popular because of the measurement needed and its subsequent pot life. Another method is to include the ingredients within the one tin but choose them such that no reaction takes place at normal temperatures. A third method is to dilute the ingredients by means of a solvent so that the reaction within the can is very slow and only speeds up after its evaporation. Oil paints, industrial storing enamels and polyester wood finishes dry by means of the chemical reaction of their ingredients.

Types of paint

Oil-bound paints (convertible)

Until the beginning of the century, nearly all paints consisted of white lead dispersed in linseed oil. In fact all natural oils of both animal and vegetable origin are tri-esters of glycerol. These are fatty acids with a molecular chain containing most commonly 18 carbon atoms.

The process of hardening is firstly evaporation of the volatile solvent, followed by polymerisation of the fatty acid molecules after the addition of oxygen. The resulting polymer is quite different from the original oil and is not soluble in the solvent, so there are no problems when brushing on later coats. They need a very long drying time, varying from 3 to 12 h, depending on temperature and humidity.

Alkyd resins (convertible)

These are again often based on linseed oil but contain a polymeric ester as a result of the reaction between glycerol and phthalic anhydride. They need a shorter drying time; in normal conditions they should be 'touch' dry in about 3 h, though gloss paints need rather longer. Three main types are used:

(a) 'long-oil' alkyds with more than 60 per cent oil;
(b) 'short-oil' alkyds with less than 40 per cent oil;
(c) the non-drying variety that are used with nitrocellulose resins.

The thixotropic alkyds are produced from the same raw materials but modified by reaction with small quantities of polyamide resin.

Paints based on alkyd resins form the major type of interior and exterior finish for woodwork; they are harder, more adherent and have better gloss and durability than the pure linseed they are derived from. Lifetimes vary between 2 and 8 years, depending on situation and exposure. The biggest cause of deterioration is sunlight which embrittles the paint, hence south-facing aspects deteriorate most quickly.

Polyurethane paints (convertible)

These can be regarded as modified alkyds and give a coating of superior hardness, though this can accelerate the destruction of the paint in external applications.

Epoxy esters of fatty acids (convertible)

These are produced by reacting epoxy resins with fatty acids and give greater water and chemical resistance than normal oil-based paints. Linseed esters are used as boat varnishes because of their great water resistance.

Emulsion paints (convertible)

The resin consists of a latex similar to rubber. It is insoluble in water which is present to the extent of about 30 per cent. A typical latex is polyvinyl acetate (PVA) and the pigment might be titanium dioxide.

Finishes are normally 'matt' (dull), 'silk' or 'satin', though some gloss paints are now available. Drying times vary according to conditions – they may be as low as one hour in a warm, dry, well-ventilated enclosure. In cold, damp conditions they may take a long time to set or fail to set at all.

Advantages of emulsion paints are that the hardened film is fairly permeable, hence the paints can be applied to slightly damp materials, such as new plaster, permitting subsequent drying of the background. PVA emulsions are alkali-resistant, hence they can be used on cement backgrounds subject to some dampness. Emulsion paints of suitable composition can be used externally and they now form an alternative to traditional oil-based paints for wood, though their rapid drying in hot conditions makes it difficult to maintain a 'wet edge'. Lifetime is 4 to 7 years depending on quality and degree of exposure.

Nitrocellulose lacquers (non-convertible)

Nitrocellulose is produced by the action of nitric acid and sulphuric acid on a form of cellulose such as wood pulp. It is highly explosive and dampers are added. The volatile material will be 70 to 80 per cent of the total, consisting of about seven different hydrocarbons. It forms a rapid-drying paint suited to such applications as spraying of motor cars and other manufactured items. Alternative lacquers with similar properties are acrylic and vinyl lacquers.

Chlorinated rubber paints (non-convertible)

Produced by treating rubber with chlorine to produce a creamy white powder for use as a binder. The solvents consist of suitable hydrocarbons. The main advantage of this type of paint is its resistance to water, acid and alkalis, which is gained at the expense of appearance.

Paint failures

Saponification

Oil-bound paints súch as alkyds may sometimes fail when used on certain building materials. When an acid and alkali react together, the result is a soap and water. This is known as saponification. Many building materials such as lime mortars and plasters, Portland cement and asbestos cement develop alkalis, especially when new. If such surfaces are coated with an oil-bound paint, particularly in the presence of even small quantities of moisture, they will cause saponification. The paint may blister in a mild attack or show yellow soapy runs in a severe attack. The problem can be avoided by allowing the background to dry completely before painting; by use of alkali-resistant primers, or by use of PVA emulsions paints as an alternative to oil-based paints.

Loss of adhesion

Loss of adhesion in walls can occur through a number of causes. The effect may lead to blistering, peeling or flaking of the paint film. Repeated condensation on certain types of paint can cause a swelling and shrinking of the binder, particularly when freshly applied. It could also be caused by defects in the surface which is being painted, particularly where gypsum plaster has dried out before hydration is completed, resulting in a powdery surface. This same fault may also cause delayed expansion of the plaster. Very smooth surfaces such as glazed tiles may suffer from loss of adhesion with certain primers. Alternatively, high suction of a surface can remove too much of the binder from a paint.

Efflorescent salts may also be deposited under the paint film, leading to peeling.

Loss of adhesion in woodwork may be caused by the following:

(a) painting while too wet;
(b) ineffective primer;
(c) inadequate preparation/keying of smooth surfaces;
(d) water penetration – for example at joints or end grain;
(e) excessive substrate movement caused by solar radiation in conjunction with a brittle or aged paint coating.

Chalking

This is the term used to describe erosion of the paint film due to inadequate binder performance. It is caused by use of paints containing either a poor quality binder or an inadequate quantity of binder.

Questions

1. Explain why it is unwise to paint new cement surfaces with an oil-bound paint, describing any visible effects. How can these defects be prevented?
2. Explain, without chemical formulae, the actions of a drying oil and an extender as normal constituents of a paint.

References

BRE Digest 106: *Painting Woodwork.*
BRE Digest 70: *Painting: Iron & Steel.*
BRE Digest 71: *Painting in Buildings 2 – Non-ferrous Metals & Coatings.*
BRE Digest 197: *Painting Walls Part 1: Choice of Paint.*
BRE Digest 198: *Painting Walls Part 2: Failures & Remedies.*
BRE Digest 182: *Natural Finishes for Exterior Timber.*
BRE Digest 261: *Painting Woodwork.*

Chapter 9

Plasters

Plasters may be defined as materials designed to provide a durable, flat, smooth, easily decorated finish to internal walls or ceilings. Plasters were traditionally based on lime or cement but in the last 30 years gypsum has become the most important binder. Gypsum plasters have the following advantages:

1. Their setting time can be precisely controlled according to function.
2. The time delay between successive coats may be very small.
3. Various surface textures and surface hardnesses are obtainable according to function.
4. Unlike cement-based plasters, they are non-shrinking (provided plastering technique is correct).
5. They have excellent fire-resistance. Set gypsum plaster contains 21 per cent water of crystallisation which vaporises slowly in a fire. This process (calcination) absorbs considerable heat, minimising the rate of temperature rise in and behind the plaster. Calcined gypsum also acts as an efficient insulating barrier in fire.

Note that, since gypsum is slightly soluble in water, gypsum plastics are not suitable for exterior uses unless very effective permanent protection is provided.

The plastering process

A maximum of three coats may be used, each having its own function:

1. render coat – to level the background;
2. floating coat – to produce a surface of uniform suction;
3. finishing coat – to provide a smooth, hard finish.

The first two coats require relatively coarse-textured plasters applied in thicknesses of up to 20 mm. The functions of these are now largely combined in a single undercoat or 'browning' coat. The finish coat utilises a much finer material of thickness up to 5 mm. Some backgrounds, such as plasterboard, provide a flat surface with uniform suction, so that a single finishing coat will suffice.

Classes of gypsum plaster BS 1191

The raw material is $CaSO_42H_2O$, calcium sulphate dihydrate, which is obtained from mines. During manufacture, some or all of the water is driven off by heat, the nature of the resultant material depending on the heating regime. Small amounts of impurities are usually present and these colour the plaster grey or pink, though they have no other significance.

BS 1191 classifies gypsum plasters as follows:

Class A. Hemihydrate $CaSO_4\frac{1}{2}H_2O$ *(plaster of Paris)*
This is produced by heating to a temperature not in excess of 200 °C. Plaster of Paris sets within 5 to 10 min of adding water, which is far too rapid to permit use in ordinary trowel trades. It is nevertheless useful for moulding purposes such as in decorative plasterwork.

Class B. Retarded hemihydrate $CaSO_4\frac{1}{2}H_2O$
These are produced from Class A plasters by the addition of a suitable set retarder such as keratin. The amount of retarder added depends on function.

Undercoat plasters tend to be slower setting than finish coat plasters to allow time for straightening. These plasters are normally designed to be used with sand in ratios of up to 3 : 1 sand : plaster. Increasing the sand content has the effect of accelerating the set, setting times being in the range 2 – 3 h.

Finish coat plasters are designed to be used neat or with the addition of up to 25 per cent by weight of hydrated lime, which accelerates the set. Setting times are in the range 1 to 1½ h.

Class B plasters should not be retempered once setting has commenced.

A most important application of Class B plasters is in premixed plasters containing lightweight aggregates which are now very widely used. 'Board finish' plasters for plasterboard are also Class B.

Class C. Anhydrite

Class C plasters are obtained by heating the raw material to a higher temperature than Class B plasters, with the result that a proportion of anhydrous calcium sulphate forms, although some hemihydrate also remains. The anhydrous component is so slow to set that an accelerator such as alum is added. The presence of two compounds gives Class C plasters a 'double set' – an initial set and then a slow final set, so that the material can be retempered with more water during the first half an hour after adding the water, though it should be applied as soon as possible after mixing and sets completely in $1\frac{1}{2}$ h. An important current use of Class C plasters is a finishing coat on a sand/cement backing (trade name Sirapite).

Class D. Anhydrite (Keene's cement)

This is harder burnt than Class C, resulting in a higher proportion of anhydrite. The plaster set must again be accelerated and stiffening, as in Class C plasters, is continuous. The final product has superior strength, smoothness and hardness compared with other types and is used for arrises and surfaces such as squash court walls, where a very hard durable finish is required. It also provides an ideal base for gloss paints. On account of its strength, it should not be used on soft backings such as plasterboard or fibreboard.

Other components of plasters

Sand

Sand can be used to reduce the cost of gypsum plasters. It may be incorporated in traditional Class B material, mainly in the browning coat.

BS 1191 gives gradings of sand which are suitable for undercoats and finish coats; these sands are characterised by a relatively small range of particle sizes compared with, say, concreting sands (Table 9.1), most particles being in the size range 0.3 – 1 mm.

Type I sands may be used in undercoat plaster in the ratios 1 : $1\frac{1}{2}$, 1 : 2, 1 : 3 plaster: sand by volume for backgrounds of progressively decreasing strength. If the finer type II sands are used, the sand proportion should be reduced by one-third. Sands must be clean, since fine clayey material reduces strength, while salts affect setting time and tend to produce efflorescence. Some ready-mixed Class B plasters are obtainable ('Thistle').

Table 9.1 Particle size gradings of plastering sands

BS sieve	Type I	Type II
5 mm	100	100
2.36 mm	90–100	90–100
1.18 mm	70–100	70–100
600 μm	40–80	40–100
300 μm	5–40	5–50
150 μm	0–10	0–10

Lightweight aggregates

Low density aggregates, such as expanded perlite (produced from siliceous volcanic glass) and exfoliated vermiculite (produced from mica) are a most important ingredient of modern plasters, which are now very commonly premixed. Some advantages of these plasters are as follows:

1. Transporting and handling costs of the plaster are reduced.
2. The lower density fresh material requires less effort to mix and apply and can be used in thicker coats without sagging.
3. The thermal insulation of walls or ceilings is improved and the internal surface temperature increased, thereby improving 'U' values and reducing the risk of surface condensation and pattern staining.
4. Fire performance of structures is improved.

Lime

Lime may be used in quantities up to 25 per cent of gypsum in finish coats of ordinary Class B and C plasters. It improves the working properties ('fattiness') of the fresh material and in Class C plasters counteracts acidity due to accelerators, hence it may help reduce corrosion of embedded metals. Non-hydraulic limes must be used and should be soaked in water for one day before use.

Factors affecting the choice of plaster

These may be conveniently described under the headings undercoat and finish coat, although the two components are not completely independent – for example strong, hard finishing coats also require a reasonably strong undercoat.

Undercoat

The most important factor affecting choice of undercoat is background suction – that is, the tendency of the background to absorb water from the plaster coating.

Some suction is desirable, since it removes excess water from the plaster, the pores which are responsible for suction also increasing adhesion of the plaster by a mechanical keying effect.

Excess suction is a disadvantage because it results in premature stiffening of the plaster, giving too little time for levelling and may lead to poor adhesion.

Very low suction is equally a problem, owing to lack of pores which improve adhesion.

Table 9.2 indicates plasters which may be used for backgrounds of varying types. The properties of premixed lightweight undercoat plaster can be varied according to function – for example, bonding plaster contains vermiculite aggregate and produces a relatively dense plaster with good adhesion. 'Browning' plaster contains perlite, while 'high suction background' plaster contains, in addition, cellulose additives to improve water retention.

Table 9.2 Undercoat plasters and their applications

Suction	Examples	Lightweight gypsum plaster	Gypsum plaster/sand mixes
Low	Dense concrete. No-fines concrete. Engineering bricks	Bonding	1 : $1\frac{1}{2}$ plaster : sand (stronger backgrounds) 1 : 2 plaster : sand (weaker backgrounds)
Medium	Ordinary clay bricks	Browning	1 : 2 plaster : sand
High	Some stock bricks. Aerated autoclaved concrete blocks	High suction background browning	1 : 3 plaster : sand

Raking of joints in low suction brickwork or hacking of dense concrete will improve adhesion to backgrounds in the low suction group. Treatment with PVA bonding agents both reduces water absorption of high suction backgrounds and improves adhesion of low suction backgrounds, such as high-strength concrete. Cement/sand/lime plasters form an alternative group of undercoat materials, though these have the disadvantage that finish coat application must be delayed for some days to allow curing and shrinking of the undercoat. One possible advantage of cement-based plasters is that they form a barrier to efflorescent salts if these are present in substantial quantities in the background. It is important, when using cement-based undercoats, that their strength does not exceed that of the background, otherwise shrinkage may result in breakdown of the background surface.

Finish coat

This will be selected primarily according to the surface hardness requirement, which will in turn depend on the situation within the building and the function of the building. The most demanding situations are projections in corridors and doorways of public buildings for which the hardest plasters are required. Table 9.3 indicates the gypsum plaster type most appropriate to various situations. Of the plasters listed, the lightweight variety form the largest part of the current market. These do not have the hardness of dense plasters but are nevertheless quite resilient, since impacts are absorbed by localised indentation of the lightweight undercoat.

Table 9.3 Finish coat plasters and their applications

Function		Plaster type	Comments
Very hard smooth surface		Class D (anhydrite) finish plaster	Strong undercoat needed. Lightweight types not suitable
Hard surface		Class C (anhydrite) finish plaster	Normally on cement/sand or class B/sand backing
Ordinary purposes	Max. fire resistance and insulation	Lightweight Class B plaster	Used on lightweight undercoat
	Alternative	Class B plaster	Used on class B/sand undercoat

One-coat plasters

Plasters are now available which serve as both undercoat and finishing coat, thereby saving the craftsman's time. A typical product consists of a white, high purity Class B gypsum plaster combined with perlite and other additives. The material must be machine mixed. After application, the material is straightened and then left for about 1 h to stiffen. The surface is then wetted and trowelled to a smooth finish. The main problem is that the cost of the material is considerably higher than that of the more common gypsum plasters.

Plasterboards

These consist of an aerated gypsum core sandwiched between and bonded to strong paper liners. Most boards have one ivory-coloured surface for direct decoration and one grey-coloured surface, which has better adhesion properties for plastering. Plasterboards with a foil backing for improved thermal insulation or with a polythene backing for improved vapour resistance are also obtainable.

Boards may be used either as an internal lining to solid or cavity walls or nailed to a timber frame to form walls, partitions or ceilings. Various sizes and thicknesses are obtainable (Table 9.4).

Table 9.4 Examples of thickness and sizes obtainable in gypsum plasterboards

Type	Length (mm)	Width (mm)	Thickness (mm)
Laths	1200	406	9.5 or 12.7
Baseboards	1200	914	9.5
Wallboard	2400	1200	9.5 or 12.7
Plank	2400	600	19.0

Laths and baseboards are specifically designed for a plastered finish and, provided joints are staggered, they are less likely to result in cracks at joints than wallboards. Planks are intended primarily for fire-resistance applications. Various edges are obtainable according to function – for example, tapered edges are suitable for smooth, seamless joints on boards to be decorated direct (dry lining), square edges are suitable for plastering and rounded edges, as in laths, give a good bond to the filler which is used between adjacent pieces. For plastered finishes, all joints except those in laths must be reinforced with some form of scrim tape to prevent cracking. Correct procedure is essential in respect of joint treatment to obtain the best finished effect and to avoid cracking.

Where plastering is to be carried out, this may be in one or two coats and a neat Class B 'board finish' plaster is normally used. The thickness applied is quite small – in the region of 5 mm – and it is important that drying out is prevented until setting is complete, otherwise a soft, powdery surface will result.

In spite of their paper surfaces, plasterboards provide good fire protection, being designated as Class 0 in Building Regulations.

Common defects in plastering

These may be associated with background problems, inadequate or incorrect surface preparation, incorrect use of materials or incorrect plastering technique. The main problems are as follows:

Cracking

Cracks occur when movement of the plaster in excess of its strain capacity occurs. Gypsum plasters are non-shrinking but may still be subject to tensile stress if the background moves. Examples are:

1. *Background shrinkage*. This may result if the background is very wet when the plaster is applied. The plaster then cracks at concave corners or following a definite line of cracks in the background. The only practicable remedy is to fill the cracks and disguise with a suitable decorative finish.
2. *Undercoat shrinkage*. Cement-based undercoats may result in numerous hairline cracks if not given sufficient time to shrink before the finish coat is applied. An excess of lime in the finishing coat may have the same effect. These cracks may be filled or simply obscured using a suitable wallpaper.
3. *Plasterboard finishes*. This type of cracking is widespread, usually following plasterboard joints. The extent of cracking is reduced by used of laths or baseboard, movement then being spread over more joints than in larger sheets. Causes include undersized joists, inadequately fixed or restrained joists, poor nailing technique, omission of scrim tape, inadequate joint filling or simply severe impact or vibration of the structure. Fine cracks can be covered by a textured finish but deeper cracks should be cut out and filled. Where background movement is the cause of the cracking, it will be likely to recur.
4. *Structural movement*. This leads to well-defined cracks which follow a continuous line through the structure, plaster cracking in the same position on each side of solid walls. Cracks tend to be concentrated at weak points such as above doorways or windows. Before cutting out and filling, it is essential to establish and rectify the cause of the movement.

Loss of adhesion

This results when a strong finishing coat is applied to a weak backing coat, especially if the backing is inadequately 'scratched' to form a mechanical key or if it is still 'green'. The problem is uncommon, except with sand/cement backings. Both coats must be replaced unless the problem is caused by a green backing; if this is the case, it should be allowed to harden, loose material removed and then the finish coat reapplied.

The problem will occur with plasterboard if too much lime is added or, in two-coat work, if too much sand is used in the undercoat. The plaster must be stripped off and replaced. If the exposed surface is damaged or uneven, the plasterboard also must be replaced.

Dry out

This occurs if plaster dries before the water becomes chemically bound by setting. It occurs if thin coats are applied to dry backgrounds such as plasterboard, especially in hot, dry weather. The result is a soft powdery surface which may be difficult to paint on paper. Defective plaster should be stripped and replaced.

Efflorescence
British Standard 1191 limits the amount of efflorescent salts in gypsum plasters but salts may be present in the background or in sand (when used) if not clean. Salt deposits may appear on drying of plaster, especially if the background is wet during plastering. Deposition may also result subsequently if a plastered area becomes wet due to a leak. The salts crystallise below the surface of emulsion paints, causing loss of adhesion. They can be removed by brushing, once plaster is dry, and will not recur provided the plaster does not become rewetted.

Questions

1. Give four advantages of gypsum plasters compared with lime or cement alternatives.
2. Describe the composition, properties and uses of the four main classes of gypsum plaster.
3. Suggest why lightweight premixed gypsum plasters have become very popular in recent years.
4. Explain how the choice of plaster for a given situation will depend on:
   (a) the suction of the background;
   (b) the requirements of the finished surface.
5. Explain the reasons for traditional plastering being carried out in three stages. Give situations in which two or one coat work may be acceptable.
6. (a) Describe the various types of plasterboard which are available, giving applications of each.
   (b) Give reasons for cracking in skim coats to plasterboard and suggest how the risk of cracking can be minimised.
7. Give possible causes of adhesion of the finishing coat on:
   (a) solid backgrounds;
   (b) plasterboard backgrounds.
   Give steps which may be taken to avoid and to rectify the problem in each case.

References

British Gypsum White Book – Technical manual of building products.
BS 1191: 1973, *Gypsum Building Plasters*.

Answers to numerical questions

Chapter 1 Concrete

8. Zone 2
10. (a) 5.1 per cent
(b) 9.3 per cent
11. Compacting factor 0.93
13.

1 (a) 0.43	1 (b) 0.56	1 (c) 0.50
2 (a) 0.48	2 (b) 0.44	2 (c) 0.41
3 (a) 0.50	3 (b) 0.54	3 (c) 0.45

14.

Cement	20.5 kg
Water	9 litre
Fine aggregate	31.25 kg
Coarse aggregate	58 kg

15.

Cement	3.5 kg
Water	1.4 litre
Fine aggregate	4.15 kg
Coarse aggregate	15.7 kg

16. Standard deviation = 3.6 N/mm^2
Required characteristic strength is not being reached.
17. The results are satisfactory.
18. Water/cement ratio = 0.51

Chapter 2 Bricks

4. The brick is of Engineering 'A' classification.

Chapter 3 Dampness in buildings

3. Porosity = 67 per cent
4. Solid density = 2364 kg/m^3

Chapter 4

6. Carbon equivalent = 0.473 per cent.

Chapter 5

10. (a) Actual stress = 3.67 N/mm^2 (satisfactory)
(b) Maximum deflection = 4.6 mm (within permissible limits).

Index

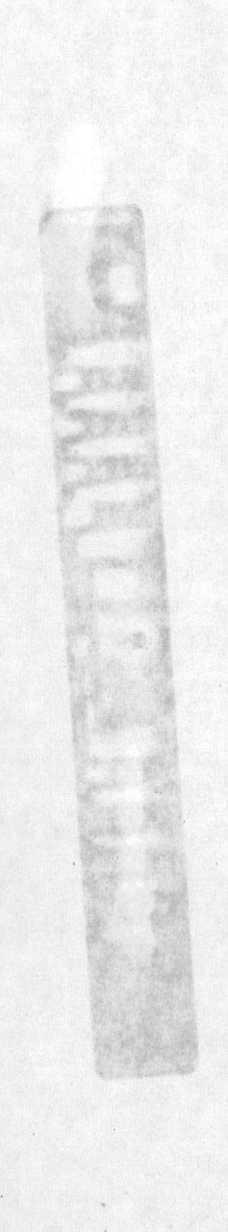